Praise for *Wellness Witchery*

"This book is a joy to read, with potions, teas, baths, and tonics to soothe, invigorate, and heal you inside and out. By learning to work with plant allies and using formulas and exercises to improve specific mood disorders, you can discover how to reach your highest potential. … Laurel uses practical advice, step-by-step exercises, and guided meditations to help her readers manifest their goals and create a life of joy, abundance, and peace."

—Dean Jones, host of the *Calling the Quarters* podcast

"*Wellness Witchery* is the perfect adjunct to a Witchcraft practice, with tons of information and suggestions on how to connect with plants on both the practical and magical level. Author Laurel Woodward guides the reader to better physical, mental, and emotional health while honoring both the natural world and our own inner healer. Magic indeed."

—Deborah Blake, author of *The Everyday Witch's Coven*
and *The Eclectic Witch's Book of Shadows*

"*Wellness Witchery* is the healing balm needed in a world that can sometimes feel uncertain. Brew a cup of tea and lose yourself in the pages of Woodward's book as you learn to nurture your soul through self-care rituals, meditative practices, spells, exercises, and recipes to induce calm and restoration. The author's wisdom is evident throughout every page, so keep a pen handy and don't be afraid to dog-ear the pages, as *Wellness Witchery* is the go-to to nourish the spirit."

—Monica Crosson, author of *Wild Magical Soul*

"*Wellness Witchery* is an essential compendium of medicinal recipes and an invaluable guide for those seeking to harness the power of plant healing and infuse their lives with magic."

—Lisanna Wallance, herbalist, chef, author of *The Natural Witch's Cookb*

"Laurel Woodward has crafted a guide to empower the reader on their journey mental, physical, and spiritual well-being. She draws upon both the practical and t magickal worlds to navigate the changing times that we all face. Laurel is a kind a caring voice in a world that isn't always as caring as we would like it to be. Her wo

is well researched and full of useful exercises, formulas, rituals, and more. She's even shared healthy recipes that are comforting and take into consideration dietary restrictions. This book will be a soothing balm for your witchy soul."

—Mickie Mueller, author of *The Witch's Mirror*
and *Llewellyn's Little Book of Halloween*

"In *Wellness Witchery*, you will find a plethora of knowledge, recipes, and insight to seamlessly integrate wellness magic into your practice. Once again, expert Laurel Woodward has crafted an amazing resource jam-packed with accessible how-tos and well-researched recipes for wellness. Wherever you are on your herbal and magical journey, *Wellness Witchery* is an instant must-have for your magical library!"

—Julia Halina Hadas, author of *WitchCraft Cocktails*
and *The Modern Witchcraft Book of Astrology*

"*Wellness Witchery* is an exquisite treat. It is relevant, practical, diverse, magical, entertaining, and incredibly informative. With over twenty years of practice and experience, Laurel Woodward compiles an endless variety of topics ranging from dishes to elixirs and spells, baths, and teas, to all kinds of easy-to-follow formulas for the herbal practitioner and every Green Witch out there looking for a very complete compendium on herbal and natural magic."

—Elhoim Leafar, author of *Manifestation Magic* and *Dream Witchery*

WELLNESS WITCHERY

About the Author

Laurel Woodward (Portland, OR) has been a witch for twenty years and is also a tarot reader. She has written for magazines and ezines on the subjects of healthy living, organic gardening, sustainable living, and the magick of tapping into the creative energy of the natural world. You can visit her at liminallandscapes.com.

LAUREL WOODWARD

WELLNESS WITCHERY

A *Magickal* Approach
TO Nourishing the
Body, Mind & Spirit

Llewellyn Worldwide
Woodbury, Minnesota

First Edition
First Printing, 2023

Cover design by Cassie Willett

Llewellyn is a registered trademark of Llewellyn Worldwide Ltd.

Photography is used for illustrative purposes only. The persons depicted may not endorse or represent the book's subject.

Library of Congress Cataloging-in-Publication Data (Pending)
ISBN: 978-0-7387-7534-0

Llewellyn Worldwide Ltd. does not participate in, endorse, or have any authority or responsibility concerning private business transactions between our authors and the public.

All mail addressed to the author is forwarded, but the publisher cannot, unless specifically instructed by the author, give out an address or phone number.

Any internet references contained in this work are current at publication time, but the publisher cannot guarantee that a specific location will continue to be maintained. Please refer to the publisher's website for links to authors' websites and other sources.

Llewellyn Publications
A Division of Llewellyn Worldwide Ltd.
2143 Wooddale Drive
Woodbury, MN 55125-2989
www.llewellyn.com

Printed in the United States of America

Also by Laurel Woodward

Backyard Garden Witchery: Creating Magickal Space Outside Your Door

Kitchen Witchery: Unlocking the Magick in Everyday Ingredients

Acknowledgments

A good editor is an absolute gift, and I have two amazing women to thank. First and foremost is the talented Heather Greene. Thank you for your keen insight, kind words, and personal support. It was your creative vision, expert advice, and gentle guidance that turned a troubled manuscript into a work fit to publish. Thank you for helping me turn content into the lovely book it now is. The second is my production editor, Lauryn Heineman. I am so lucky to have you on my team. Thank you for answering all my questions with explanations I could understand and for challenging statements and directing me to research content and citations that were questionable.

I'd also like to thank the amazing team at Llewellyn Worldwide. A big thank-you to everyone in production who helped transform a manuscript into this beautiful book.

Thank you to the booksellers and librarians who support my efforts. A shout-out to the staff of the Washington County library system. A big thank-you to Barbara Peters and Patrick King from the Poisoned Pen Bookstore and Megan Love Smith from Crystal Lake Public Library. Thank you to my fabulous friend Britta Nicholson. Thank you for all the lovely hours of tea and conversation that helped to keep me sane during the last trying year.

And last, thank you to my husband, who makes my writing possible.

Contents

PART 3: APOTHECARY FOR WELLNESS

Exercise and Formula List

Exercises, Baths, and Spells

Kitchen Witchery Recipes

Herbal Formulas

Essential Oil Recipes

Disclaimer

Never use a plant unless you are 100 percent sure of its identity. Misidentifying a plant may result in injury, illness, and even death. Not all the plants are friendly. Some are very poisonous. Experimenting with these plants can be dangerous. Some are dangerous in large doses or with extended use. Others may be harmful to pregnant women, to children, or to people with certain types of medical conditions. All should be treated with respect. The information in this book is not a substitute for medical treatment. Please consult your doctor before self-medicating.

INTRODUCTION

I am a wife, a mother of four, and a witch who uses food, herbs, and spices to make my life the best it can be. My practice as a kitchen witch is rooted in herbal study. For the past twenty years I have been studying and working with the ingredients in my pantry, the spices in my cabinets, and the plants in my yard. For me a study of witchcraft and a study of herbcraft go hand in hand.

I use herbs and oils daily for food and drink, for first aid, to modify mood, and in my magickal practice. As the second year of the COVID pandemic came to an end, I realized that the focus of my magickal practice had shifted. Instead of working bold rituals with a sunny focus on empowerment and prosperity, I was working simpler rituals to ease worry and lighten mood. Instinctively, I had embraced the antianxiety powers of the natural nervines growing in my environment. California poppy (*Eschscholzia californica*), chamomile (*Matricaria recutita*), hawthorn (*Crataegus monogyna*), lavender (*Lavandula* spp.), lemon balm (*Melissa officinalis*), mimosa (*Albizia julibrissin*), motherwort (*Leonurus cardiaca*), passionflower (*Passiflora* spp.), and vervain (*Verbena* spp.) had become main ingredients in many of my formulas.

The new normal the pandemic enforced not only changed routine but, for many of us, introduced a state of worry and fear. And it wasn't just COVID wreaking its havoc on health, schedules, and food supplies, but also the increasing social unrest, the radicalized political climate, and the looming threat of climate change that contributed heavily to my darkened worldview. As COVID lingered, I came to the realization that in shutting out the outside world, I'd also neglected my friendships and slipped into a role as a hermit. All my social interactions had trickled down to almost none. Even my telephone conversations had fallen away. No longer was my world a sunny place, my vision bright with hope. The wolf was at the door, it seemed, and the future was uncertain.

To counteract my darkening outlook, I had instinctively evolved my practice into work with a focus on being kinder to myself. I'd revived a daily morning meditation exercise that often included watching the winter sunrise. I'd embraced nurturing, nutrient-rich foods and forced myself to exercise for at least twenty minutes each day. When the weather was good, instead of spending the time doing chores, I'd slip away to spend a couple of quiet hours walking through the woods, and in the evenings I spent sacred time soaking in a scented bath.

Implementing a self-care practice and focusing on the immediate moments of all that was good and constant in my small corner of the world not only fought off the threat of doom and gloom but allowed the kindling of a brighter outlook, one that was filled with gratitude and wonder. I rediscovered that eating a healthy diet and exercising still made my body feel good. Getting a good night's sleep, though sometimes difficult, was still fortifying. The simple act of unplugging, setting down the tablet, silencing the phone, and stepping out into the beauty and preciousness of nature still worked its restorative magick. The secret was to just do it.

Times of change are hard on everyone. New realities emerge. We learn to adapt. Life might eventually be different, but we can still fill it with the things we love and the small things that make us happy. In doing so, we make it feel less hollow. We can create space to devote the time and energy needed to manifest what we yearn for in the depth of our soul. When we set aside time for self-care ritual, we reprogram the mind and find our way through the chaos of the world to the sacredness of the immediate moment.

It is my hope that by reading about my experience with plant allies, you may form some of your own experiences as you integrate a magickal mindset into daily living to help you feel better and live better, as you learn to meditate, eat, and spell your way to a higher quality of life.

Plants are fascinating. Many have ancient histories full of magickal stories and lore. Each and every one holds an amazing energy. When we get to know a plant, it ceases to be a mere ingredient and becomes a magickal ally with energy to realize our intentions.

In these pages is a magickal guide, a reflection of my own magickal practice to bring magick to the mundane. You will meet plant allies and learn how to nurture a relationship with them. You will be introduced to meditations and mood-lifting exercises to empower your own practice. Included are scores of recipes and formulas to help you become a happier, healthier, more magickal you.

Part 1
The Wonderful World of Plant Allies

Chapter 1

THE POWER OF PLANTS

Each and every plant in your home and yard holds knowledge to broaden your practice and expand your work. Each has its own personality and its own talents. The peace lily that lives beside my desk is a friendly specimen that keeps me company, a complete opposite of the thorny blackberry bramble that guards the boundary of my yard.

Plants help filter the air. They take in carbon dioxide and release oxygen. Plants provide us with food to nourish our bodies and medicines to heal and comfort. They give us ingredients for herbal formulas to dress candles, burn as incense, and brew into infusions to drink, to wash with, and to add to our bathwater.

Over the course of my magickal journey, I have found it is the plants that grow in and around my yard that fuel my practice and inspire me the most. Each has become a teacher and a friend. The only cost is effort, attention, and time. When I come across an unfamiliar plant, there is a thrill in the discovery. I look at each as if meeting a new friend. I photograph and identify what kind of plant it is. Then I research how it is used and how it was used in the past. I record its stories in my journal, finding the information both fascinating and rewarding. It is a habit that has evolved my spiritual practice.

Twenty years ago when I first started on this path, I spent my free time foraging the shelves at my local occult shop and hunting for new treasures to bring home and inspire my studies. I ended up with boxes of herbs I knew little about. It wasn't until I bought seeds, successfully sprouted them, and began spending time in my garden caring for each plant that I came to truly understand the power they held. Each observation, each interaction, fed a relationship and deepened my awareness until the plant was no longer an ingredient but had become a magickal ally with resources to heal or empower.

Our Western view has crippled our relationship with plants. We need to rethink their place in the world to understand that they are sentient beings, each engaged in a complex relationship within the ecosystem in which they live. To the shaman, a plant ally relationship is not about chemistry, as healer and author Eliot Cowan explains in an interview: "In recent times, our culture has basically looked to plants as healing agents in terms of their chemical properties. That is a relatively recent development in the history of humanity. In previous times when people turned to plants as agents of healing they were not primarily concerned with chemical constituents, but rather they saw plants as living beings, as highly aware, having feelings and as well disposed to helping people. It was that living awareness and good disposition to help people that people turned to plants as the primary source for the element of healing potentials."[1]

Curious scientists across the world are beginning to look at plants in a new light. In 2019, a group of scientists documented the response of beach evening primrose (*Oenothera drummondii*) as pollinators approached and concluded that plants respond to the sounds they "hear."[2]

Through her studies and encounters with nature, research associate professor Monica Gagliano concluded "that learning, memory, and decision-making are not the exclusive province of animals."[3] In her book *Thus Spoke the Plant,* Dr. Gagliano details her experiences and how they changed her view of the world: "When I finally

1. Bridgitte Jackson-Buckley, "What Is Plant Spirit Medicine?" *Gaia*, April 26, 2017, https://www.gaia.com/article/what-plant-spirit-medicine.

2. Marine Veits, et al., "Flowers Respond to Pollinator Sound within Minutes by Increasing Nectar Sugar Concentration," *Ecology Letters* 22, no. 9 (September 2019): 1483–92, doi:10.1111/ele.13331.

3. Monica Gagliano, *Thus Spoke the Plant: A Remarkable Journey of Groundbreaking Scientific Discoveries and Personal Encounters with Plants* (Berkeley, CA: North Atlantic Books, 2018), 160.

understood all this, the quality of my surprise was magically transformed from a sense of disbelief born of anthropocentric conceit into a feeling of awe. It was a sense of elated wonder inspired by something sublime, something magnificent that engenders a deep reverence for life. It is awe that inspires the freedom for very different questions to be asked, questions that don't need to be answered in order to renew our sense of ecological intimacy and kinship with the nonhuman living world."[4]

German forester Peter Wohlleben made a similar discovery while working in his forest. He began to see each tree as a highly sensitive individual, living cooperatively in a community, nurturing each other. He discovered that trees communicate, remember, and even make decisions in order to survive. In an interview for *Yale Environment 360*, Wohlleben explains, "Trees also send chemical signals through the air when they are attacked by insects. Nearby trees receive these messages and have time to prepare their defenses." He continues, "Plants process information just as animals do, but for the most part they do this much more slowly."[5]

In her new book, *Finding the Mother Tree*, scientist Dr. Suzanne Simard explores the ways trees interact and communicate through underground fungal networks and that trees are able to "perceive and connect and relate with an ancient intricacy and wisdom that can no longer be denied. … The old and young are perceiving, communicating, and responding to one another by emitting chemical signals. *Chemical signals identical to our own neurotransmitters. Signals created by ions cascading across fungal membranes.*"[6]

Plants are so much more than mere ingredients. Just like the other life forms on this planet, plant life is part of the fabric of the planet's consciousness, and just like our relationship with the other denizens that share our world, they have been greatly overlooked.

· · · · · · · · · · · · · · · ·

4. Gagliano, *Thus Spoke the Plant*, 71.

5. Richard Schiffman, "Are Trees Sentient Beings? Certainly, Says German Forester," *Yale Environment 360*, Yale School of Environment, November 16, 2016, https://e360.yale.edu/features/are_trees_sentient_peter _wohlleben.

6. Suzanne Simard, *Finding the Mother Tree* (New York: Alfred A. Knopf, 2021), 4–5. Author's italics.

The Potent Power of Your Local Plants

In her book *The Earth Path,* Starhawk writes, "A Witch must not only be familiar with the mystic planes of existence beyond the physical realm; she should also be familiar with the trees and plants and birds and animals of her own backyard, be able to name them, know their uses and habits and what part each plays in the whole."[7] The plants of your yard are part of your local energy web. When we become familiar with the local flora and fauna and build a relationship with its individuals, we also create a bond with the local energy systems, and we ourselves become part of the local energy web—and that is very powerful. As we work with these energy systems, a great awakening that opens our perception and touches the very center of our being begins.

As you begin the work, you will experience a shift that you feel deep within you as the moment around you swells and reality expands and gains dimension. What was fleeting slows and gains depth to become rich and multilayered and filled with meaning. Suddenly, things are not so separate but linked, and life becomes magickal as you become aware of the synchronicities happening all around you and feel the presence of the other energies that are nearby.

Many of your plant neighbors can be allies if you take time to get to know them. Each has its own personality, and just like people, some are friendlier and more helpful than others. Yet each and every one is a complex conscious being from the loftiest tree to the lowliest weed, and if you spend time and give them attention, you will find each is waiting with a unique lesson.

Exercise
Identify a Plant Ally

You will need:

notebook

pen or pencil

. . . .

7. Starhawk, *The Earth Path: Grounding Your Spirit in the Rhythms of Nature* (San Francisco, CA: HarperCollins, 2004), 7.

camera (optional)

offering of rainwater, a small amount of ash from a ritual fire, or a handful of leaf mold

For this exercise you need to cut out the modern distractions. Turn off your electronic devices or leave them inside. Collect the items you are taking and go to where
the plants are. This could be indoors or outdoors. Settle into a comfortable position.
State your intention. You might use a phrase like "I meet my ally" or "My plant ally
reveals itself." Then draw a few breaths as you draw in your awareness and let your
thoughts quiet. You will pick up more signals if you place yourself in a receptive
state. Close your eyes and notice your breath. Sit with your breath, noticing as you
draw it in through your nose and deep into your chest. Move your awareness to your
center. Do you feel a sense of expansion? Move your awareness to what you feel on
your skin. Does the sun warm your face and arms, or is a breeze softly cooling it?
You should begin to feel a wondrously exhilarating shift of being right there, awake
and oh so aware in your own skin.

As the moment grows deeper, open your eyes and engage your other senses. Shift
your awareness to what you see, hear, and smell. Sit with your expanding awareness.
Spend several breaths in stillness as you listen, feel, and observe, and then cast out
your awareness or move your focus to a large area around you. Notice everything.
If you feel drawn to an area, get up and go closer. Let your eyes light on anything
that draws them. When you find a plant that calls to you or stands out in some way,
examine it. Do you know what kind of plant it is? If you don't, settle comfortably in
front of it and photograph it or sketch it so that you will be able to identify it later.
When we take the time to sketch a plant, we are getting to know it more intimately
as we replicate its features onto our page. If you are certain it isn't a plant with irri-
tating properties, you might ask the plant if you can take a clipping and press it in
the pages of your notebook to help you identify it later. There are a lot of good plant
identification apps. Pl@ntNet, iNaturalist, and PlantSnap are a few well-regarded
ones that are free to use.

If you know what kind of plant it is, make note of it in your journal and spend
some time with the plant, noticing how it makes you feel as you observe it. Before

you leave, thank the plant and offer it the gift of friendship that you brought. Say goodbye and that you will return soon.

Later, do some research. Keep notes in your notebook about the plant's history and lore. Note the ways the plant is used in medicine and magick. Note its growing habit and the conditions it needs to thrive.

Cultivate a Relationship with Your Ally

Our relationships with allies grow and develop just as our other relationships do. The more effort you put into it, the stronger your relationship will become. Nurture your connection by spending time with your ally. Treat it as you would a friend. The more familiar you are with it, the better of a friend it will become. Visit it. Talk to it. Learn what it needs to thrive and provide for its needs. Plants bond with us when we show them love.

Look up your ally's history and lore. Not only is this information fascinating, but it will give you insight into how the plant was used in the past. Look to how it was represented in stories and art. Often these symbols carry over into its modern correspondences.

I have many plant allies that I interact with, having learned their habits by caring for them, observing them, learning about them, and experimenting with them throughout the year. Each and every plant brings a wisdom that can be applied to your practice. Some are very friendly and reveal their wisdom easily. Others are secretive and grant their wisdom only after intensive research and experimentation.

When it is time to harvest, only take the amount of material you need. Never take more than a third, or you will risk harming the plant's health. If you plan on foraging on someone's land, be sure to get his or her permission first. Be kind to the plants and the earth. Unless you are foraging for invasive species like dandelions or burdock, it's a good idea not to uproot any plant. Take care not to trample colonies, and never harm an endangered or protected species.

Always thank the plant and tell it what you are going to do with the portion you are taking. When we talk with our allies and share gratitude, the relationship shifts into a partnership and the plant's input becomes greater. Leave your ally an offering to show your gratitude. A glass of rain or spring water, a bit of compost, a handful of ash from a ritual fire, or some crushed eggshells all are good choices.

Plant Magick

Plants contain a multitude of resources to help us live happy, abundant lives, but just like any neighbor, we need to be on friendly terms to truly reap the benefits. Natural healers will tell you that in order to gain the help of a plant, you must first develop a relationship. This is why, when it comes to traditional medicine, healers get big results while pharmaceutical studies might get little. In an interview herbalist and author Eliot Cowan explains that traditional cultures are concerned with the chemicals in a plant but focus on nurturing relationship "so that the plant feels free to share its medicine." He shared, "The plant people don't have mouths and voice boxes, so they find another way to speak to us and inform us, and that is predominantly through dreams."[8]

Plants have a lot to teach us if we only take the time to open to them. A rich tapestry of lore and power opens to you when you form an alliance with a local plant. When you spend time working with an individual plant, the interaction fosters a relationship in which the plant ceases to be an ingredient and becomes a unique spirit ally, a friend. As you develop this relationship and learn its habit, you will become aware of its place in the local web of life, and as you incorporate it into your own practice, you will deepen your connection to that web.

Nurture a Conscious Relationship

When we step out of modern life's busyness and take time to immerse ourselves in the natural world, we wake to a deeper existence and gain the ability to receive and respond to messages that are sent our way. One of the ways to forge this connection is to open your senses to plants growing around your home.

· · · · · · · · · · · · · · · ·

8. Erin Everett, "Plant Healing, Fire Wisdom," *Bee and Tree* (blog), January 3, 2017, https://www.beeandtree .org/2017/01/03/plant-healing-fire-wisdom-an-interview-with-plant-spirit-medicine-author-eliot-cowan/.

Exercise
Communicate with Your Plant Ally

You will need:
notebook
pen or pencil
offering

For this exercise you need to cut out the modern distractions. Turn off or leave your electronic devices inside. Collect your pen and notebook and settle comfortably beside the plant you identified as an ally in the previous exercise.

State your intention. You might say something like "I get to know my plant ally," "I become friends with my plant ally," or "We are having a friendly chat so that we may get to know each other."

Draw a breath and close your eyes as you draw your focus in. Breathe as you focus on how it feels for your spirit to be there, in that moment, in your body. Draw a measured breath and follow your breath with your awareness into your center. Your center may be in the area of your heart, or you may feel it lower in your belly. As you follow your breath, sit with your expanding awareness.

When your perception grows to the point of becoming sharply focused, open your eyes and move your focus to the plant. Fix your awareness on it. Listen with your heart. Note everything your senses pick up. Spend several breaths in stillness as you observe. Take note of anything that draws your attention. Next move your focus to your sense of hearing and spend several breaths listening. Note any messages, visions, scents, or feelings that come up.

When the time feels right, call out a greeting. You can do this in your mind or out loud. Introduce yourself and spend a few quiet moments watching and listening for a response. Say anything positive that you feel prompted to say. Then spend a few moments listening and watching for a response. Be aware of any feelings you experience. Plants often speak to us through impressions. Take note of any sensations, emotions, and thoughts that come up.

When you are ready to end your visit, note everything you experienced in your notebook. Thank the plant and offer it the gift you brought. Say goodbye and that you will return soon.

Spend time with your ally. Tend to it as you provide for its needs. Talk to it—plants respond to our attentions. Notice its growing habit throughout the seasons. Experiment with your plant ally and take notes. Note its effects on your magick. Record all your own personal responses to it. The more you work with the plant, the more you will get to know it.

Chapter 2

PRACTICAL HERBAL APPLICATIONS

Down through the ages, healers turned to local plants to treat illness. They amassed a healing tradition of folk remedies and lore. Now science is confirming that many of those same remedies are medicines fit to treat modern illness. Chamomile does indeed calm the nerves. Hawthorn does improve circulation. Lavender does soothe the psyche.

Herbcraft has been in use for thousands of years. The knowledge is waiting. The journey begins when you decide to gather your own medicine and initiate a relationship with the plants in your yard.

How to Dry and Store Your Herbs and Herbal Blends

Inspect the herbs you harvested and remove any discolored leaves. Wash them in cool water and then gently shake off the excess moisture, patting it dry with a clean cloth. Gather leafy herbs in small bundles and secure the ends with string or a rubber band. If you are drying herbs with small flowers or seedheads, enclose the bundles in small, individual paper bags to help prevent the flowers and seeds from dropping as they dry.

Label each bundle with the name of the herb and the date. Then hang the bundles upside down in a cool, shady place with good airflow. This allows for the plant's essential oils to concentrate in the leaves. Make sure to keep the bundles evenly spaced to encourage ventilation. Immediately discard any herbs that show signs of molding. Mold can be deadly!

When your herbs have dried, store them whole in airtight containers such as zip-lock bags or small glass jars with tight-fitting lids. Whole herbs retain their natural oils much longer than an herb that has been crushed or ground.

When making an herbal blend, mix together all the ingredients and store the blend in a clean, dry jar with a tight-fitting lid. Label the jar with the date and the name of the formula. If there is room, write your intention.

Infusions

Making an infusion is the process of pouring hot water over herbal matter and letting it steep for 10 minutes or so. The mug or pot holding the infusion is covered while it is steeping so that the plant's essential oils do not escape with the steam. After the allotted time, the herbal matter is strained out and the leftover liquid is ready for use. When you make a cup of tea, you are using the infusion method.

Basic Method to Brew an Infusion

Heat water until it comes to a boil. Measure 1 tablespoon of herbal mixture per each cup of water into a tea strainer and tell it what you want it to do. Place the strainer in a mug or a heatproof bowl and pour the hot water over the herb. Cover the mug or bowl with a lid or a towel to prevent the essential oils from escaping with the steam. Let the infusion steep for up to 10 minutes. Remove the strainer and discard the herbal matter. Taste the liquid. Some herbs are bitter; others have a sour flavor. If you don't care for the taste, flavor the drink with lemon juice or sweeten with honey.

The Ritual of Drinking Tea

Every morning I get up and one of the first things I do is put the kettle on. Making a cup of tea and quietly sipping it is my morning ritual to get myself ready for the day. When I am forced to skip or hurry through this process, I feel discombobulated and like things just happen around me instead of being focused through me.

It is through ritual that we transform the mundane into an act of magick. Through ritual we align thought and action to manifest intention. So it is with the making and drinking of tea.

Teas are very healing in themselves, but when we change the process of making and drinking tea from a passive one into a focused, directed event, the act becomes *more*. The herbs in the tea are powerful, but the real magick comes from you. When you are present to take in the sensory input and the pleasure of the experience as you breathe in the aroma, feel the steam dampen your face, notice the warmth of the brew in your mouth, feel it as it spreads throughout your body, and then visualize it doing whatever it was you willed it to do. This is when the true magick happens. When we give the process our full attention and notice our reaction to the power of the herb, of being soothed or uplifted or empowered, the action is multiplied.

Begin by crafting your intention, and then hold it in your mind as you gather the ingredients. Tell each ingredient what you would like it to bring to your tea as you measure it out. You can hold your intention as a thought or vocalize it with a whisper, a song, or a chant.

When the tea is ready to drink, pour some into your mug and settle comfortably. Let your mind quiet so that there is only you and tea. Take a deep breath as you breathe in the scent of the tea. Lift the cup to your lips as you open your senses to how it feels being right there in that moment. Savor the flavor and as you swallow, visualize the liquid as healing energy sliding down your throat into your stomach. Take another sip as you visualize the warm, healing energy glowing at your center. See it moving out to do whatever it is that you programmed it to do.

Decoction

A decoction is a heating method used to make the antioxidants, minerals, and essential oils of roots, bark, and seeds available. A decoction is prepared by placing water and plant matter in a pan and bringing the contents to a gentle boil. The heat is then reduced, and the pan is covered and left to simmer for a determined amount of time before being allowed to cool. The plant matter is strained out and the leftover liquid, or decoction, is ready for use.

Basic Method to Brew a Decoction

Measure 4 cups of water and 4 to 6 tablespoons of herbal matter into a saucepan. Heat to a slow simmer and cover partially. Simmer until the liquid has been reduced by half. Turn the heat off. At this point you can add any leaves or flowers needed for the formula. Cover and set aside for several hours. Strain the liquid and drink, or pour it into a clean jar with a tight-fitting lid and store in the refrigerator for up to 24 hours.

Flower Essence

Soaking flowers in spring water and using the power of the sun infuses the liquid with a flower's essence. The plant matter is then strained out and the liquid, or the mother essence, is bottled with a high-quality brandy or gin that is at least 80 proof. Dr. Edward Bach is known for creating the first line of flower essences in 1935 to support his patient's emotions.

Basic Method to Make a Flower Essence

You will have to begin by making a mother essence. Choose a sunny day. Fill a glass bowl with 8 ounces (1 cup) of spring water. Place your bowl in sunny place and float your flowers in the water, facing upward, to cover the surface. Allow the flowers to infuse the water for up to 4 hours. Avoid having any shadow fall across the bowl's surface.

Pour the liquid through a strainer into a jar filled with 1¼ cups brandy. The ratio should be about 40 percent essence and 60 percent brandy. Seal the jar and label. Then store in a cool, dark place.

Use your mother essence to make a stock essence by filling a small bottle with equal parts spring water and brandy. Add 6 to 10 drops of your mother essence and use as needed.

Cold Infused Oil

A cold oil infusion is the method of macerating herbs and flowers in oil to infuse the oil with scent, flavor, and other herbal goodness. Fresh or dry herbs are washed and completely dried before being gently bruised to release their oils. The bruised herbs are then placed in a clean, dry jar and oil is pour over the herb to fill the jar to the top. The jar is then fitted with a tight lid and allowed to sit for an indicated time. During the macerating process, it is important to check the jar to make sure the oil is still at the top and all the herbal matter is submerged. Give the jar a shake as you reinforce your intention. After the allotted time, strain out the herbal matter and store the oil in a clean jar with a tight-fitting lid. Label the jar with name and date and, if there is room, include your intention.

Basic Method to Make a Cold Infused Oil

If you are using fresh herbs, you will need to fresh-wilt them first to reduce their moisture content. To do this, take your clean fresh herbs and lay them out on the kitchen countertop in a single layer. Cover with a dishtowel and let them sit for several hours or overnight.

Fill a small clean jar partway with the herbs, dried or fresh. Pour oil over them to cover and fill the jar to the top. I almost always use olive oil. Seal the jar and shake to make sure there are no trapped air bubbles. Set it on a shelf for several weeks. The recipe will determine if this should be in the sun or in a dark cupboard. Visit the jar daily and give it a shake. After the allotted time (this time will change depending upon the herbs being infused), you will need to remove the herbal matter from the oil. Cover a bowl with a doubled layer of cheesecloth and pour the oil through it. You may need to do this twice. Then wring the oil out of the herb in the cloth and pour the oil into a clean jar with a tight-fitting lid. Label the jar and store it in a cool, dry place. Watch out for any signs of spoilage and discard any spoiled batches.

Tincture

A tincture uses alcohol as a solvent to extract the herbal goodness. The alcohol dissolves the active properties of the plant matter and acts as a preservative, allowing the tincture to retain its effectiveness for a much longer time. Fresh or dried leaves, flowers, roots, barks, or berries are placed in a canning jar to fill it a third of the way full. The jar is then filled with a high-proof alcohol (80 to 100 proof) such as gin or vodka to cover the herbs and fill the jar to the top. The jar is then sealed with a tight-fitting lid and stored in a cool place out of direct sunlight. It is important to check on the jar to make sure the alcohol is still at the top and all the herbal matter is submerged. If not, add alcohol to avoid oxidation. During each check, shake your tincture as you reinforce your intention. After the allotted time, strain the tincture through a cheesecloth and store it in a brown glass bottle. Label the bottle with the name and date and, if there is room, include your intention.

Basic Method to Make a Tincture

Prep your herbs by chopping them finely. If you are using fresh herbs, you will need to fresh-wilt them first to reduce their moisture content. To do this, take your clean fresh herbs and lay them out on the kitchen countertop in a single layer. Cover with a dishtowel and let them sit for several hours or overnight.

Put the chopped bits into a clean dry jar with a tight-fitting lid. Pour alcohol over the herbal bits to completely cover by 2 inches. Seal the jar and place it in a cool, dark place. Visit it daily to give it a shake and inspect it to see if you need to add more alcohol to bring it back to its 2-inch coverage mark. After 4 to 6 weeks, strain the tincture through a cheesecloth into a bowl. Wring the herb in the cheesecloth to express any remaining liquid and dispose of the herbal matter. Sweeten the liquid with honey. Carefully pour the liquid into a brown glass bottle and label with name and date. Store in a cool, dark place out of direct sunlight. Use up the tincture within a year.

Herbal Simple Syrup

Dissolve sugar in an infusion to preserve the herbal goodness and make it readily available. The ingredients are placed in a saucepan and brought to a boil. The liquid is stirred as it simmers so that the sugar dissolves. After about 1 minute, the pan is removed from the heat and the liquid allowed to cool. The herbal matter is then strained out and the liquid poured into a clean jar.

Simple syrups are usually made with white sugar. Simple syrups made with maple syrup or honey will not last as long. Elderberry, hibiscus, and lavender are popular herbal syrups.

Basic Method to Make a Simple Syrup

Place 4 cups of water in a saucepan. Add 1 cup of herbs and bring to a simmer. Partially cover the pan with a lid and simmer until the liquid has been reduced by half. Remove the pan from heat and strain out your herbs. Measure the liquid; you should have about 2 cups. Pour the liquid back into the pan and add half the amount of sweetener. If you have 2 cups of liquid, you will stir in 1 cup of honey or sugar. Cook the mixture for 3 more minutes. Pour the liquid into a jar. Store in the refrigerator for up to 2 weeks.

Working with Essential Oils

Essential oils are natural aromatic compounds found in the seeds, bark, stems, roots, leaves, and flowers that have been extracted usually by distillation, and on average they are 50 to 75 percent more powerful than the oil when in the plant itself. Essential oils can be worn, but as they are so strong, they must be diluted, or carried, by a base oil before being used topically. If you plan to apply an essential oil to your skin, blend it with a carrier oil to avoid skin irritation. Choose a carrier oil that complements the energy you are working with and use 1 ounce (which equals 2 tablespoons) for every 14 drops of essential oils. Test out the blend on a small patch of skin and wait a few hours to check for irritation before applying it more liberally. If the patch turns red or becomes itchy, do not use the blend on your skin.

Carrier Oils

A carrier oil is a base oil used to carry the energy of essential oils so the stronger oils won't irritate the skin. While sweet almond and jojoba oil are the old tried and true standards, I use olive oil and sweet almond oil for the base of most of my blends. Not only do they both have long histories as ritual anointing oils, but they hold magickal energy to complement a whole array of intentions.

Today there are many oils to choose from. Check out the oils available where you do your shopping. Many grocery markets now carry exotic oils like avocado, walnut, hazelnut, and macadamia alongside their olive oil choices. Consider the oil's corresponding energies. Choose one with energy to support your intention. If the blend you are creating is something you are going to wear, give the oil a sniff to see if you like its scent. Some oils have strong aromas that can be overwhelming.

The following is a list of recommended carrier oils along with their correspondences and associations.

Apricot Kernel Oil: Attraction, beauty, emotional issues, and love. This oil is associated with Venus and the element water.

Avocado Oil: Aphrodisiacs, beauty, clear sight, fertility, health, love, and youth. This oil is associated with Venus and the element water.

Castor Oil: Absorbing negativity, fertility, healing, and protection. Castor oil is associated with Mars and the element fire.

Coconut Oil: Beauty, clear thinking, moon magick, healing, protection, purification, and transformations. Coconut oil is associated with the moon and the element water.

Grapeseed Oil: Abundance, dreams, fertility, garden magick, mental powers, and money. Grapeseed oil is associated with the moon and the element water.

Hemp Seed Oil: Healing, love, meditation, and psychic abilities. Hemp seed oil is associated with the moon, Saturn, and the element water.

Jojoba Oil: Abundance, beauty, and healing. Jojoba oil is associated with the moon and the element water. Jojoba has a long shelf life.

Olive Oil: Fertility, healing, love, lust, peace, potency, prosperity, and protection. Olive oil is associated with the sun and the element fire.

Rosehip Seed Oil: Beauty, friendship, healing, and love. Rosehip seed oil is associated with Venus and the element water.

Sesame Oil: Luck, opportunity, riches, and wealth. Sesame seed oil is associated with Ganesha, the sun, and the element fire.

Sunflower Oil: Abundance, beginnings, confidence, fertility, protection, and success. Sunflower oil is associated with the sun and the element fire.

Sweet Almond Oil: Communication, connection to spirit, love, money, riches, and wisdom. Sweet almond oil is associated with Mercury and the element air.

Not all oils are created equal. When possible, choose an organic oil that is cold-pressed or expeller-pressed to ensure there are no residual solvents and toxins and that the oil hasn't been heated to a high temperature during manufacturing, as this negatively alters the molecular composition of the fatty acids. Avoid oils rendered by using harsh chemical solvents.

When making any blend you are not going to use right away, avoid using canola, corn, flaxseed, safflower, or soy as your carrier oil. These oils are unstable and tend to turn rancid quickly when exposed to sunlight or heat.

Some Helpful Tips for Crafting Herbal Formulas and Oil Blends

Keep the following best practices in mind when crafting your own herbals and oil blends.

- Start small. Save money and ingredients by crafting your brews in small quantities as you begin to experiment with them and get to know them. When you have determined which ones you use and enjoy, make bigger batches.
- Match the jar to the batch size and fill it to the top so there is no airspace for mold to grow in. For example, a small jelly jar holds 4 ounces or ½ cup, a ½-pint jar holds 8 ounces or 1 cup, and a pint jar holds 16 ounces or 2 cups.
- Use the best quality ingredients available.
- Always label your creation with the name and the date it was made, and if there is room on the label, add your intention.
- At the first sight of mold, throw out your mixture. Mold can be deadly.
- If you are crafting an herbal formula that you are going to store, use dried herbs to avoid mold issues.
- When working with oils, avoid introducing water into your jars, as it will encourage mold growth and ruin your potions.
- As you begin working with essential oils, begin with simple formulas that use three or fewer oils.

- Use a different dropper for each oil to avoid contaminating it, compromising its energy, and ruining its scent.
- Discontinue using an oil immediately if you experience any sort of negative reaction.

Chapter 3

BASIC SELF-CARE APPLICATIONS FOR EVERY DAY

Use these comforting practices to alleviate stress, elevate your mood, restore your energy, and enhance your overall sense of well-being.

The Magick of a Bath

There is nothing quite as restoring as a nice soak after a hectic day. The energy of water is very healing. Add a simple ritual scented with herbs and oils, and bath time becomes magickal.

When you take time to relax in a tub of water with natural scents, salts, herbs, and oils, the bath becomes a baptism in natural energies to cleanse, calm, heal, unhex, rejuvenate, and empower. A ritual bath can cleanse our energy of negativity, frustration, anxiety, and anger to modify or lift mood and renew spirit.

A handful of salt is a traditional spiritual cleanser. Leaves, flowers, and herbs are tossed in by the handful to lend their healing energies. Flowers can be floated on the surface. A handful of rose petals or jasmine will induce feelings of love. A handful of bay leaves will aid in victory. A handful of mugwort will boost intuition and clear sight.

To avoid a messy cleanup, stuff your herbs into a sachet or tie them up in a bit of netting before you toss them into the tub. Even an old stocking can be used to keep the plant matter from going down the drain. Or you can skip the mess altogether by brewing up a magickal infusion to add healing herbal energy to your bathwater.

Basic Bath Salts

Mix together in a wide-mouth glass jar:

> 1 cup sea salt
> 1 cup Epsom salts
> ½ cup baking soda

Shake to mix. Store the salts in a glass jar with a plastic lid. Salt is corrosive. It causes things to rust. If you do use a metal lid, slide a piece of plastic wrap over the top to seal the jar before you put the lid on to avoid contact with metal.

To use, add ½ cup of the basic bath salts mixture to each tub of water and soak. Salt not only clears energy, but it also draws impurities out from your body and works to heal and deodorize it too. If you have sensitive skin, you might want to have a quick rinse after your soak.

Exercise
Ritual Bath of Renewal

For a ritual bath, the tub becomes a ritual space. Before you begin, clean the space and gather everything you need for the ritual. Make sure you have an uninterrupted block of time. Turn off your electronic devices. Craft your intention, and when you are ready to begin, set the atmosphere by lighting candles or incense. Both work as a cue to tell the mind to get ready to meditate.

The bath itself is a meditation. Get into the tub and draw your attention in. Follow your breath until your attention has fixed on the moment. State your intention. Visualize as you work with the energy of the water. See it clearing, healing, or energizing your mind, body, and spirit.

You will need:

neroli or grapefruit essential oil

½ cup basic bath salts

1 white candle

matches

Fill the bath. Add 7 drops of the essential oil to ½ cup of basic bath salts. Pour the salt mixture under the running water. Place the candle where you can comfortably see it and light it. Undress and get into the water. Lie back and let your muscles relax. Breathe, and with your breath draw your attention in. When your focus has become sharply fixed on the moment, visualize the water glowing with healing light. Splash the water over yourself. See it restoring your energy field, adding to it, building it. If you are really feeling weighed down, completely immerse yourself by dunking your head under the water before repeating the following incantation:

> *All that is negative washes from me.*
> *It washes away and I am free.*
> *Peace and calmness now fill my center.*
> *I am renewed. I am revived. I am free to be me.*

When you pull the plug, visualize all the negativity flowing down the drain. When you step out, say,

> *What is past, is past,*
> *I accept the opportunity to become the positive,*
> *hopeful, loving me I am supposed to be.*
> *I am renewed, I am renewed.*

If the urge strikes, tweak the phrases to better suit you. Words have power. Our brains believe what they hear. This is why affirmations are so effective.

Exercise
Relaxing Footbath

If you don't have a tub or simply don't want to take a bath, soaking your feet in an herbal infusion is an effective way to soak up some herbal healing power. Make the soak a meditation and it will become transforming.

You will need:
basin large enough to comfortably rest both of your feet in
hot water
infusion of herbs or essential oils

Make sure you have an uninterrupted block of time. Craft your intention. Turn off your electronic devices. Fill your basin with hot water. Add the herbal infusion or essential oils to the water. Set the atmosphere by lighting candles or incense.

Sit down in a comfortable chair and place your feet in the basin. Close your eyes and relax. Follow your breath until your attention has fixed on the moment. State your intention. Visualize the basin glowing with energy. See it filling your feet, moving up your legs and up into your body. See it clearing, healing, or energizing your mind, body, and spirit.

Soak as long as you'd like.

Simmer Pots

A simmer pot is just that: a pot filled with water and fragrant fruits and spices that are warmed to fill the home with comforting scents. Fill a small pot halfway with water and heat to a boil. Turn the heat down to a simmer and add your ingredients. Stir the pot clockwise to attract something or counterclockwise to banish. Check on the pot every 20 minutes or so and add more water to maintain the water level. Here are some simmer pots to try:

Celebrate: Cinnamon sticks, cranberries, an orange cut into segments, a
handful of pine needles, and a star anise pod

Cheer: Lemon or grapefruit peals or slices, cedar twigs, bay leaves, and rosemary

Cozy: Cinnamon sticks, cloves, and rosemary sprigs

Fresh Forest Air: Cedar twigs, eucalyptus leaves, and pine needles

Love: Cinnamon sticks, cloves, lavender sprigs, and nutmeg

Nostalgic: Apple peels or slices, cinnamon sticks, and 2 teaspoons vanilla extract

Sacred Smoke

Burning herbs and resins is an age-old ritual practiced by a multitude of cultures down through the ages. We burn incense to move the mind into a mystical state. We burn it to carry our intentions up into the universe. We burn it to clear away negative energy and move what has become stagnant.

Incense, herbs, and resins are used to create ambiance at the beginning of ritual. The scent is a powerful trigger to enable the mind to shift realities or slip into a centered awareness. The scent creates an ambiance that can calm nerves, balance emotions, and elevate mood. You can burn loose herbal blends on a charcoal disk to create the same effect. Place the disk in a firesafe dish and light it. Drop a pinch of herbs on it to fill a room with fragrant smoke. Here are some basic herbs and their uses to get you started:

Cedar: Healing, protection, purification, enhancing communication, and summoning

Juniper: Instilling comfort, protection, and exorcism

Lavender: Instilling calmness and promoting happiness

Mugwort: Enhancing psychic sight and deflecting malevolent thoughts

Sage: Cleansing, purification, and dispelling fear and negativity

Sweetgrass: Balance, cleansing, and purification

Chapter 4

PRACTICAL SKILLS TO BOOST WELL-BEING

Here are a few practical skills I rely on. They cost nothing except a bit of effort and time, but once you master them, you will be able to navigate your thoughts out of the mire of worry and hang on to a positive outlook.

The Conscious Breath

Conscious, or mindful, breathing is all about learning to be present by focusing on the breath and following its flow in and out of the body. When one focuses or meditates on the breath as it enters and leaves the body, the mind falls silent, the psyche calms, and awareness expands. This is because the breath, the brain, and the body are all connected. Not only does your breath oxygenate your blood to relax muscles and lower blood pressure, but it also influences your brain's emotional control regions.[9]

Learning to breathe consciously is a skill that will allow you to switch on your inner calm. In the article "Rewrite Your Anxious Brain," Dr. Evian Gordon talks

. . . .

9. Anup Sharma et al., "A Breathing-Based Meditation Intervention for Patients with Major Depressive Disorder Following Inadequate Response to Antidepressants: A Randomized Pilot Study," *Journal of Clinical Psychiatry* 78, no. 1(2017): e59–e63, doi:10.4088/JCP.16m10819; David DiSalvo, "How Breathing Calms Your Brain," *Psychology Today*, December 31, 2017, https://www.psychologytoday.com/us/blog/neuronarrative/201712 /how-breathing-calms-your-brain.

about the conscious breath: "Exhaling triggers the parasympathetic nervous system. It's the single most effective way to put the brakes on the fight-or flight response."[10] Mastering the technique will give you tools to alleviate worry, quiet panic, and even cool anger.

Exercise
Mindful Breathing

With your spine straight, slowly draw a deep, even breath in to the count of three. Focus on your breath. Follow it as it enters your body. Notice how your chest expands and rises. Notice how your body feels. Don't allow other thoughts to distract you. Keep your mind solely focused on what it feels like in this moment. When your lungs are fully expanded, hold the breath for the count of three. Then slowly release it, exhaling out to the count of three. This is the "conscious breath." By mastering this technique, you will gain the ability to quiet anxiety and expand your awareness.

Do it again. Inhale. Focus on your breath as you draw air into your lungs. This time notice how the muscles of your body feel. Starting with your head, face, and jaw, will your muscles to relax. If you are holding any tension, release it as you exhale. You may want to open your mouth and reposition your jaw to release the tension. When you have relaxed your head and face, move your attention down to your neck and shoulders. Will those muscles to relax. Breathe and concentrate on your body and how it feels. If a thought interferes, just notice it and let it go as you gently move your attention back to your breath. Relax your back and pelvis and when those areas have relaxed move your attention down to your legs and feet. When your body is completely relaxed, you will begin to feel light and floaty. Sit for a while with your breath and notice how it feels to be right there in that moment. As you sit with the moment, reality will begin to shift and grow sharper as your awareness expands. All your sensory input will intensify, making the moment feel truly wonderful.

Couple this technique with visualization and you will be able to take all kinds of magickal journeys.

· · · · · · · · · · · · · · · · · ·

10. Ginny Graves, "Rewire Your Anxious Brain," *Real Simple*, November 13, 2020, 10.

Learn to Visualize

Visualization is the ability to conjure up images in your mind's eye. It is a form of self-hypnosis, a tool many can learn to use to help foster healing. By providing suggestion combined with positive images, visualization can form a mind-body connection that fosters the healing process on a physical level. Through conscious awareness of our thoughts, we are able to focus our experiences in the desired directions and change reality. All it takes is learning to see images the way you wish them to be in your mind's eye.

Exercise
Image Recall

When I first began working with visualization techniques, I had a very difficult time trying to conjure up and hold an image in my mind. One afternoon over lunch with a magickal friend, I mentioned my difficulties and my friend helped me right there at the table by running me through this exercise. She said, "You are making this way too hard. It's simple. Just look at your plate. Good, now close your eyes and picture your plate in your mind's eye. Try to recall as many details as you can. Now bring in the other senses. What do you smell? Hear? Feel? Taste?" And just like that, the simple exercise opened the door for me.

You will need:
quiet moment with no distractions
object to rebuild in your mind

Settle in a comfortable position and place the item where you can comfortably gaze at it. With your spine straight, close your eyes and draw a conscious breath. Let your thoughts quiet as you focus on your breath. Breathe it in to the count of three, hold it to the count of three, and then exhale to the count of three. Draw another breath and follow it as it enters your body. Repeat until your thoughts have quieted. When you have become present and focused on the immediate moment, open your eyes and gaze at the object. Notice it in as much detail as you are able. Take in the color, shape, and texture. Think about how it would feel it you held it. Bring in your other senses and consider how the object would sound, taste, or smell. When you have focused on it for a full minute, close your eyes and rebuild the image on the screen of your mind.

Don't fret if you only dredge up a few bits of it. Visualization takes practice. Try the exercise again. See how much better you do. The more you practice this exercise, the better you will become at it.

Adopt a Meditation Practice

Meditation is the act of shifting concentration inward. Through this shift, thought becomes still so that the mind may enter a deep state of concentration as awareness expands. When we adopt daily meditation, we are granted life-changing skills. The practice of meditation changes both the workings of brain and consciousness as it opens up access to layers of consciousness in which profound changes in the perception of reality and the self occur.

New studies have shown that adopting a daily meditation practice shifts our mind into a mindfulness behavior that affords calm emotional responses, heightened awareness, and an appreciation of one's day-to-day life.[11] By practicing meditation and learning to redirect thought back to the present moment, we train our mind and gain the ability to consciously relax, end a worried thought loop, and gain control over our emotional responses. We become present and happy and—what's more—we begin to access latent abilities and come into our power.[12]

. . . .

11. Antonio Crego et al., "Relationships between Mindfulness, Purpose in Life, Happiness, Anxiety, and Depression: Testing a Mediation Model in a Sample of Women," *International Journal of Environmental Research and Public Health* 18, no. 3 (February 2021): 935, doi:10.3390/ijerph18030925; Xiao Ma et al., "The Effect of Diaphragmatic Breathing on Attention, Negative Affect and Stress in Healthy Adults," *Frontiers in Psychology* 8, no. 874 (2017): n.p., doi:10.3389/fpsyg.2017.00874.

12. Zongpai Zhang et al., "Longitudinal Effects of Meditation on Brain Resting-State Functional Connectivity," *Brain Sciences* 11, no. 10 (September 2021): 1263, doi:10.3390/brainsci11101263.

Exercise
A Guided Meditation to Instill Inner Peace

You will need:

20 minutes

a quiet place where you will not be disturbed

Turn off your digital devices. Settle into the meditative position you find most comfortable. You might sit in a chair, sit on the floor, or even recline. The important thing is that you are comfortable and your spine is straight.

Start by taking a conscious breath. Breathe in to the count of three, and hold for the count of three, then slowly exhale to the count of three. Do this twice more, and then on the exhalation of the third breath, shift your attention to the top of your head and consciously relax your scalp and tips of your ears. Relax your face as you allow your eyelids to relax and release. Let go of all the tension in your cheeks and jaw. Open your mouth if you need to in order to allow it to relax and soften. Breathe, and as the breath fills your lungs, peace begins to fill your center. You feel it as a glowing energy that fills your chest and brings you comfort. Use the ability to visualize by seeing this energy glow and grow brighter. Breathe and as your breath fills your body, notice the energy grow and get brighter as it sends a peaceful feeling flowing through your chest, over your shoulders, into your neck, and down your arms. The warm feeling loosens and relaxes each muscle as it flows through your body. It relaxes and softens until there is no tension held anywhere … All is relaxed.

With your next breath you notice a soft white energy has begun to form just above you. You move your awareness to it as it gathers to press around you. It is the infinite creative energy of the universe drawing to you … It gathers and swirls around you, like a gentle cloud moving all around your body. With cool light, this energy softly encompasses you in a great cocoon. You feel lighter and more relaxed as the loving energy nurtures and revitalizes the energy of your aura, filling you with a pleasant floaty feeling. All your worries melt away. You feel so relaxed, you smile, and as you bask in the glow of the healing energy, your heart fills with gratitude for all the positive things happening in your life. You are happy. You are healthy. You are safe. Peace is yours. Peace in yours. Peace is yours.

Relax in the glowing light as long as you would like to. When you are ready to enter this reality, wiggle your fingers and toes, before you slowly open your eyes.

Discover the Power of Gratitude

Many modern people spend a lot of time and energy longing for things they do not have. This longing creates a lot of dissatisfaction. If we set our sights on the goodness of life, we elude the doldrums and become appreciative. It is in these small moments of sitting with a heart filled with gratitude that we can experience the swell of joy. Having a heart filled with gratitude nourishes the soul. The simple act of being grateful can transform you into a happier person, and in turn will make others happy to be around you.

Exercise
Keep a Gratitude Journal

Nurturing gratitude is nurturing happiness. Regularly expressing gratitude cultivates a positive attitude.

You will need:
notebook or journal
pen
15 minutes every day to do this exercise

Schedule in a time when you can write for 15 minutes each day. First thing in the morning as you drink your coffee or last thing at night as you get ready for bed work well. Open your journal and write down something you are grateful for and why, or write about a positive experience and how it affected the way you felt. Allow yourself to be grateful for what you have. We have so many things to be thankful for, and yet they are often overlooked as we set our attention on longing for the things we want. Give thanks for the positive people in your life. Give thanks for your health, for the food in your kitchen, for the comforts of your home.

When you have finished with your entry, draw a meditative breath or two as you allow your feelings of gratitude to fill your heart. When you are ready, smile and thank the universe for all that is positive in your life.

Exercise
Employ an Affirmation to Embrace Positivity

At the beginning of 2021, I adopted the habit of looking in the mirror each morning and smiling as I said, "Today is a beautiful day!" Though it was only a simple gesture, when performed purposefully and repeated every morning, the affirmation served as an anchor to make the business of my day more manageable and so much more positive.

Words have power! Using an affirmation is a way to reprogram the subconscious to think differently and to automatically react in a more positive way. The word *affirmation* comes from the Latin *affirmare*, which simply means "to make steady" or "strengthen."[13] When we affirm something positive, taking the time to believe it as we say it out loud, it works on our mood and outlook on a subconscious level. Simply put, your brain believes what it hears.

It's so simple to do. In the morning while you are brushing your teeth or fixing your hair, pause to look at yourself in the mirror and smile. Smiling itself is a trigger to boost your mood and lower stress.[14] Say your affirmation and believe it. Repeat your affirmation throughout the day to reinforce it.

The positive language of an affirmation has the power to elevate mood and change outlook. Craft your own affirmation using positive language set in the present tense. For example, statements such as "I am happy," "I have all that I need," "Today is a good day," "All good things come to me," "I am healthy, wealthy, and

13. Online Etymology Dictionary, "affirmation (n.)," accessed November 23, 2022, https://www.etymonline.com/word/affirmation#etymonline_v_26048.

14. Nicole Spector, "Smiling Can Trick Your Brain into Happiness—and Boost Your Health," NBC News, November 28, 2017, https://www.nbcnews.com/better/health/smiling-can-trick-your-brain-happiness-boost-your-health-ncna822591.

wise," and "Creative energy surges through me" are all powerful affirmations that can help you keep your positive mindset.

Recurring patterns mold our subconscious. They create patterns of thought that result in predictable behaviors. Our mindset determines how we relate to the world. By crafting an affirmation and saying it to ourselves daily, we gain another tool to create positivity.

Chapter 5

ADDING THE MAGICK

You've written your formula and collected your items. Now it's time to add the magick. It is important to remember the first part of that magickal energy comes from *you*. The thoughts coursing through your mind and your actions of gathering, chopping, mixing, and grinding all become a part of the energy structure of the formula. Be present. Fix your thoughts so that they influence the work you are doing. Fuel the process with the energy of your body, with your breath, with your voice. Focus your intention into the formula so that it becomes more than just a mixture.

To Set an Intention

An intention is a power phrase that represents your goal. A powerful intention is one that is clear and concise. It is something you can focus on and believe in. When you set an intention at the start of making any formula, your intention directs your will and energy so that the work is focused on manifesting your goal.

As you begin to make a formula, think about what you want the formula to accomplish. The answer is your intention. Simplify it into a clear, concise statement as though you have already gained it. An intention to heal would be stated as "I am well" or "She is healed." An intention to empower would sound like "I am blessed," "I am happy," "I am whole," "It is mine," "Victory is mine," or "I succeed."

A compelling intention would be something like "She likes me," "She accepts this," or "We all get along."

While the herbs in a formula contain properties to accomplish your goal, part of the energy comes from you. It is fueled by your concentrated thought and will, by the motion of your actions as you gather, measure, and stir. State your intention and then pour positive energy directly into the formula as you craft it. Your observations and beliefs influence its power. Focus on your intention as you gather the ingredients. Compound this power by voicing it. Speak to each herb as you work with it. Tell each herb what you want it to contribute to the formula and thank it for its goodness. I include this step for several reasons. Adding your voice strengthens the magickal programming. It also acts as a psychological trigger. The brain believes what it hears. When we voice something, the words act as a form of self-hypnosis to gain a desired reaction. And remember, you are crafting these recipes for your wellness. Don't craft them half-heartedly. Invest your energy. This is your time to weave your energy, will, and intent, with the energy of the ingredients to make it magickal. You can chant or even sing if you'd like. Do whatever feels right to empower your magickal creation. The more engaged you become in the process, the more energy your formula will have to align with your goal.

When you have finished, concentrate the energy into the formula by writing your intention out on the label. Words have power.

Consider the Other Energies Present

Magickal energy is everywhere, in every aspect of the universe. It is in objects. It is in the hour. It is in the day of the week. Magickal energy is in the moon and the sun and the stars. It is in the earth, the air, fire, and water. Learning to sense it, name it, and apply it is magickal knowledge that will fuel your formulas and make them more predictable. When you consciously acknowledge the energies that are present and align your intention with them, the energies support and fuel your work, transforming the effort into an act of real magick!

The Magick Moon

At its most basic, moon magick can be broken down to this: If the moon is waxing, you should call what you desire. If it is waning, you should push away what you wish to banish. Or as Pliny the Elder, the first-century Roman naturalist, noted in his *Natural History*, the moon "replenishes the earth; when she approaches it, she fills all bodies, while, when she recedes, she empties them."[15] Apply this law when you craft your formulas to align the moon's energy to your work.

The New Moon

This is the beginning of the moon cycle when the first sliver of moon is visible in the night sky. This is the time when the moon's energy is beginning to build for gain and increase. Use its energy to invoke new beginnings and inspire new projects with creative energy. Set an intention to plant the seed for things you want to manifest later in the month.

A second new moon in a month is called a black moon, which is more powerful than the first in the cycle. Intentions set at this time will manifest more quickly.

The Waxing Moon

This is when the moon appears to be growing larger in the sky. This moon holds energy to heal and grow. Use it to build self-esteem, enhance beauty, and empower work for growth and development. When the moon is waxing, work to build up whatever it is you are striving to create. Use this moon to manifest anything you wish to bring into your life. If you had set an intention at the new moon, now is the time to do the work to move your plan forward.

The Full Moon

This is when the maximum surface of the moon is illuminated. Now is the time to manifest your desires, as this is when the moon is at the height of its power. Under its light you can work practical magicks to build, summon, create, grow, and expand. Use this moon's energy to draw opportunity and positive energy into your life. The seeds planted at the new moon should be coming to fruition under the light of the full moon.

. . . .

15. Pliny the Elder, *Natural History: The Empire in the Encyclopedia*, trans. John Bostock and Henry T. Riley (London: H. G. Bohn, 1855; Perseus Digital Library), bk. 2, ch. 102, http://www.perseus.tufts.edu/hopper/text?doc=Perseus%3Atext%3A1999.02.0137%3Abook%3D2%3Achapter%3D102.

The blue moon is the name for the second full moon in a month. It is a powerful time to manifest spells begun at the new moon.

The Waning Moon

This is when the moon appears to decrease, and as the energy shifts, so does our focus. Now instead of drawing something to ourselves, we use the energy to push away things from our life. This moon will support efforts to bind, banish, release, and cleanse. Use this moon's energy to banish negative influences, addictive behaviors, and harmful energies. Do work for protection, to remove problems, to neutralize your adversaries, or protect you, your home, and your loved ones. Now is also a good time for reflection, meditation, and study.

The Dark Moon

This is when there is no moon visible in the night sky. The dark moon is a deeply magickal liminal phase associated with the womb. It is often a time of rest and reflection, as this is when the moon is at its lowest point of power. The energy of this moon is quiet and very receptive. The dark moon will support work to release, banish, clear away, and break a curse, as well as hex work.

The Energy of Each Day

The days of the week are named after the seven luminaries, or the planets that were visible to the naked eye: the sun, the moon, Mars, Mercury, Jupiter, Venus, and Saturn. When Rome fell, the names evolved from dies Solis, dies Lunae, dies Martis, dies Mercurii, dies Jovis, dies Veneris, and dies Saturni to reflect local language and gods.[16] Today in English the days are named after the sun, the moon, Tiw (the Anglo-Saxon god of war), Woden (the Anglo-Saxon god-king), Thor (the Norse god of storms), Frigga (Norse goddess of the home), and Saturn (the Roman god kept this day).

. . . .

16. "Origin of Day Names," *Old Farmer's Almanac*, November 12, 2021, https://www.almanac.com/origin-day -names.

Sunday

Sunday was named after the sun god Sol or Helios. The phrase for the day is "The sky is the limit!" Use this strong, vibrant, harmonious energy to bolster good health, manifest your dreams, advance your career, and fortify personal achievements. Sunday's strong masculine energy makes anything possible. Sundays are generous power days. Use the energy for work to increase happiness, health, and general prosperity.

Monday

Monday belongs to the moon and is ruled by the moon goddesses Luna and Selene. The phrase for the day is "It's a mystic Monday." Work today to bolster well-being, expand your intuition, instill harmony, attract love, or inspire your inner muse. Work some bath magick, craft a potion, or do some divination. Monday's fertile feminine energy is all about intuition and emotion. Use it to grant clarity and fuel aspirations of the heart.

Tuesday

Named after the planet Mars (Aries) in Roman times, Tuesday's phrase for the day is "We are the warriors!" Tuesday brims with strong masculine warrior energy for leadership, strength, courage, passion, and combat. Tuesdays are all about action. Use this energy to support work for success through action. Tuesday holds a fiery energy to empower baking and candle magick and to work with sacred smoke. Use this force to fix problems, deal with trouble, launch a new venture, or drive off an attack.

Wednesday

Wednesday, as dies Mercurii, was named after the planet Mercury (Hermes). The phrase for the day is "To pursue knowledge and practice wisdom." Wednesday's energy will benefit any work of expression. Write that speech, work on your essay, write in your journal, or send that letter off to a friend. Use the energy to send, enhance, or fix any communication. It will empower all work regarding messages, study, and travel.

Thursday

Thursday was once named after the planet Jupiter (Zeus). The phrase for the day is "Good fortune smiles upon me!" Craft a healing formula, work in your garden, and invest some time nurturing your spirituality. Thursdays brim with benevolent energy to manifest healing, abundance, and growth. This day's energy supports work for increase. Use it to manifest good health, prosperity, expansion, success, and luck.

Friday

In ancient Rome, Friday was named after the planet Venus (Aphrodite). The phrase for the day is "Beauty, joy, and love be with you." Take a beauty bath, craft a new scent, work in your garden, or bake a sweet treat for someone you love. Fridays brim with love energy for relationships, family, attraction, and beauty. Use this energy to fuel work for affection, friendship, trust, healing, and protection.

Saturday

Saturday was named after the planet Saturn (Cronus). The phrase for the day is "Forgive, learn the lesson, and forge ahead." Saturn has a reputation for setting boundaries and healing through tricky life lessons. Work to release and renew. Use this energy to aid the sick, restore what is blocked, find peace, or deal with issues that are restricting you. Saturday's energy will fortify any work around the home. Work in the garden, fix things around the house, or complete a forgotten chore. Saturn will also support work for self-preservation. Use this energy to fuel work for protection, remove an obstacle, or bind a troublemaker.

Part 2

Formulas and Exercises to Improve Specific Mood Disorders

Chapter 6

POSITIVITY

The best way I know to embrace positivity is to narrow my vision to my small corner of the world, be present, and let my heart swell with gratitude for all the good things around me. When I hold gratitude, my outlook becomes brighter. It is a very simple shift, but it holds a powerful magick. Just let go of all the chaos in the big world picture. Move your focus to the good things in your life. Be present to savor the pleasurable moments: the wonderful scent and flavor of your morning coffee; the luxury of a long, hot shower; the comfort of your kitchen at mealtime; the amazing beauty of nature outside your door.

Five Must-Have Herbs for Positivity
Chamomile, hawthorn, lavender, lemon balm, and rose

Five Must-Have Essential Oils for Positivity
Frankincense, grapefruit, sweet orange, peppermint, and pine

Gratitude

When we are distracted, life happens around us. When we are present, we can soak in the wonder and beauty we encounter. Being present to take in the good things around us cultivates a spirit of gratitude. Holding gratitude nourishes the soul and creates space for peace to grow. It is in these small moments of sitting with a heart filled with gratitude that we can experience the swell of joy, as we elude the doldrums and set our sights on the goodness of life. Several studies have shown that the simple act of being grateful can transform one into a happier person.[17] This, in turn, makes others happy to be around you. Holding gratitude deepens spirituality, as it allows space to acknowledge and connect with deity and expands awareness of all that is magickal at work in your daily life just out of sight.

Exercise

Gratitude Meditation

It is difficult to be in a bad mood if you are holding gratitude in your heart. When we make it a regular practice to appreciate the good things in life, no matter how big or small, it improves our well-being and reduces the effects of stress.

You will need:
candle
matches
journal
pen

. . . .

17. Robert A. Emmons and Michael E. McCullough, "Counting Blessings versus Burdens: An Experimental Investigation of Gratitude and Subjective Well-Being in Daily Life," *Journal of Personality and Social Psychology* 84, no. 2 (February 2003): 377–89, doi:10.1037//0022-3514.84.2.377; Jeffrey J. Froh, William J. Sefick, and Robert A. Emmons, "Counting Blessings in Early Adolescents: An Experimental Study of Gratitude and Subjective Well-Being," *Journal of School Psychology* 46, no. 2 (April 2008): 213–33, doi:10.1016/j.jsp .2007.03.005; Álvaro Tala, "Gracias por todo: Una revisión sobre la gratitud desde la neurobiología a la clínica [Thanks for everything: a review on gratitude from neurobiology to clinic]," *Revista Medica de Chile* 147, no. 6 (2019): 755–61, doi:10.4067/S0034-98872019000600755.

Settle into a comfortable position and set the candle where you can view it. Light the candle and take a deep breath. Draw your thoughts in. When you are present, open your journal and make a list of everything you are thankful for. Take a moment to thank whoever is responsible for providing you with that blessing. You may write it down or say it out loud.

When you are ready to conclude the exercise, take a deep breath and close your eyes. Bring your focus to your center and let your mind fall quiet. Graciously acknowledge all the good things in your life and smile. Count your blessings and let your heart swell.

When you are bursting with joy, say,

Thank you for all that I have,
all that I am,
and all the potential I have to be.
Help me to be the person I am meant to be
as I put forth the effort to make this day a magickal one.

Smile as you sit with the good feeling.

When we express gratitude, our outlook shifts to hopeful and we in turn become positive, attracting the best things the day has to offer.

As you go about your day, keep your eyes open for reasons to say thank you. Make a conscious effort to respond when people do good things, whether for you or others. Tell the person you recognize their good deed and give a sincere thank-you.

SPOTLIGHT INGREDIENT
Lavender

Clarity, communication, healing, love, protection, sleep, and transformations

Lavender is an edible, attractive herb with pleasant-smelling aromatic oils that hold the power to soothe anxiety and lift mood. It is used to treat symptoms of stress such as irritably, insomnia, nervous stomach, and muscle tension. Its bitter, peppery flavor earned it a reputation as a seasoning. Lavender is an ingredient in the famous French spice mix herbes de Provence and is used to flavor everything from meats to jellies.

Lavender is also known for its powers of love and protection. It was baked into breads and sweet treats to inspire affections, hung to ward the home, burned to protect against the evil eye, and used to cure illness attributed to sorcery and malicious elves.[18]

When shopping for lavender, choose a culinary-grade product if you intend to ingest it. Other types may not be safe to eat.

Lemon Lavender Shortbread Cookies

Serve this at any friendly gathering to sweeten mood and elicit happiness.

Makes about 25 cookies.

You will need:

parchment paper

2½ cups flour (or 1-to-1 gluten-free replacement plus 2 Tablespoons corn starch)

½ teaspoon salt

½ teaspoon baking powder

2 teaspoons dried lavender, ground into bits

1¼ cups unsalted butter, softened

¼ cup honey

1 cup sugar, plus more to garnish

1 egg

2 teaspoons vanilla extract

2 teaspoons lemon juice

In a medium bowl, combine the flour, salt, baking powder, and lavender. In a mixing bowl, cream together the butter, honey, sugar, and egg. Scrape down the sides of the bowl with a spatula, then beat in the vanilla and lemon juice. Stir the dry ingredients into the wet ingredients, and as you mix, tell the batter what you want it to do. Mix to form a cookie dough. Spoon the dough onto a sheet of parchment

. . . .

18. Nancy Arrowsmith, *Essential Herbal Wisdom: A Complete Exploration of 50 Remarkable Herbs* (Woodbury, MN: Llewellyn Publications, 2009), 438–40.

paper and press to form into a log that is 2 inches in diameter. Fold the parchment over the dough and seal in a plastic bag. Place the bag of dough in the refrigerator to chill for at least 1 hour or overnight.

To bake, preheat your oven to 350 degrees Fahrenheit. Line a baking sheet with parchment paper and set aside. Open the dough and slice into ½-inch rounds. Place the rounds on the parchment-covered baking sheet. Sprinkle with sugar and bake 15 to 18 minutes, or until cookies are aromatic and golden in color. Serve to cheer. Nibble one with tea to shore up your positivity for the day. Share with a friend to improve outlook and brighten conversation.

For a fancier cookie, prick the edges with a fork to create a pattern, press with a stamp, or roll out the dough and cut into shapes.

Lavender Infused Honey

This infused honey is the perfect sweetener when you need an uplifting dose of positive energy. Makes 1 cup.

You will need:
2 Tablespoons dried lavender buds
2 Tablespoons dried rose petals
1 cup honey, preferably local, raw, unfiltered, and pesticide-free

Place dried flowers into a clean, dry jar with a tight-fitting lid. Cover the flowers with honey. Fill the jar to the top to not leave any air pockets for mold to grow in. Seal tightly and label the jar with the date and the name of the brew. If there is room, write your intention. Place the jar in a dark place for 4 weeks. Be sure to check on it every few days and give it a gentle shake as you reinforce your intention. Then strain the honey into a clean bottle. Use within 6 months of label date. Discard if any signs of mold appear. Add a spoonful to sweeten teas and to add cheery energy. Drizzle the honey over toast to sweeten mood and outlook. Use it topically on small burns and bites to accelerate healing, or take it during cold season to treat a sore throat.

Feel-Good Floral Infused Sugar

You will need:

2 Tablespoons dried violet flowers

2 Tablespoons dried lavender

2 Tablespoons dried rose petals

16-ounce jar with a tight-fitting lid

1½ cups sugar

In a small bowl, mix the flowers together to combine. To a clean, dry jar, add ¼ of the flower mixture. Top with sugar and add another layer of dried flowers. Top with sugar and repeat until all the flower mixture is covered in sugar. Seal the jar with the lid and shake to mix the floral mixture throughout the sugar. Label the jar with name and date and, if there is room, add your intention. Set the jar on a cool, dark shelf for 3 or 4 weeks. Use the sugar to sweeten tea or coffee to add energy for a positive outlook. Add it to whipping cream and use it to top fresh fruit for a posh and luxurious treat to brighten mood and bring cheer. Or measure a couple of spoons of the floral sugar into a small bowl. Add several drops of olive oil and mix to incorporate. Use the mixture as a sugar scrub for soft, vibrant skin.

Recipes to Encourage Positivity

Festive Autumn Berry Rum Cocktail

Enliven fall and winter celebrations with this festive drink. Begin the preparation in the morning to allow the mixture to infuse and develop the best flavor. This recipe makes 4 cocktails.

You will need:

3 Tablespoons hawthorn berries (dried or fresh)

4 Tablespoons cranberries (dried or fresh)

3 Tablespoons dried rose petals

4 cups water

1 orange, cut into thin slices

1 cinnamon stick

1 teaspoon grated lemon peel

¼ cup sugar

2 cups rum

Place the berries and rose petals in a large pan and cover with 4 cups of water. Set aside to infuse for up to 3 hours. Add the orange, cinnamon stick, and lemon peel. Bring the mixture to a boil, then reduce the heat and simmer until liquid reduces by half. Stir in the sugar until dissolved. Remove from heat and let cool. Cover the pot and let sit until ready to serve. For ideal flavor cook the mixture at least 4 hours ahead of time to allow flavors to concentrate. Pour the mixture through a fine sieve, reserving the liquid. Mix rum into the infused liquid and chill. Serve the cocktails garnished with orange slices and whole cranberries to enhance celebrations and induce a feeling of festivity. Sip them with friends to encourage happiness and comradery.

Hawthorn Berry Hibiscus Decoction

This bright summer drink is brimming with revitalizing properties to improve mood and inspire an upbeat attitude. This recipe makes 4 servings.

You will need:

4 cups water

2 Tablespoons dried hawthorn berries

2 Tablespoons dried hibiscus flowers

2 Tablespoons of honey

½ lemon

Measure water into a saucepan and add the berries and flowers. Heat to a simmer, then cover the pan and simmer the mixture for about 20 minutes. Turn the heat off and allow the liquid to steep for an additional 30 minutes. Strain out the plant matter, reserving the liquid. Stir the honey into the liquid and add a squeeze of fresh lemon juice. Serve over ice. Sip for a refreshing drink to perk up mood and instill an optimistic point of view. Add a sprig of pineapple sage to inspire kindness or mint to inspire creative thought.

Lemon Verbena Spritzer for Positivity

You will need:

spray bottle

2 cups water

1 handful lemon verbena, fresh or dried

Heat 2 cups of water until it comes to a boil. Remove the pan from heat and drop in a handful of lemon verbena. Cover the pan to prevent steam from escaping, and let the infusion steep for up to 10 minutes. Strain out the herbal matter and let the liquid cool. Pour the infusion into a spray bottle. Mist yourself to inspire an optimistic view. Spray the air above you and feel the mist gently shower you with positive energy. Breathe in the scent and allow your heart to open to adopt a brighter outlook. Spritz to help mitigate post-traumatic shock.

Positivity Bath

You will need:

4 cups water

½ cup fresh lemon verbena

¼ cup fresh orange peel pieces

1 handful fresh rose petals

Heat 4 cups of water until it comes to a boil. Add the lemon verbena and orange peel to the pan and remove from heat. Cover pan and let steep for up to 10 minutes. Strain out the plant matter and add the liquid to bathwater. Float the rose petals on the water and get in to soak. Let your heart open and fill with gratitude as you relax. Set your thoughts on all the positive things going on in your life and smile.

When you have reached a meditative state, say,

Here and now I release all that is negative as I enter the flow of All That Is.
My thoughts and emotions transform as my heart fills with loving kindness.
Pure power surges through me, filling my center with divine love.
I draw it tight as my being fills with joyous gratitude.

It transforms my attitude,
so that I am happy. I am joyous. I am love.
It is positive to be me.
Thanks be to thee.

Say this three times. When you step from the tub and pull the plug, visualize all the negativity going down the drain.

Herbal Formulas to Encourage Positivity

See page 18 for infusion brewing guidance.

Floral Happiness Infusion

You will need:

2 parts dried rose petals

2 parts dried chamomile

2 parts dried hawthorn leaf and/or flower

1 part dried lavender

1 part dried lemon balm

1 part dried passionflower

1 part dried skullcap

Sip the infusion to brighten mood and encourage a brighter outlook.

Energizing Blend

You will need:

1 part dried holy basil

3 parts green tea

2 parts dried violet leaf

Sip an infusion of this blend to boost energy, mood, and cognition.

Cheering Verbena and Borage Brew

You will need:

2 parts dried lemon verbena

1 part dried borage flowers

Drink an infusion to reduce fatigue, lift spirits, and encourage a cheerful outlook.

Make Me Smile Tea

You will need:

2 parts dried skullcap

3 parts dried lemon balm

1 part dried chamomile

1 part dried lavender

Drink to lift mood and encourage happiness.

Essential Oil Formulas to Encourage Positivity

The World Is Mine

You will need:

6 drops frankincense essential oil

3 drops grapefruit essential oil

3 drops peppermint essential oil

Mix the essential oils into a carrier oil of your choice and wear it as a scent to embrace your best self. Add the blend to a spray bottle of water and use it as a spritzer to boost self-esteem.

Calm and Confident

You will need:

5 drops chamomile essential oil

5 drops grapefruit essential oil

5 drops lavender essential oil

Add the blend to a spray bottle of water and use to spritz the air above you to boost confidence. Mix the oils into 1 tablespoon castile soap and add to bathwater for a luxurious soak to balance emotions and inspire self-esteem.

Happiness Blend

You will need:

7 drops neroli essential oil

3 drops chamomile essential oil

2 drops lavender essential oil

1 drop sweet orange essential oil

Mix the oils into a small bowl of salt. Pour the mixture under running water for a luxurious bath to instill feelings of happiness and raise vibration.

Feel-Good Oil Blend

You will need:

3 drops cedarwood essential oil

3 drops bergamot essential oil

3 drops lavender essential oil

3 drops rose essential oil

Mix the essential oils together and blend into 1 tablespoon of a carrier oil of your choice. Wear the blend as a scent to lift mood and encourage a brighter outlook. Add the blend to a spray bottle of water and use it to spritz a room to restore a calming ambiance.

Mood-Lifting Blend

You will need:

4 drops sweet orange oil essential oil

2 drops cardamom essential oil

2 drops cinnamon essential oil

Blend the essential oils together and burn in a tea light warmer to enhance mental well-being, or add the blend to a spray bottle of water and use it to mist a room to lighten mood. Mix the essential oils into a carrier oil of your choice to make a massage oil to banish anger and lighten mood.

Mood-Adjusting Blend

You will need:

4 drops grapefruit essential oil

2 drops cardamom essential oil

2 drops frankincense essential oil

2 drops pine essential oil

Mix the essential oils together and burn in a diffuser to chase away anger and restore peace. Blend them into 1 tablespoon of a carrier oil of your choice to make a massage oil to work into muscles to lift thought and encourage a brighter outlook. Add the blend to a spray bottle of water and use it to spritz a room to gain positivity.

New Point of View Blend

You will need:

3 drops coriander essential oil

2 drops clove essential oil

2 drops pine essential oil

Blend the oils into 1 tablespoon of coconut oil. Rub it into your skin to bolster your spirit before venturing out into the world. Burn the oils in a diffuser to stymie worry. Mix the blend into a dish of salt and pour it into bathwater for a relaxing and uplifting soak to foster an optimistic outlook.

Fresh Perspective Blend

You will need:

6 drops jasmine essential oil

2 drops basil essential oil

2 drops lemon essential oil

Blend the oils into 1 tablespoon of your favorite carrier and wear it as scent to inspire a fresh outlook. Add the oil blend to a spray bottle of water and use to spritz the air above you to stimulate creative thought, or burn it in a diffuser to open perception.

See the Positive Blend

You will need:

5 drops myrrh essential oil

5 drops sandalwood essential oil

3 drops clary sage oil essential oil

Blend the oils together and burn in a diffuser to gain positive insight. Add the blend to a small dish of salt and add it to a bath to shed negativity and embrace an optimistic outlook.

Positive Energy Way-Opening Blend

You will need:

5 drops nutmeg essential oil

5 drops bergamot essential oil

1 Tablespoon sesame seed oil

Blend the oils together and burn in a diffuser to usher in energy for opportunities. Massage the oil into your hands to find your way around obstacles. Wear it as scent to enhance well-being and regain a positive outlook.

Gently into the World I Go

You will need:

5 drops vanilla essential oil

5 drops ylang-ylang essential oil

5 drops rose essential oil

Blend the oils together and burn in a diffuser to foster positive emotions. Mix the blend into 1 tablespoon of your favorite carrier and wear it as scent to inspire feelings of kindness.

Chapter 7

ANXIETY AND STRESS

I don't know anyone who is not feeling some kind of stress right now. The world is in a chaotic state. The news is full of angry people, radical politics, war, and fears over climate change and food security. There is drought and famine and outbreaks of viruses like COVID and mpox. And it's not just the news. The high cost of living is stressing budgets and limiting options.

There is a lot of strife out there. It's enough to make anyone feel anxious. I carry the tension in my jaw, shoulders, and stomach. When I become aware of it, I draw a few breaths and relax my jaw and shoulders, but it takes a remedy like an herbal tea or a long, hot bath to ease a headache or calm a nervous stomach. Here are some of my favorite stress-relieving practices and formulas.

Five Must-Have Herbs to Alleviate Anxiety

California poppy, chamomile, lemon balm, passionflower, and St. John's wort

Five Must-Have Essential Oils to Alleviate Anxiety

Cedarwood, frankincense, lavender, melissa, and vetiver

Restorative Breathing

Breathing is a vital function that not only provides oxygen to the blood and to the brain but also allows us to control our emotions. Our breath, our thoughts, and our emotions are interconnected so that when we control the breath, we are also able to control the others. By simply focusing on the breath as it enters and leaves the body, the mind is able to fall silent as the psyche calms and awareness expands.

Slowly draw a deep, even breath in to the count of three. Focus on your breath. Follow it as it enters your body. Notice how your chest expands and rises. Notice how your body feels. Don't allow other thoughts to distract you. Keep your mind solely focused on what it feels like in this moment. When your lungs are fully expanded, hold the breath to the count of three. Then slowly release it, exhaling out to the count of three. This is the meditative, mindful, or conscious breath.

Do it again. Inhale. Focus on your breath as you draw air into your lungs. Notice as your chest expands. Allow the muscles in your head, face, neck, and shoulders to relax. If you are holding any tension, release it as you exhale. If a thought interferes, just notice it and let it go as you gently move your attention back to your breath.

Soon you will notice a deep sense of relaxation fill your limbs as your awareness begins to sharpen and expand. This is the meditative breath, and the more you practice the technique, the easier it will become.

SPOTLIGHT INGREDIENT

Lemon Balm

Friendship, happiness, healing, love, peace, and success

Lemon balm is an aromatic herb in the mint family. It is a nervine with the power to calm worry, soothe the spirit, and even ease a nervous stomach. Lemon balm's pleasant scent and flavor make it easy to brew and cook with. Add a spoon of lemon balm to your morning tea for a boost of gentle uplifting energy. Add lemon balm to pesto and pasta dishes or mince the leaves and add to bread, muffin, and cookie recipes.

A Simple Lemon Balm Infusion

You will need:

lemon balm, fresh or dried

Heat water until it comes to a boil. Measure 1 tablespoon of dried lemon balm into a tea strainer, or chop the fresh herb and use 3 tablespoons. Place the strainer in a mug. Pour 1 cup of hot water over the herb and cover to prevent steam from escaping. Let the infusion steep for up to 10 minutes. Remove the strainer. Sweeten with honey if you don't care for the flavor.

This infusion is calming. Sip it to relieve anxiety, balance emotions, and improve outlook. Serve it to console melancholy or comfort the brokenhearted. Use it as a toner to improve complexion. Or add the infusion to bathwater and soak to treat sunburn and accelerate the healing of skin irritations.

Simple Syrup for a Bright Outlook

Brew up a week's supply of lemon balm syrup to inspire a cheerful outlook. This recipe yields 1½ cups.

You will need:

1 cup fresh lemon balm leaves

1 cup water

1 cup honey or sugar

Rinse the lemon balm and place it in a saucepan. Cover it with water and bring to a simmer. Stir in the honey or sugar until dissolved. Remove from heat, cover the pan, and let the mix infuse for 30 minutes. Strain out the herb and pour the liquid into a clean jar with a tight-fitting lid. Take a spoonful whenever you feel sad or stressed. Stir a spoon or two into your morning tea to improve your outlook. Stir into an herbal sleepy tea to concentrate relaxation powers. Use the syrup to sweeten iced tea or lemonade and add energy for happiness. Add a spoonful to a glass of sparkling water for a refreshing lift. Store in the refrigerator for up to 1 month.

Be Chill Ice Cubes

You will need:

ice cube tray

1 part fresh lemon balm

1 part fresh mint

1 part fresh chamomile

Cut the herbs into small pieces. Fill each depression halfway with the herbal matter. Carefully pour water over the herbal bits to fill. Place in the freezer until solid. Float the ice in a glass of tea to add a calm, uplifting refreshment. Float in water and sip to revitalize. Run an ice cube over your face to alleviate fatigue.

Lemon Balm Poppy Seed Cookies

This recipe makes 16 cookies.

You will need:

1½ cups flour, or gluten free 1-to-1 flour replacement

½ teaspoon baking soda

1 teaspoon cream of tartar

½ teaspoon salt

2 Tablespoons poppy seeds

½ cup butter, softened

½ cup maple syrup or sugar

1 egg

1 Tablespoon lemon juice

1½ teaspoons almond extract

½ cup finely chopped fresh lemon balm

Preheat the oven to 375 degrees Fahrenheit. Line a baking sheet with parchment paper. In a small bowl, stir together the flour, baking soda, cream of tartar, salt, and poppy seeds. In a mixing bowl, cream together the butter and sugar. Add the eggs, lemon juice, almond extract, and lemon balm and mix to combine.

Stir the dry ingredients into the butter mixture. Mix until incorporated. Drop dough by the spoonful onto prepared cookie sheet. Press to flatten to ½-inch thickness and place the cookie sheet in freezer for 15 minutes.

Bake for 14 minutes, or until the edges of the cookies are golden. Snack on a cookie whenever you need a gentle lift. Serve at a friendly get-together to add to the feel-good energy.

Recipes to Calm Anxiety

Cup of Warm Comfort

This blend uses chrysanthemums. While all chrysanthemums are edible, some varieties taste better than others. All hold energy to foster joy and encourage a positive outlook.

You will need:

1 part green tea
1 part dried lemon balm
1 part dried hawthorn leaves
1 part dried chrysanthemum flowers

Mix together all ingredients and store in a clean, dry jar with a tight-fitting lid. Label the jar with the date and the name of the brew. If there is room, write your intention.

To use, heat water until it comes to a boil. Measure 1 tablespoon of the herbal mixture into a tea strainer and tell it what you want it to do. Place the strainer in a mug. Pour 1 cup of hot water over the herb and cover to prevent steam from escaping. Let the infusion steep for up to 10 minutes. Remove the strainer. Flavor the infusion with lemon juice or sweeten with honey if you don't care for the flavor. Sip to soothe a frazzled psyche, calm the spirit, and lift mood. Drink a glass whenever you need to ease anxiety or elevate your outlook.

Motherwort Infused Vinegar

Motherwort is a bitter herb that aids digestion and can be used to improve gut health. Herbalists Steven Foster and James Duke write in *A Field Guide to Medicinal Plants* that motherwort is found "to have antispasmodic, hypotensive, sedative, cardiotonic, diuretic, antioxidant, immuno-stimulating, and cancer-preventative activities."[19] Add it to vinegar and you get an age-old medicine to soothe a stress-induced upset stomach.

For this recipe, you'll need a jar with a tight-fitting nonreactive lid, as vinegar corrodes metal. If you only have a metal lid, use a rubber band to hold wax paper under the metal lid and act as a barrier.

You will need:
enough chopped fresh motherwort to almost fill a jar
unfiltered apple cider vinegar
jar with a tight-fitting nonreactive lid

Make sure the motherwort is clean and dry. Water will spoil the potion. Take a canning jar and loosely pack it with the chopped motherwort until the jar it is ¾ of the way filled. Add vinegar to the top and seal tightly, using wax paper underneath the lid if it's made of metal. Say your intention out loud and give the jar a shake.

Label the jar with the name of the herb and the date and, if there is room, add your intention. Place the jar in your pantry or set it somewhere it will be out of direct sunlight. Visit the jar to give it an occasional shake as you reinforce your intention. After 2 weeks, strain out the herbal matter by placing a cheesecloth or clean cotton dishcloth inside a colander and setting inside a bowl. Let the vinegar drain through the cloth, then squeeze the remaining liquid out of the plant matter as you thank the plant for the valuable essence it has given to you.

Pour the vinegar into a clean, dry bottle or jar and label again. Store in a cool, dark place. Discard after 6 months. Take a spoonful as a morning tonic. Stir a spoon of infused vinegar into a glass of water and drink it to balance a nervous stomach. Drizzle it over a salad or add it to salad dressing to add medicinal powers.

. . . .

19. Steven Foster and James A. Duke, *A Field Guide to Medicinal Plants: Eastern and Central North America* (Boston, MA: Houghton Mifflin, 1990), 182.

Eucalyptus Sugar Scrub

This sugar scrub will help balance and moisturize your skin as it gently exfoliates. Breathe deeply as you rub it into your skin to renew your youthful glow and shed your worries.

You will need:

½ cup turbinado sugar

10 drops eucalyptus essential oil

5 drops lavender essential oil

5 drops peppermint essential oil

2 Tablespoons melted coconut oil

Measure the sugar into a jar and mix in the oils. Seal with a tight-fitting lid. To use, scoop a small portion into your palm. Wet the fingers of your other hand and use them to scoop up a bit of the scrub. Do breath work to breathe out worry and breathe in peace as you gently massage the scrub into your skin. Message the scrub into your face and neck to gently exfoliate as you visualize shedding your worries. Rinse thoroughly with warm water and pat dry.

De-stress with an Herbal Milk Bath

Let your hair down with this historical remedy.

You will need:

1 or more candles

matches

6 drops clary sage essential oil

4 drops lavender essential oil

¼ cup milk

Set out the candle(s) to create a relaxing ambiance. Measure the essential oils into the milk and pour the mixture into the tub under the running water. Turn off your electronic devices. Light the candles, turn off the overhead lights, and get into the tub. Lie back in the water and draw several deep breaths as you draw your attention in. Follow your breath until your attention has fixed on the moment. Shift your attention to the top of your head and consciously relax your scalp and the tips of your ears. Relax your face and jaw. Open your mouth if you need to in order to allow it to relax and soften. Relax the muscles of your neck and shoulders. Draw another breath and relax your arms. Relax your back. Breathe and relax your legs and feet. Relax and breathe until there is no tension held anywhere. If a thought interferes, just notice it and let it go as you return your focus back to your body in the tub of water. Spend as much time as you like relaxing in the luxurious water.

Herbal Formulas to Alleviate Stress and Calm Anxiety

See page 18 for infusion brewing guidance.

Nerve Tonic Tea

You will need:

1 part dried catnip

1 part dried California poppy

1 part dried lavender

2 parts dried lemon balm

2 parts dried skullcap

Sip an infusion of these herbs to alleviate nervous tension and quiet racing thoughts. Sip before bedtime to induce sleep.

Infusion to Banish Restlessness

You will need:

1 part dried California poppy

2 parts dried lemon balm

1 part dried hawthorn leaves

Sip an infusion of these herbs to help banish worry and lift outlook. Pour an infusion into bathwater and soak to banish body aches and relax nervous tension.

Stomach Soother

Catnip is an herb that lifts mood and soothes both the psyche and the stomach. If, like me, you channel your stress into your stomach, try sipping a warm catnip infusion to simultaneously relieve anxiety and remedy digestive troubles.

You will need:

1 part dried catnip

1 part dried peppermint

3 parts dried chamomile

Sip an infusion of these herbs to relax an irritable stomach. Breathe deep and sip to melt away nervous tension.

Stress-Soothing Formula

The gentle action of these herbs works to reduce anxiety and lift outlook.

You will need:

4 parts dried chamomile

4 parts dried feverfew

1 part dried rosemary

1 part dried peppermint

Drink these herbs in an infusion to soothe away worry and quiet troubled thoughts. Drink 1 hour before bedtime to induce a sleepy feeling.

Stress-Reducing Blend

You will need:

1 part dried holy basil

2 parts dried rose

Sip an infusion made from this blend to relieve stress, cheer the heart, and restore a positive outlook. Serve it to the downhearted to comfort. Pour it into bathwater and soak to improve mood and reinstate hope.

Be Calm Brew

You will need:

1 part hops

2 parts California poppy

1 part passionflower leaf

Flavor this infusion with lemon juice or sweeten with honey if you don't care for the flavor. Drink it to soothe anxious feelings and ease worried thoughts.

Peace Be Mine Blend

You will need:

1 part dried passionflower

3 parts dried vervain

Sip this infusion to ease anxiety and quiet a worried mind. Add the infusion to bathwater to relax and unwind.

Tension Relief Blend

You will need:

1 part dried vervain

2 parts dried lemon balm

1 part dried skullcap

Sip an infusion of this blend to calm nerves and instill a peaceful disposition. Drink it to strengthen the nervous system and relieve tension headaches. Add it to bathwater and soak to remedy nervous exhaustion.

Oil Formulas to Alleviate Stress and Calm Anxiety

Breathe in the Calm

You will need:

5 drops myrrh essential oil

5 drops patchouli essential oil

5 drops pine essential oil

Blend the essential oils into 1 tablespoon of your favorite carrier oil and wear it as a scent to calm anxious feelings. Rub the oil into your wrists and lift them to your nose to breathe in the scent when you need a dose of calm.

Blend to Soothe and Elevate

You will need:
4 drops lavender essential oil
4 drops melissa essential oil
4 drops rose essential oil

Blend the oils into 1 tablespoon of your favorite carrier oil and wear it as scent to lift spirits. Add it to water for a footbath to restore energy and soothe the senses. Use it in a hair rinse to clear away anger and resentment.

Keep It Together Blend

You will need:
8 drops sweet orange essential oil
6 drops clary sage essential oil
2 drops chamomile essential oil

Blend essential oil with a carrier oil and wear to remain even keeled. Burn the blend in a tea light warmer to enhance mental well-being, or add it to a spray bottle of water and use it to mist a room to ease nervousness or dispel anxiety. Mix the blend into coconut oil for a salve that will banish worry and lighten mood.

Thought-Refresher Blend

You will need:
5 drops bergamot essential oil
5 drops lavender essential oil
5 drops oregano essential oil

Blend the oils together and burn them in a diffuser to overcome stress. Or mix the oil blend into 1 tablespoon of your favorite carrier and wear it as scent to calm racing thoughts and turn them optimistic. Mix the blend into 1 tablespoon of castile soap and add to bathwater for a luxurious bath to inspire action and vanquish feelings of apathy and lethargy.

Strength Be Mine Oil Blend

You will need:

5 drops bergamot essential oil

5 drops lavender essential oil

2 drops juniper berry essential oil

1 drop patchouli essential oil

Mix the essential oils into 1 tablespoon of your favorite carrier oil and use it as a massage oil to work into tense muscles when you need the resolve to deal with things you've been avoiding. Add the blend to a spray bottle of water and use to spritz a room to clear away anxiety. Burn the blend in a diffuser to restore peace and banish tension. Or add a few drops to a small dish of salt and add to it bathwater to chase away a tension headache.

Frustration-Releasing Oil Blend

You will need:

6 drops cinnamon essential oil

4 drops frankincense essential oil

4 drops sweet orange essential oil

Blend the essential oils together and burn in a tea light warmer to enhance mental well-being, or add the blend to a spray bottle of water and use it to mist a room. Mix the blend into coconut oil for a salve to banish frustrations and lighten mood.

Peace Is Mine Oil Blend

You will need:

5 drops jasmine essential oil

3 drops lemon essential oil

2 drops vetiver essential oil

Blend the oils together and burn in a diffuser to relax the mind and release nervous tension. Mix the oil blend into 1 tablespoon of castile soap and pour under running bathwater for a restorative soak. Dunk your head underwater to soothe away hurt feelings and elevate your outlook. Add the blend to washwater and use it to clean counters and floors to lift vibration and improve energy flow.

Blend to Fade Worry

You will need:

5 drops cedarwood essential oil

4 drops jasmine essential oil

3 drops vetiver essential oil

1 drop ylang-ylang essential oil

Blend the oils and burn in a diffuser to find comfort when your soul is troubled. Blend the oils into your favorite carrier and wear it as scent to avoid becoming anxious. Rub the blend into pulse points and breathe in the scent. Allow your chest to open and your worries to fade.

De-stress Me Now Blend

You will need:

4 drops vetiver essential oil

3 drops lavender essential oil

3 drops sweet orange essential oil

2 drops cedarwood essential oil

Blend the oils together and mix into 1 tablespoon of your favorite carrier. Wear it as scent to feel calm. Mix the blend into a small dish of salt and add it to bathwater for soak to quiet racing thoughts and encourage serenity.

Anxiety-Buster Blend

You will need:

6 drops clary sage essential oil

5 drops bergamot essential oil

4 drops juniper berry essential oil

3 drops patchouli essential oil

3 drops sweet orange essential oil

Blend the essential oils together and burn in a diffuser to enhance mental well-being. Mix the blend into a carrier and wear it as scent to reduce anxiety and shore up optimism. Add the blend to a spray bottle of water and use to mist a room to lift mood and elevate outlook. Mix the blend into coconut oil for a salve to lighten mood and restore a hopeful outlook.

Chapter 8

ANGER, BAD MOODS, AND DARK FEELINGS

Sometimes it's hard to be optimistic when there is so much anger and hatred in the news. Bad moods and anger are catchy. When we are exposed to a negative emotion, we often reflect it back. When anger or a bad mood threatens, brew up some magickal self-care to regain your positivity and hang on to your optimistic outlook.

> ### Five Must-Have Herbs to Banish Anger
> *Catnip, feverfew, lavender, passionflower, and St. John's wort*
>
> ### Five Must-Have Essential Oils to Banish Anger
> *Cedarwood, chamomile, frankincense, lavender, and neroli*

Shift Your Self-Talk

We each have thoughts running through our heads, a running dialogue that can be depressing or uplifting. These dialogues color our outlook and affect our mood. Notice when these thought loops begin and nudge them back to the positive. When you shift your thoughts to the positive, your whole reality shifts.

Next time you notice that your thoughts have turned negative, take control. Breathe out and give yourself a shake to free yourself from the thought loop. Close your eyes and draw a slow, even breath. As you inhale, say silently or aloud, "Be." Then as you exhale say, "Gone."

Stick the thought in a bubble or a balloon and visualize it floating away. See it float up into the sky. When it is gone, return your awareness to your breath.

If the negative thought still comes back, release it again, saying, "Be ... gone," and watch as it again floats away. Continue the imagery until your thoughts are calm.

SPOTLIGHT FOOD
Blueberries

Abundance, health, legal matters, luck, memory, money, prosperity, and protection

I love fresh berries and blueberries are one of my favorites. They are so good for you. Blueberries are a good source of vitamins C and K, manganese, and fiber. They are loaded with nutrients to fight free radicals that cause aging, cell damage, and cognitive decline.[20] A 2017 study concluded that eating flavonoid-rich food like blueberries improves positive moods within two hours of consumption.[21]

Blueberry Spinach Salad

This recipe makes 2 servings.

For the salad:
2 cups chopped spinach
1 cup fresh blueberries
4 ounces goat cheese, crumbled
½ cup sliced almonds

. . . .

20. B. N. Ames et al., "Oxidants, Antioxidants, and the Degenerative Diseases of Aging," *Proceedings of the National Academy of Sciences of the United States of America* 90, no. 17 (September 1993): 7915–22, doi:10.1073/pnas.90.17.7915.

21. Sundus Khalid et al., "Effects of Acute Blueberry Flavonoids on Mood in Children and Young Adults," *Nutrients* 9, no. 2 (February 2017): 158, doi:10.3390/nu9020158.

For the dressing:
½ cup olive oil
¼ cup fresh lemon juice
1 Tablespoon dijon mustard
2 Tablespoons honey
1 shallot, chopped
salt and pepper to taste

Divide the spinach between 2 plates. Top each with the blueberries, goat cheese, and almonds.

To make the dressing, measure the oil, lemon juice, mustard, and honey into a large-mouth jar. Add the shallot and salt and pepper and allow the dressing to stand for 30 minutes before serving. Shake and pour over the salads or serve alongside. Store any leftover dressing in your refrigerator for up to 1 week.

Blueberry Smoothie

Start your day with a nutrient-dense smoothie. This recipe makes 2 servings.

You will need:
1 cup blueberries
1 cup orange juice
1 banana

In a food processor or blender, whiz blueberries, orange juice, and banana until smooth. Pour into glasses and drink to fortify your mood.

Blueberry Cornmeal Cake

This simple rustic cake is wonderful as a dessert or a quick grab-and-go snack. This recipe makes 1 single-layer 10-inch cake.

You will need:
½ cup sugar
½ cup butter, soft
2 eggs
½ cup olive oil

½ cup maple syrup

1 Tablespoon vanilla extract

¾ cup sour cream

¾ cup ricotta

1½ cups flour, or gluten free 1-to-1 flour replacement

¾ cup cornmeal

2¼ teaspoons baking powder

1 teaspoon baking soda

1½ teaspoons salt

1 cup blueberries

1 Tablespoon coarse sugar

Preheat your oven to 350 degrees Fahrenheit. Spray a round 10-inch cake pan with cooking spray and dust with flour. In a mixing bowl, cream together the sugar and butter. Scrape down the sides of the bowl and them beat in the eggs, adding one at a time. Scrape down the sides of the bowl, then add the oil, syrup, and vanilla. Mix well. Stir in the sour cream and ricotta, stirring only to combine. Add the flour, cornmeal, baking powder, baking soda, and salt into a separate bowl and stir together to mix. Add the flour mixture to the ingredients in the mixing bowl and stir to only combine. Spoon the batter into the prepared cake pan and top with the blueberries. Sprinkle the top with the coarse sugar and bake about 70 minutes or until a wooden pick comes out clean. Let the cake cool for 15 minutes, then invert it onto a plate before carefully flipping it right-side up onto a cake platter. Serve to comfort or instill feelings of cheer and pleasure. Eat a piece to nurture yourself, enjoy the moment, or lift mood.

Recipes to Banish a Bad Mood

Brew to Ease Troubled Thoughts

You will need:

3 bay leaves

1 cinnamon stick

Pour an infusion of bay leaves and the cinnamon stick into a mug and sweeten with honey to taste. Hold the mug up to your face and breathe in the scent to calm troubled thoughts or wake intuition. Drink to alleviate stress or to calm a nervous stomach. Drink at the onset of a cold to ease symptoms. Add the infusion to bathwater to aid relaxation and help relieve muscle aches. Fill a spray bottle with the infusion and spritz yourself to awaken creativity.

Violet Leaf Infused Massage Oil

You will need:

violet leaves

olive oil or sweet almond oil

Fill a small canning jar with clean, dry violet leaves. Cover with oil, filling the jar to the top and leaving no air pocket for mold to grow in. Seal the jar and shake to mix. Place it on a dimly lit shelf. Allow the oil to steep for 4 weeks. Be sure to check on it every few days and give it a gentle shake as you reinforce your intention. When it is ready, strain out the herbal matter and store the oil in a clean bottle. Label the bottle with the name, the date, and your intention. Massage the oil into the skin to heal hurt feelings. Rub over your third eye to enhance psychic abilities. Blend a spoon of violet leaf oil into a small dish of salt and pour into bathwater for a soak to sweeten attitude and reduce anger and grief.

Spell: Banish an Unwanted Condition

As the light of the moon wanes, the energy shifts to support work to banish conditions you no longer desire. Be it a harmful relationship, a bad habit, or even a stubborn health issue, the energy of this moon will fuel your work to free yourself.

You will need:

black candle

matches

small piece of paper

pen

piece of yarn, string, or thread

jar with a lid

1 handful rue

sea salt

firesafe dish

Light the candle and come to center. Write or draw a symbol of what you would like to banish on the paper. Lean over the page and tell it what you want it to do. Blow across it. Roll the paper away from you to create a little scroll. Tie up the scroll tightly with string. Put it in a jar, drop in the rue, and cover it with sea salt. Seal the jar and set it where you can see it. Whenever it catches your eye, send energy to the jar to banish the condition from your life.

At the next dark moon, open the jar. Remove the scroll. The rue and the salt have been working to neutralize the power it held over you. Finish it off by lighting it with a match as you hold it over a firesafe dish. When the scroll has caught fire, drop it in the disk and watch as it burns. When it is reduced to ash, take the ash and the jar with salt and the rue and dump them at a crossroads. Leave an offering for the energy there to keep watch over the spell remains. When you are finished, walk away without looking back.

Old-Fashioned Milfoil Tea

Milfoil tea is an aromatic and tangy infusion used traditionally to treat melancholy.

You will need:
⅓ cup fresh yarrow flowers and leaves, or 2 Tablespoons dried
1 spoonful of honey

Place the yarrow in a pot and pour 2 cups of hot water over the top. Cover to prevent the steam from escaping and let the infusion steep for up to 5 minutes. Strain out the herb and stir a spoonful of honey into the liquid to sweeten. Sip the infusion to combat sadness. Drink it to improve outlook.

Energy-Clearing Bath

Rinse away the negative with a comforting bath. Pour the water over your head as you visualize your negative thoughts and bad mood washing away. This bath will also help you wash away the chaos of the outside world.

You will need:
1 Tablespoon chamomile
½ cup basic bath salts (see page 28)
clove essential oil

peppermint essential oil

lemon essential oil

1 white candle

eucalyptus essential oil

matches or a lighter

To begin, brew a cup of chamomile tea by infusing chamomile in 1 cup of hot water. Mix ½ cup of the basic bath salts with 2 drops each of clove oil and peppermint oil and 5 drops of lemon essential oil. Run the bath and strew the salt mixture under the running faucet. Anoint the candle with eucalyptus oil. Light the candle and get into the tub. Watch the flame as you sip your cup of chamomile tea. When your cup is empty, draw a couple of conscious breaths as you exhale the negative emotions you are feeling. Be sure to completely submerge to clear your energy.

Herbal Formulas to Banish Anger, Bad Moods, and Dark Feelings

See page 18 for infusion brewing guidance.

Be Happy Tea

Combine St. John's wort with California poppy for a feel-good infusion to lift spirits and chase away negativity.

You will need:

1 part dried St. John's wort

1 part dried California poppy

Sip a cup of tea made from these herbs before traveling to alleviate fears. Pour it into your bath and soak to unwind and clear away hostilities. Serve it to someone who is tightly wound to help them relax and find perspective. Drink a cup before giving a speech or facing a crowd to soothe nervousness.

Rosemary Rescue Remedy

You will need:

2 Tablespoons fresh chopped rosemary

1 cup water

Drink this infusion to improve circulation and enhance cognitive function. Drink a cup to remedy a headache or stimulate digestion and kidney function. Pour a cooled infusion into a spray bottle and use it to spritz away negativity and chase away gloomy thoughts. Pour the infusion into your bathwater and soak to revive a weary spirit.

Troubled Thoughts Be Gone Infusion

You will need:

1 part dried catnip

1 part dried lavender

1 part dried passionflower

Sip an infusion of these herbs to quiet thoughts, ease anxiety, or bring clarity to a misunderstanding.

Brew to Calm a Restless Spirit

You will need:

1 part dried St. John's wort

1 part dried lavender

1 part dried yarrow

Sip these herbs in a tea to relieve anxiety and soothe a restless spirit. Add an infusion to bathwater or to a footbath to treat nerve pain and hasten wound healing.

Infused Calm

This infusion is a gently calming formula with a pleasant citrusy flavor.

You will need:

1 part dried skullcap

1 part dried lemon balm

1 part dried lemon verbena

1 part dried linden flowers

Drink this blend to encourage a calm and positive state of being.

Keep My Cool

You will need:

5 parts dried peppermint

1 part clove

1 part cinnamon

1 part ginger

Drink a tea of these herbs to defuse anger. Add it to a spray bottle with water and spritz to balance emotions. Add it to bathwater and soak to strengthen resolve to break bad habits and overcome destructive behaviors.

Essential Oil Formulas to Banish the Negative

Headache-Banishing Blend

You will need:

3 drops bay essential oil

3 drops cypress essential oil

3 drops grapefruit essential oil

3 drops juniper berry essential oil

Blend the essential oils into the carrier oil of your choice and massage the oil into your neck, shoulders, upper arms, and feet for a de-stressing therapy to chase away a tension headache.

Fear Be Gone Blend

You will need:

5 drops bergamot essential oil

5 drops chamomile essential oil

5 drops neroli essential oil

5 drops sweet orange essential oil

Blend the oils into 1 tablespoon of your favorite carrier oil and wear it as scent to remain calm when facing new situations or to boost performance. Or mix the blend into a small dish of salt and add it to bathwater for an evening soak to chase away troubled thoughts and restore peace.

Blend to Banish Panic

You will need:

2 drops ylang-ylang essential oil

6 drops frankincense essential oil

2 drops lavender essential oil

Blend the oils into 1 tablespoon of your favorite carrier oil and rub it into your skin to avoid feeling overwhelmed. Wear the blend as a scent to avoid becoming panicky.

Blend to Guard Against Anger

You will need:

3 drops clary sage essential oil

3 drops lavender essential oil

3 drops sandalwood essential oil

Blend the essential oils into the carrier oil of your choice and wear it as scent to keep your cool. Add the oil blend to a small dish of salt and dump it into bathwater. Soak to banish resentment and frustration.

I Will Not Get Angry Blend

You will need:

5 drops coriander essential oil

5 drops bergamot essential oil

5 drops lavender essential oil

Mix the essential oils together and blend into 1 tablespoon of a carrier oil of your choice. Wear it as a scent to guard mood and resist becoming angry. Burn it in a diffuser to help you remain cool. Mix the oil blend into a dish of salt and pour it into bathwater for a relaxing and uplifting soak to restore peace of mind.

Blend to Diffuse Anger

You will need:

3 drops lavender essential oil

2 drops chamomile essential oil

2 drops ylang-ylang essential oil

Mix the oils and burn in a diffuser to release anger. Add the oil blend to a small dish of salt and dump it into bathwater to banish resentment and worry. Add the blend to washwater and use it to clean an area after an argument.

Aggravation-Banishing Blend

You will need:

7 drops rose essential oil

3 drops tea tree essential oil

5 drops vetiver essential oil

Blend the oils together and burn in a diffuser to overcome a stress situation. Or mix the oil blend into 1 tablespoon of your favorite carrier oil and wear it as a scent to calm racing thoughts and vanquish fears.

Blend to Banish a Bad Mood

You will need:

8 drops lavender essential oil

4 drops chamomile essential oil

2 drops frankincense essential oil

Mix the essential oils together and blend into 1 tablespoon of a carrier oil of your choice. Wear it as a scent to guard mood and resist becoming angry. Burn it in a diffuser to help you remain cool. Mix the oil blend into a dish of salt and pour it into bathwater for a relaxing and uplifting soak to restore peace of mind.

Blend to Banish Depression

You will need:

7 drops frankincense essential oil

7 drops lavender essential oil

5 drops sweet orange essential oil

3 drops clary sage essential oil

Burn this oil blend in a diffuser to lift mood and ease anxiety. Or blend the oils into 1 tablespoon of your favorite carrier oil and wear it as a scent to keep your outlook optimistic.

Blend to Release Negative Thoughts

You will need:

4 drops grapefruit essential oil

2 drops juniper berry essential oil

2 drops pine essential oil

Mix the oils into your favorite carrier and wear it as a scent to lift spirits and direct your thoughts forward instead of dwelling on the past. Add the oil blend to 1 tablespoon of castile soap for a soothing bath to calm frazzled nerves and banish worry.

Blend to End a Negative Thought Loop

You will need:

5 drops chamomile essential oil

5 drops neroli essential oil

5 drops sweet orange essential oil

Blend the oils into 1 tablespoon of your favorite carrier oil and wear it as a scent to remain calm when facing new situations or to boost performance. Or mix the blend into a small dish of salt and add it to bathwater for an evening soak to chase away troubled thoughts and restore peace.

Chapter 9

SADNESS

At some point, each of us experiences a period of feeling low. Just like death and loss, sorrow is a part of life. Sometimes bad things happen to bring it. Other times our feelings of sadness are triggered by something we are unaware of. Bad news, worrying about things we cannot control, stressful situations, loneliness, and even bad weather can bring on a bout of the blues. When your mood sinks, acknowledge it and take time out for a mood-lifting self-care ritual.

Five Must-Have Herbs to Ease Sadness
Lavender, lemon balm, mimosa, passionflower, and St. John's wort

Five Must-Have Essential Oils Ease Sadness
Cypress, frankincense, lavender, sweet orange, and vetiver

Go for a Meditative Walk or Jog

You don't have to sit in a yoga pose to meditate. Meditation can be done while you are walking through nature or jogging with your feet pounding out a repetitive beat. All it takes is being present with a mind that is engaged and focused on the moment.

For this exercise, turn off your phone and leave behind your other digital devices. The goal is to be free from distraction so that you may fully engage in the experience.

Begin your walk. Breathe deeply and open your mind to your senses. Focus on what you can feel, see, smell, and hear. Be intensely present. Notice everything. If something catches your attention, pause to take it in. Engage in the exchange. Allow yourself to respond with joy and curiosity. Take in all that is beautiful. Respond to the beauty with happiness and wonder. Breathe deeply, and with each breath, feel the energy swell. Feel the joy or peace flow through your core to energize your body and calm your spirit. Spend as much time as you are able soaking in the beauty of the natural world.

SPOTLIGHT INGREDIENTS
Hawthorn and Mimosa

Hawthorn: *Cleansing, cheer, faery magick, healing, protection, and wishes*

Mimosa: *Calming, cheerful, ease trauma, emotional balance, finding joy, hex breaking, love, and peace*

My yard is dominated by hawthorn and mimosa. The mimosa stands in the center of the front yard, shading most of it for most of the day. The hawthorns grow on the edge, with new ones sprouting wherever the berries fall. Both are medicine plants that I use in my formulas and my magickal practice.

Mimosa acts as a mild antidepressant. The bark and the flowers are used to make infusions and tinctures to improve mood, elevate outlook, and reduce brain fog. Hawthorn acts as a mild sedative. The leaves and berries of hawthorn increase circulation to reduce nervous tension. When combined, they create an uplifting feel-good formula to reduce anxiety, improve mood, and elevate outlook.

Hawthorn and Mimosa Infusion

When my mimosa tree blooms, I collect the honey-scented flowers and use them fresh with formulas to cheer and lighten mood. Jean Willoughby writes in her book *Nature's Remedies* that brewing an infusion of hawthorn leaves and mimosa flowers is helpful to "alleviate the heavy-hearted feeling many of us experience during difficult times."[22]

You will need:
2 cups water

¼ cup fresh hawthorn leaves and flowers

¼ cup fresh mimosa flowers (California poppies can be substituted)

honey to sweeten

Heat the water. Into a medium-size bowl, tear the leaves to help release their oils. As you tear them, say something like,

Plant of virtue, instill your healing energy to this brew.

Place the leaves in the bowl. Add the hawthorn and mimosa flowers and say something like,

Lovely flowers, add your power to this brew. With your gentle essence, infuse this potion with energy to cheer and comfort.

When the water comes to a boil, remove it from the heat and pour it over the plant matter. Cover and let it infuse for at least 4 hours. Strain out the herbal bits and sweeten the liquid with a spoonful of honey to taste. Pour over ice and drink over the next few hours to boost outlook and refresh mood.

Mimosa Hawthorn Happiness Tea

This infusion is a tried-and-true mood lifter. Brew up a batch whenever you need to adjust your outlook.

You will need:
1 pound young, green mimosa branches

1 pound hawthorn leaves and/or dried berries

. . . .
22. Jean Willoughby, *Nature's Remedies: An Illustrated Guide to Healing Herbs* (San Francisco, CA: Chronicle Books, 2016), 64.

Take a sharp knife and scrape the bark from the mimosa branches. Cut the bark into 1-inch pieces and lay the pieces out on a counter to dry overnight (this may take up to 3 days). Place the dried mimosa bark and hawthorn in a clean, dry jar and fix with a tight-fitting lid. Label the jar with the date and the name of the blend. If there is room, write your intention.

To use, heat 2 cups of water to a boil. Measure out 2 tablespoons of the herbal mixture and crush it to release the oils. Add the herbal mixture to the pan of water and reduce heat to a simmer. Cook for 1 minute, then turn off heat. Cover the pan to prevent steam from escaping and let the infusion steep for 20 minutes. Strain the liquid into a mug. Flavor it with lemon juice or sweeten with honey if you don't care for the flavor. Drink this tea to reduce brain fog and encourage a cheerful outlook. Drink it to lift mood and encourage happiness. Serve it to someone who is grieving to cheer and comfort them.

Mimosa Tincture to Heal a Broken Heart

You will need:

fresh mimosa flowers to loosely fill your jar
80–100-proof vodka to fill your jar

To begin, prep the flowers by removing anything that might be stuck to them and pulling off the stems. Put the flowers into a clean jar as you clean them. Pour the vodka over the flowers to fill. Make sure the flowers are completely covered. Seal the jar with a tight-fitting lid and place it in a spot where you will see it but also where it will be out of direct sunlight. Shake your tincture several times a week, checking to make sure the flowers are still completely submerged and the alcohol level is still at the top. Add alcohol if needed to avoid oxidation. After 6 weeks, strain the tincture through a cheesecloth into a bowl. Wring out the cheesecloth to express all the liquid, then dispose of the flowers. Pour the liquid into a brown glass bottle and label it. Take a spoonful whenever you need to improve your outlook. Add a spoonful to a glass of iced tea to lift sprits. Give a spoonful to cheer or comfort someone. Store the bottle in a cool, dark cabinet. Discard after 1 year.

Mimosa Flower Essence

You will need:

2 parts spring water

1 part fresh mimosa flowers

2 parts brandy or gin that is at least 80-proof alcohol

Pour the spring water into a glass bowl and add the flowers so that they float on the surface. Place the bowl in a sunny spot so that the solar energy can warm the liquid. Keep in mind there is lore that states no shadow should fall over the bowl during this time. After 4 or 5 hours, strain the flowers from the liquid. Pour the liquid into a clean bottle to fill halfway. Fill the bottle the rest of the way with the alcohol and label it. Store the bottle in a cool, dark place.

To alleviate sadness, take 2 to 4 drops by opening your mouth and dropping them onto your tongue. Add a spoonful of essence to a bottle of water and shake to mix. Take a sip up to 4 times a day to balance emotions and restore a positive outlook.

Hawthorn Leaf Acceptance Bath

You will need:

1 handful hawthorn leaves, dried or fresh

1 handful rose petals, dried or fresh

Fill a saucepan halfway with water and heat until it comes to a boil. Add the leaves and petals and reduce to simmer. Simmer on low for 5 minutes. Remove from heat and let the mixture cool. Strain out the herbal matter to make cleanup easier or add the entire mixture to a tub of bathwater to add gentle uplifting energy for acceptance. Get into the tub and relax. Visualize the water glowing with light, filling you with peace and love. As the light grows, let go of whatever is troubling you. Say in your mind or out loud,

I let go of (what you wish to release).

or

I make peace with (what you wish to accept).

Breathe out loudly as you breathe the thing out of your body, out of your thoughts, and out of your life. Say it as many times as you need to as you breathe deeply until you have let go of all the anger, resentment, or worry and there is only calmness at your center.

Recipes to Raise Spirits

Rose Petal Tea for Grief Relief

You will need:

2 cups water

1 cup fresh rose petals

honey to taste

Measure 2 cups of water into a pan and heat to a simmer. Drop in petals, cover, and simmer for 5 minutes. Strain out the petals and pour the liquid into a mug. Add honey to taste and sip to encourage acceptance. Pour the infusion over ice and drink to see past issues and embrace opportunity to heal. Pour into bathwater and soak to calm inner turmoil or soften a hardened heart.

Violet Syrup

You will need:

½ cup fresh violets

1 cup water

1 cup sugar

Rinse the violets and then separate each flower from its calyx, the green base, by twisting the petals off. Discard the green parts and place the flower parts in a clean canning jar.

Bring 1 cup of water to boil. Pour the hot water over the flower petals and set the jar on the counter for 24 hours. Pour the jar of violets and water into a medium saucepan. Stir in sugar and cook over medium heat until the sugar is completely dissolved. Strain out the flower bits and pour the syrup into a clean glass jar. Use the syrup to sweeten teas to add gladness. Serve it to lift the spirits of someone who is melancholy. Drizzle the syrup over cereal or fruit to brighten outlook. Store it in the refrigerator for up to 6 months.

Calm Acceptance Tincture

You will need:

1 part fresh motherwort, chopped into bits

1 part fresh lavender, chopped into bits

1 part fresh lemon balm, chopped into bits

80–100-proof vodka to fill your jar

2 or 3 Tablespoons honey

Loosely fill a clean, dry jar with tight-fitting lid with the herbs. Pour the vodka over the herbs to fill. The herbs need to be completely covered. Place the jar in a spot where you will see it but also where it will be out of direct sunlight. Shake your tincture several times a week, checking to make sure the herbs are still completely submerged and the alcohol level is still at the top. Add alcohol if needed to avoid oxidation. After six weeks, strain the tincture through a cheesecloth into a bowl. Dispose of the herbs. Sweeten the tincture with honey. Carefully pour the liquid into a brown glass bottle and label it with the tincture name and the date. Take a spoon-ful whenever you need help accepting something you are resisting. Take a spoonful to elevate your outlook. Give a spoonful to comfort someone. Use up the tincture within 1 year.

Gentle Support Massage Oil

You will need:

rose petals

sweet almond oil

Fill a small jar with fresh rose petals and cover with oil. Fill to the top, leaving no air pocket for mold to grow in. Seal the jar and shake to mix. Place it on a dimly lit shelf. Allow the oil to steep for 4 weeks. Be sure to check on it every few days and give it a gentle shake as you reinforce your intention. When it is ready, strain out the herbal matter and store the oil in a clean bottle. Label the bottle with the name, the date, and your intention. Strain out the plant material and sniff. The oil should be sweetly scented. Use it as a massage oil to soothe anxiety and support emotions. Roses have properties to soothe irritation and help the mind and body release grief. Use the oil as a foot massage oil to relax. Add oil to a small dish of salt and add it to bathwater to restore balance or your outlook. Discard after 6 months or at the first sign of mold.

Herbal Formulas to Lift Mood

See page 18 for infusion brewing guidance.

Consolation Tea

You will need:

2 parts dried chamomile flowers

2 parts dried hawthorn leaves and flowers

1 part dried rose petals

1 part dried lavender flowers

Sip an infusion of these herbs restore a positive outlook. Serve it to the down-hearted to comfort them. Pour the infusion into bathwater and soak to improve mood and reinstate hope.

Heart-Opening Tea

You will need:

1 part dried motherwort

2 parts dried hawthorn leaves and flowers

2 parts dried linden flowers

1 part dried yarrow

Drink this tea to support all matters of the heart. Brew up a batch when you need help breaking away from the troubles of the world and refocusing on the positive things happening in your community.

Cheer Up Brew

Use this blend to help overcome grief or when you wake up in a funk and need help lifting your outlook.

You will need:

3 parts dried lemon balm

2 parts dried hawthorn berries

1 part dried linden flowers

1 part dried rose petals

Sip the infusion for a relaxing brew that will gently ease sorrow and encourage peace. Sip it before bed to ease anxiety and encourage rest.

Gentle Calm Lift Blend

You will need:

2 parts green tea

2 parts dried passionflower leaf

1 part dried holy basil

1 part dried St. John's wort

Drink an infusion of this blend to restore a positive outlook.

Instant Mood-Lifter Blend

You will need:

4 parts dried skullcap

4 parts dried lemon balm

2 parts dried St. John's wort

1 part dried hibiscus flowers

Drink an infusion of this blend to lift mood and encourage happiness.

Flower Power Tea

You will need:

1 part dried rose petals

1 part dried chamomile

1 part dried lavender

1 part dried yarrow flowers

Sip an infusion to lift mood and adopt a brighter outlook. Serve at a friendly luncheon to brighten the day and inspire cheer. Serve to someone who is suffering to help them heal.

Blues-Busting Infusion

You will need:

3 parts dried lemon balm

1 part dried mint

1 part dried yarrow

Sip this infusion to brighten mood and encourage a positive outlook. Drink up to 3 cups a day when you feel a cold coming on to help the body overcome illness. Add an infusion to bathwater and soak to rid yourself of negativity.

Essential Oil Formulas to Lift Mood

Blend to Console the Grief-Stricken

You will need:

3 drops cypress essential oil

2 drops bergamot essential oil

2 drops oregano essential oil

Blend the oils the into 1 tablespoon castile soap or a small dish of salt. Add the mixture to bathwater and soak to help heal grief. Relax and breathe in the scents to reduce anxiety and improve mood.

Emotional Healing Blend

Juniper berry oil holds a calming and supportive energy to help a sense of well-being.

You will need:

3 drops juniper berry essential oil

2 drops clove essential oil

Blend the oils into 1 tablespoon of your favorite carrier and wear it as a scent to balance mood. Burn the blend in a diffuser to encourage emotional healing. Add the oil blend to a spoonful of castile soap and add it to bathwater to release past hurts and embrace acceptance.

Good Times Blend

You will need:

4 drops lavender essential oil

2 drops grapefruit essential oil

2 drops pine oil essential oil

Blend the oils into your favorite carrier and wear it as a scent to lift mood and become receptive for adventure. Burn the oil blend in a diffuser to lighten mood and instill cheer. Or add it to a small dish of salt and dump it into bathwater to chase away the doldrums and instill feelings of happiness.

Blend to Heal Past Hurts

You will need:

5 drops rose essential oil

3 drops thyme essential oil

3 drops yarrow essential oil

Blend the oils into 1 tablespoon of your favorite carrier and wear it as a scent to banish negativity and promote courage. Use the blend to anoint an amulet and wear it to find courage when facing adversity and to keep your thoughts cool and focused. Add the blend to 1 tablespoon of castile soap and dump it under running bathwater. Get in and soak to release anger, heal past hurts, and soothe aggravation.

Sorrow Be Gone Blend

You will need:

5 drops cypress

3 drops patchouli

3 drops sandalwood

Blend the oils into 1 tablespoon castile soap or a small dish of salt. Add the mixture to bathwater and soak to help heal grief. Relax and breathe in the scents to encourage acceptance.

Calm Acceptance

You will need:

5 drops sandalwood essential oil

5 drops frankincense essential oil

5 drops myrrh essential oil

Blend the oils together and burn in a diffuser to banish negativity and sorrow, or use the blend during meditation to gain insight or foster spiritual growth. Add the blend to a small dish of salt and add it to bathwater to shed negativity and embrace an optimistic outlook.

Optimism Blend

You will need:

4 drops sandalwood essential oil

3 drops melissa essential oil

2 drops jasmine essential oil

1 drop vetiver essential oil

1 drop clary sage essential oil

1 drop ylang-ylang essential oil

Blend the oils into your favorite carrier and wear it as a scent to lift mood and shore up optimism. Burn the oil blend in a diffuser to promote acceptance. Or add it to a small dish of salt and add it to bathwater to chase away the doldrums and instill feelings of peace.

Gloom-Buster Blend

You will need:

10 drops lavender essential oil

4 drops sweet orange essential oil

3 drops clary sage essential oil

3 drops frankincense essential oil

3 drops pine essential oil

2 drops rose essential oil

1 drop ylang-ylang

Blend the oils into your favorite carrier and wear it as a scent to lift mood and elevate outlook. Mix the blend into a small dish of salt and add it to bathwater to banish the blues and instill feelings of peace.

Chapter 10

REVITALIZING AND RESTORING

When you are feeling down, it's sometimes hard to find the motivation to make a healthy meal or get your body moving. Sometimes we all just need a rest day to replenish our energy stores. When low energy strikes, try some of these self-care practices to get yourself back on track.

Five Must-Have Herbs to Heal and Restore

Bay leaves, chamomile, cocoa, lemon verbena, and peppermint

Five Must-Have Essential Oils to Heal and Restore

Bergamot, cinnamon, eucalyptus, frankincense, and lemon

Mindfully Greet the Day

Adopting a morning ritual into our daily routine allows us to program our attitude to face the day ahead. This can be done by greeting the morning sun or even while still in bed. The important part is to take a moment to let thoughts quiet and the heart become receptive. Remember, meditation is a form of self-hypnosis. By developing a meditation practice, you create a zone for personal ritual. This is the true magick.

Repeat this while visualizing the love of the universe gathering in a warm, loving sphere of acceptance around you:

I greet the sunrise (day) with a joyous heart.
I am blessed. I am blessed. I am truly blessed.
Grant me the will and wisdom to be the best I can be,
a blessing to everyone I meet.
As I hold joy in my heart and spread the love,
thanks be to thee.

SPOTLIGHT INGREDIENT
Dark Green Leafy Vegetables
Abundance, clear thinking, good health, healing, and vitality

Dark cruciferous veggies are good for you. They provide nutrients our bodies need to keep our immune and detoxification systems running right. Not getting enough fruits and vegetables in your daily diet affects health and increases your risk of anxiety disorders.[23]

It's easier to feel good if your health is good, and there is no dispute that good health requires eating a healthy diet, exercising, and getting adequate sleep. Making diet, exercise, and sleep a priority gives your body what it needs to heal while reducing your risk of a variety of illnesses. Working more fresh fruits, lettuces, and vegetables into your meal plan will increase your overall sense of well-being, because when we eat food that supports bodily functions, it also balances emotions and gives us feel-good energy throughout the day. You don't have to eat your greens plain. You can sneak them into your morning egg scramble or whiz them into a smoothie.

· · · · · · · · · · · · · · · ·

23. Karen M. Davison et al., "Nutritional Factors, Physical Health and Immigrant Status Are Associated with Anxiety Disorders among Middle-Aged and Older Adults: Findings from Baseline Data of the Canadian Longitudinal Study on Aging (CLSA)," *International Journal of Environmental Research and Public Health* 17, no. 5 (2020): 1493, https://doi.org/10.3390/ijerph17051493.

Steamed Eggs with Sautéed Greens

To select your greens, look at what is in season. I use what I grow, which is spinach, bok choi, kale, Swiss chard, collard greens, and beet greens. This recipe makes 2 servings.

You will need:

2 Tablespoons olive oil

½ cup chopped onion

1 clove of garlic, crushed

4 cups chopped greens, stems removed from larger leaves like chard

½ teaspoon cumin

½ teaspoon paprika

pinch of cayenne pepper

salt and pepper to taste

4 eggs

crumbled feta or queso fresco

In a large sauté pan, heat the olive oil over medium heat. Add the onion pieces and turn to coat. Sauté until the onion is clear, about 5 to 7 minutes. Add the garlic and cook 1 more minute, then add the greens and spices, turning to coat. Cook until wilted and soft. Take a spoon and press the greens to create one depression for each egg. Carefully break an egg into each depression. Cover the pan and lower the heat to medium low. Cook for 5 minutes for a runny yolk or 6 minutes for a jammy yolk.

Serve hot with a topping of cheese.

Green Drink

This drink is so refreshing that it makes me feel positively sparkly after I've downed it. Green drinks brim with energy for vitality and success. Spinach is loaded with nutrients to fuel vitality and boost cognitive function. Drink a glass to empower your health, fuel your energy, and empower your mind.

You will need:

1 cup coconut water

1 cup ice

1 cup spinach

¼ cup holy basil or lemon balm (optional)

Put the ingredients into a blender and whiz until drinkable. Drink a glass to empower your day. Drink a green drink anytime you need a quick pick-me-up.

Swiss Chard Galette

Swiss chard is loaded with nutrients to power your energy, brighten thought, and reduce inflammation and blood pressure. Make this savory galette to inspire a good mood.

You will need:

3 Tablespoons olive oil

1 cup chopped onion

1 clove garlic, crushed

2 packed cups chopped Swiss chard leaves, stems removed

½ teaspoon Worcestershire sauce

1 Tablespoon dijon mustard

salt and pepper to taste

2 cups fresh ricotta

1 cup grated parmesan

¼ cup chopped lemon balm

1 galette dough (see the following recipe)

4 ounces goat cheese, crumbled

1 beaten egg mixed with 1 Tablespoon water to glaze

In a large sauté pan, pour in olive oil. Add the onion and cook over medium-low heat until clear. Add the garlic and cook until it has become golden brown. Add the Swiss chard leaves and sauté until the leaves are very soft and wilted, about 5 minutes. Stir in Worcestershire sauce and mustard, then remove from the heat and allow the mixture to cool. Season to taste with salt and pepper.

In a large bowl combine the ricotta, parmesan, and lemon balm. Mix to thoroughly combine. Set aside.

Preheat your oven to 400 degrees Fahrenheit. Line a large, clean work surface with parchment paper and set the dough on it. Roll out the dough as you would to fill a 9½- inch pie pan. Transfer the dough to a baking sheet by inverting it onto the tray and peeling off the parchment paper. Spread the ricotta mixture in a large circle in the center of the dough, leaving a 2-inch border along the outside edge. Top the ricotta with the Swiss chard mixture and the goat cheese. Fold the dough up over the filling to create a border that is an inch or so wide. If the dough tears, pinch it back together. Brush the top of the dough with egg wash and bake 45 to 50 minutes, until the crust is golden brown. Remove from the oven and let cool for 10 to 15 minutes before slicing. This will allow it to set up for easier slicing.

Galette Dough

This recipe makes enough dough to make one 9½-inch galette.

You will need:

2 cups flour, or gluten-free 1-to-1 flour replacement

1 teaspoon sugar

½ teaspoon salt

11 Tablespoons cold butter, cut into small pieces

8 or 9 Tablespoons cold water

In a mixing bowl, stir together the flour, sugar, and salt. Cut in the cold butter until it is evenly distributed. Add the cold water 1 tablespoon at a time and mix until the dough comes together. Gather the dough with your hands and shape it into a disk. Wrap the disk tightly in plastic wrap and refrigerate for at least 1 hour or overnight.

Remove the dough from the refrigerator and let it warm up for 10 to 15 minutes.

Recipes for Restoration

Fresh Minty Tea

Peppermint's sweet, pungent scent works to calm and refresh. Peppermint can soothe a troubled stomach, ease a tension headache, and help focus thought. Brew up a mug of this sweet tea whenever you need a comforting pick-me-up.

You will need:

1 cup fresh peppermint leaves

1 Tablespoon honey

ice

1 or 2 lemon slices

Heat 2 cups of water to a boil. Toss in the peppermint and remove from heat. Stir in the honey. Cover and let the liquid steep for 10 minutes. Strain out the herb and set aside the liquid to come to room temperature. Pour the cooled infusion into an ice-filled glass. Drop a slice of lemon or two into the glass and sip to brighten mood and restore energy.

Energizing Room Refresher

Restore your mood with the power of scent.

You will need:

¼ cup witch hazel extract

1 teaspoon vanilla extract, or 15 drops vanilla essential oil

4 drops sweet orange essential oil

small spray bottle

Place the witch hazel, vanilla, and sweet orange oil into the spray bottle. Put on the top to seal and shake to mix. Spritz the air in a room to energize and refresh. Avoid getting the spray near your face or eyes.

Revitalizing Foot Spray

You will need:

5 drops tea tree essential oil

7 drops sandalwood essential oil

5 drops lavender

¼ cup witch hazel

Measure ingredients into a small spray bottle and shake to mix. Spray it on tired feet to vanquish feelings of apathy and lethargy. Use it anytime you need to quickly revive your energy.

Simple Mint Spritzer to Wake and Energize

You will need:

1 handful fresh mint

Heat 2 cups of water until it comes to a boil. Remove the pan from heat. Take the mint in your hand and tell it what you want it to do, then drop it into the pan of hot water. Cover the pan to prevent the steam from escaping. Let the infusion steep for up to 10 minutes. Strain out the herb and set the liquid aside to cool.

Use the infusion as a refreshing hair rinse to lift the spirits and inspire creative thought. Add it to a footbath to relax the anxious and refresh the weary. Or use the infusion to fill a spray bottle and spritz the room to refresh the energy. Spray the air above you and feel the mist gently shower you with positive energy. Breathe in the scent and allow your heart to open to adopt a brighter outlook. Spritz yourself to awaken creativity, open the mind, and improve cognitive powers. Mist your place of business to attract customers and make them feel positive.

St. John's Wort Healing Massage Oil

You will need:

St. John's wort flowers

olive oil

Place the flowers in a small canning jar with a tight-fitting lid. Pour in the oil to completely cover the flowers, leaving no room for air. Cover with oil and seal the jar.

Set the jar on a sunny shelf and let it macerate until the oil becomes a rich red, about 5 weeks. Strain out the herb and rub the oil into aching muscles and varicose veins. Use it as a massage oil to help treat shingles or nerve pain. Rub the oil into aching joints or a sore back to reduce discomfort. Rub it into scar tissue or a mild sunburn to accelerate healing.

Smear the oil across the forehead to deepen spirituality during meditation. Use it as a magickal oil to anoint candles to empower abundance spells. Discard the oil after 6 months or at the first signs of mold.

Uplifting Restorative Bath

You will need:

¼ cup sea salt

5 drops eucalyptus essential oil

3 drops bay essential oil

In a small bowl, mix together the salt and oils. Pour the salt mixture under running bathwater and get in. Breathe in the scents and relax. Fix your thoughts on the lovely sensation of being right there in that moment in your skin. Let all your troubled thoughts and tension melt away as you remember the joy of simple pleasures. If your thoughts stray, reinforce your need to be present by immersing your head under the water. Visualize the intruding thoughts rinsing away.

Herbal Formulas to Revive and Restore

See page 18 for infusion brewing guidance.

Kindness Tea

You will need:

1 part lavender

1 part hawthorn flowers

1 part rose petals

1 part passionflower leaves

Drink this tea to lighten the heart and relax the mind. Serve it to soothe anxiety or console the brokenhearted. Add the infusion to bathwater to lift mood and calm the psyche.

Immune-Booster Formula

You will need:

1 part dried holy basil

1 part dried holy hawthorn berries or elderberries

Sip a tea made from this blend to boost energy, elevate mood, and sharpen cognition. Drink it when you are feeling run-down or at the first signs of a cold as a preventive to boost immune system function.

Rev It Up Formula

You will need:

3 parts dried ginseng

1 part dried ginger

1 part dried lavender

Drink a tea of these herbs to fuel energy levels. Sip and savor it to regain your zest for living.

Sunny Disposition Formula

You will need:

1 part green tea

1 part dried lemon balm

1 part dried St. John's wort

Drink this tea in the summer over ice to refresh your outlook. Drink it hot in the winter with a lemon slice to energize and inspire. Sip this infusion as a restorative to combat seasonal affective disorder.

Vitality-Booster Formula

You will need:

1 part green tea

3 parts dried dandelion root

1 part dried skullcap

1 part cinnamon stick

Drink a brew of this blend to restore vitality and balance energy levels. Make a batch to treat exhaustion or remedy a night's overindulgence.

Essential Oil Formulas to Revive and Restore

Revitalizing Blend

You will need:

3 drops lemon essential oil

2 drops frankincense essential oil

2 drops eucalyptus essential oil

Blend oils into 1 tablespoon of your favorite carrier oil and massage it into your feet to renew energy. Add the oil blend to a small dish of salt and add it to bathwater for an invigorating bath to wake the senses. Burn the oil blend in a diffuser to infuse a room with feelings of calm and comfort.

Restoration Blend

You will need:

4 drops rose essential oil

2 drops chamomile essential oil

3 drops bergamot essential oil

Mix the essential oils together and blend into 1 tablespoon of a carrier oil of your choice. Wear it as a scent to lift mood. Add the blend to a spray bottle of water and use it to spritz a room to inspire a cheerful outlook. Mix the oil blend into a dish of salt and pour it into bathwater for a relaxing and uplifting soak to restore peace of mind.

Blend to Fortify the Spirit

You will need:

5 drops lavender essential oil

3 drops chamomile essential oil

2 drops bergamot essential oil

Pour 1 tablespoon of your favorite carrier oil into a small dish. Add the essential oils and stir to mix. Massage the oil into your feet after an exhausting day to relax and unwind. Or burn it in a diffuser to stop racing thoughts and chase away fears. Add the oil blend to a small dish of salt and dump it under running bathwater for a restorative bath to balance your emotions and lift your mood.

Magickal Mood-Lifter Blend

You will need:

3 drops jasmine essential oil

3 drops clary sage essential oil

3 drops grapefruit essential oil

Blend the oils together and mix into 1 tablespoon of your favorite carrier oil. Wear it as a scent to restore a positive outlook. Burn the blend in a diffuser to instill calmness. Or add the oils to a small dish of salt and add it to bathwater for a relaxing soak with an uplifting scent to brighten your outlook and lift your mood.

Blend to Brighten Point of View

You will need:

2 drops cypress essential oil

2 drops frankincense essential oil

2 drops ylang-ylang essential oil

Blend the oils into 1 tablespoon of your favorite carrier and wear it to brighten your thoughts. Burn the oil blend in a diffuser to infuse a room with feelings of calm and comfort.

Inner Peace Blend

You will need:

4 drops rose essential oil

3 drops grapefruit essential oil

3 drops clary sage essential oil

Blend the oils into your favorite carrier oil and wear it to boost mood and carry peace in your heart. Breathe in the scent to open your chest, unclench your muscles, and release nervous tension. Mix the blend into a small dish of castile soap and add it to bathwater for a luxurious soak to ease anxiety and dismiss worry.

Everything Will Be Just Fine Blend

You will need:

4 drops sandalwood essential oil

2 drops ginger essential oil

2 drops cedarwood essential oil

2 drops nutmeg essential oil

Blend the oils into your favorite carrier oil and wear it to support a grounded outlook. Mix them into coconut oil and rub it into your skin to boost positive energy and reassure yourself that everything is going to be all right. Mix the oil blend into ¼ cup of salt and add it to your bathwater to rinse away worry and foster hope.

Zen Blend

You will need:

3 drops cinnamon essential oil

3 drops neroli essential oil

3 drops sandalwood essential oil

Blend the essential oils together and burn them in a tea light warmer to enhance mental well-being, or add them to a spray bottle of water and mist a room to infuse the air with a mood-lifting aroma. Add the oils to a small dish of salt and dump it under running bathwater for a bath with uplifting energy to heal and restore.

Energizing Oil Blend

You will need:

6 drops lemon essential oil

4 drops peppermint essential oil

3 drops eucalyptus essential oil

Blend the essential oils together and burn them in a tea light warmer to energize thought. Add them to a spray bottle of water and use it as a spritzer to elevate mood. Blend them into a tablespoon of coconut oil and rub it into the skin to brighten mood and foster hope. Rub it into the feet to renew motivation.

Chapter 11

RELAXATION AND SLEEP

We live in a challenging time, and it is affecting our physical and mental health.[24] According to a 2022 survey by the American Psychological Association, Americans are so stressed about rising prices, future shortages, and global uncertainty that many have lost their ability to relax. Of those surveyed, 87 percent claimed "it feels like there has been a constant stream of crises over the last two years."[25] This prolonged state of stress has made it difficult to embrace our down time, but by stepping away from the big world picture, turning off the news, and drawing our attention into focus on what is going on around us in the immediate moment, we can find our way back to a state of calm contentment.

By maintaining attention and intention, we can relax into the moment and find our way back to joy.

. . . .

24. "Inflation, War Push Stress to Alarming Levels at Two-Year COVID-19 Anniversary," American Psychological Association, March 10, 2022, https://www.apa.org/news/press/releases/2022/03/inflation-war-stress.

25. "Stress in America," American Psychological Association, March 11, 2022, https://www.apa.org/news/press/releases/stress/2022/march-2022-survival-mode.

> ## Five Must-Have Herbs for Relaxation
> *California poppy, chamomile, hops, lavender, and passionflower*
>
> ## Five Must-Have Essential Oils for Relaxation
> *Jasmine, lavender, melissa, neroli, and patchouli*

The Hypnotic Flame

Since the dawn of time, the flickering flame has been used as a meditative focus to help meditators gain the ability to sit with the immediate moment.

Exercise
Relaxation with the Help of a Hypnotic Flame

You will need:
timer
candle
matches

Set the timer for 10 minutes. Light the candle and set it in a safe place where you can comfortably view it. Assume the meditative position that is most comfortable to you. Close your eyes and draw a long, even breath in to the count of three. Hold it to the count of three and then release it to the count of three. As you begin the next breath, open your eyes and focus on the flame. As your eyes rest on the dancing flame, breathe and relax the muscles of your face and jaw. If a thought interferes, notice it and let it go as you draw your focus back to the flame.

Watch the flame and breathe. Move your attention to how the muscles of your shoulders, back, and arms feel. Release any tension they may hold. Breathe and move your attention to your hips and legs. Breathe relaxation into them as you watch the flame. Continue to relax your body until there is no tension held anywhere and your body is in a state of relaxation from the top of your head to the bottom of your feet.

Sit with the wonderful feeling as you watch the flame. Breathe and let contentment fill your heart as you enjoy the quiet moment of being present in your body.

When the timer sounds, you will find that your thoughts have cleared, your body is relaxed, and you are at peace.

SPOTLIGHT INGREDIENT
Chamomile

Chamomile is a gentle herb. It is one of the oldest medicinal herbs, used by the healers of Egypt, Greece, and Rome, who detailed its use in their medical writings.[26] Today chamomile is used topically to accelerate the healing of skin conditions and is drunk as a tea to stabilize mood, improve digestion, treat body aches, and remedy insomnia.

A cozy cup of chamomile is a great choice when you want help relaxing. Its light floral flavor and pleasant scent make drinking chamomile tea an enjoyable experience.

Just Relax Infusion

You will need:

1 part dried chamomile

1 part dried California poppy leaves and flowers

1 part dried skullcap

Mix together all the ingredients and store the blend in a clean, dry jar with a tight-fitting lid. Label the jar with the date and the name of the brew. If there is room, write your intention.

To use, heat water until it comes to a boil. Measure 1 tablespoon of the herbal mixture into a tea strainer and tell it what you want it to do. Place the strainer in a mug. Pour 1 cup of hot water over the herb and cover to prevent steam from escaping. Let the infusion steep for up to 10 minutes. Remove the strainer. Sweeten the infusion with honey if you don't care for the flavor. Sip the infusion when you need to unwind. Sip it before bedtime to deepen sleep.

. . . .

26. National Center for Complementary and Integrative Health, "Chamomile," National Institutes of Health, last modified May 2020, https://www.nccih.nih.gov/health/chamomile.

Motherwort and Chamomile Relaxation Oil

Treat yourself or a loved one to a scented massage. Rub this massage oil into muscles to relax tension and soothe stress.

You will need:

1 part dried motherwort

1 part dried chamomile

1 part olive or sweet almond oil

Place the herbs in a clean, dry jar with a tight-fitting lid. Label the jar with the date and the name of the brew. If there is room, write your intention. Cover the herbs with the oil. Be sure all the herbal matter is covered. Do not leave any air pockets for mold to grow in. Seal tightly and place in a warm, dark place. Visit the jar to give it an occasional shake as you reinforce your intention. After 4 weeks, strain out the herbal matter and store the oil in a dark-colored bottle.

Use the oil as a massage oil to loosen tight muscles and relieve stiffness. Rub it into the bottoms of your feet to release anxiety. Add a spoonful of the oil to a small dish of salt and pour it into bathwater for a soak that eases nervous tension and melts away anxiety. Discard after 6 months or at the first sign of mold.

Herbal Sleep Aid Pillow

You don't have to drink hops to feel their effects. The scent alone has the power to induce relaxation and help you fall asleep. A sachet filled with hops and placed under the pillow is a traditional sleep charm to calm the nervous system and quiet the mind.

You will need:

fabric to make a small pillow in your desired size

needle and thread

2 parts dried hops, whole

1 part dried chamomile

1 part dried lavender

Cut or fold the fabric and sew the sides together, leaving an opening large enough to stuff the herbs through. Take a hop and say something to it like,

Bless my sleep and guard it from troubled dreams.

or

Grant a sleep that is deep and restoring.

Stuff the pillow until it is full, then sew it closed. As the needle dips back and forth through the fabric, you can fortify the charm by chanting something like,

By my will, this charm is crafted.
With the blessing of hops, a deep sleep granted.

When you need help falling or staying asleep, invoke the charm by blowing across it and saying,

Charm of sleep, cast your spell.

Hold the pillow under your nose and draw three deep breaths. Then tuck the sleep aid pillow under your regular pillow and relax. You can also add sprigs of rosemary and thyme to the pillow to keep nightmares at bay.

Take Me Away Chamomile Bath

You will need:
1 part chamomile
1 part lavender
1 part rosemary
1 part oregano
1 part thyme

Measure herbs into a saucepan and cover with water. Bring to a boil. Remove the pan from heat and cover. Allow the mixture to steep for 10 minutes. Add the infusion to bathwater for an aromatic bath to relax tension and calm the mind. Add it to a footbath and soak to treat aching feet and brighten mood.

Recipes to Relax With

Drink a Glass of Warm Milk

When I was a child, my grandmother would warm me a cup of milk when I couldn't sleep. Back then it was still a common practice. Milk is loaded with tryptophan, an essential amino acid the body converts into serotonin, the mood-affecting hormone responsible for stabilizing mood, making us feel happy, and regulating our circadian rhythm, or sleep and waking.[27] We get tryptophan by eating food rich in it, such as milk, tuna, and oats. Whole milk furnishes 732 milligrams of tryptophan per quart, while 2 percent milk provides 551 milligrams per quart.[28]

Relaxing Aromatic Footbath

You will need:

2 parts rosemary

2 parts lavender sprigs

1 part hops, whole

1 part sage

Measure 4 cups of water into a saucepan and heat. Add the herbs, and when the water begins to boil, cover and reduce the heat to a simmer. Simmer for 10 minutes. Pour the mixture into a foot basin. Adjust the temperature by adding cold water to cool it. The liquid should be comfortably hot. Sit on a comfortable chair and put your feet in. Soak for as long as it is comfortable.

Aromatic Relaxation Bath

You will need:

2 Tablespoons dried bay leaves

2 Tablespoons dried motherwort

27. Angelica Bottaro, "What Is Serotonin?" VeryWell Health, last modified September 28, 2022, https://www.verywellhealth.com/what-is-serotonin-5189485.

28. Dan Brennan, ed., "Top Foods High in Tryptophan," WebMD, last modified November 3, 2020, https://www.webmd.com/diet/foods-high-in-tryptophan#2.

2 Tablespoons dried rosemary

1 or more candles

matches

Bring 2 cups of water to boil. Add the herbs, and as you add each one, tell it what you would like it to do. Reduce the heat and simmer for 3 minutes, then turn off the heat and allow the liquid to steep for 4 more minutes. Strain out the herbs and pour the infusion into running bathwater. Light the candle or candles to create a relaxing ambiance. Turn off the overhead light and get into the tub. Lie back in the water and close your eyes as you breathe in the scented air. Soak to cleanse your energy of negativity, frustration, anxiety, and anger. Submerge to rinse away the negative emotions. Or just relax and breathe in the scents to lift your mood and renew your outlook.

Sleep the Night Through Formula

I don't have insomnia. My biological clock is set to close my eyes just after nine p.m. each night. Falling asleep is not a problem. However, I am afflicted with the maddening condition of regularly waking around two a.m., suddenly awake and aware. Even when I try to empty my mind and return to sleep, my eyelids pop open on their own accord, and I am left to stare at the ceiling as time for a restorative rest slips elusively away. In this brew, motherwort, passionflower, and lavender work together as a magick formula to end the affliction and encourage a deeper sleep.

You will need:

3 parts dried motherwort

2 parts dried passionflower

1 part dried lavender

1 Tablespoon honey

Sip this tea to gain a good night's sleep. Drink it an hour before bed to keep thoughts quiet throughout the night.

Herbal Formulas to Encourage Relaxation and Rest

See page 18 for infusion brewing guidance.

Cup of Calm

You will need:

2 parts dried lemon balm

1 part dried catnip tea

1 part dried chamomile

Sip an infusion of this formula when you need to unclench your chest. Drink a cup when your thoughts are troubled to adopt a brighter prospective. Sip before bedtime to deepen sleep and induce pleasant dreams. Add an infusion to bathwater and soak to dissolve worried thoughts and brighten your mood.

A Good Night's Rest Brew

You will need:

6 parts dried passionflower

4 parts dried lemon balm

3 parts dried chamomile

1 part dried California poppy

1 part dried motherwort

Drink this blend to soothe anxious feelings and ease worried thoughts. Drink it before bedtime to calm the nervous system, banish tension, and induce sleepiness.

Restful Blend

You will need:

1 part dried skullcap

1 part dried California poppy

1 part dried hops, whole

1 part dried passionflower

Drink this tea to promote a good night's rest.

Peaceful Dreams

You will need:

1 part dried vervain

1 part dried chamomile

1 part dried St. John's wort

Drink an infusion of these herbs before bed to end nightmares. Pour it into bath-water and soak to chase away worry.

Let Me Get Some Rest Blend

You will need:

1 part dried lavender

1 part dried chamomile

1 part dried passionflower

Drink a tea of this blend to soothe anxious feelings and alleviate insomnia.

Relaxing Hops Infusion

This is a simple tea that naturally promotes relaxation.

You will need:

2 parts dried chamomile

2 parts dried lavender

2 parts dried lemon balm

1 part dried hops, whole

Drink this infusion to induce sleep, enhance dreams, or simply wind down after a difficult day. Add 1 tablespoon of dried valerian root to quiet troubled thoughts.

Tension Tamer Infusion

This lovely flower tea promotes relaxation. Drink it to ease anxiety or unwind after a long day.

You will need:

2 parts dried chamomile

1 part dried California poppy

1 part dried passionflower

Sip this infusion to breathe out feelings of nervousness or anxiety and breathe in relaxation. Share with a friend to make conversation light and cheerful. Serve to someone suffering from exhaustion to soothe and comfort.

Relaxing Awareness Blend

You will need:

4 parts dried lemon balm

1 part dried holy basil

Sip an infusion of this blend to boost relaxation, aid digestion, and enhance awareness. Sip a hot mug during the dark winter months to help eliminate seasonal depression.

Sleepy Tea

You will need:

2 parts dried chamomile

2 parts dried passionflower

1 part dried catnip

1 part dried hops, whole

1 part dried linden flowers

Drink this tea to soothe anxious feeling and ease worried thoughts.

Essential Oil Formulas to Encourage Relaxation and Rest

Rest and Relaxation Blend

You will need:

7 drops lavender essential oil

5 drops oregano essential oil

Burn this oil blend in a diffuser to induce a restful sleep. Mix into 1 tablespoon of castile soap and add it to bathwater for a comforting bath to help remedy nervous exhaustion and help you regain a positive outlook.

Take a Deep Breath Blend

You will need:

2 drops clary sage essential oil

1 drop patchouli essential oil

1 drop rose essential oil

1 drop ylang-ylang essential oil

Burn the blend in a diffuser to fill a room with a relaxing scent. Blend the oils together and mix them into a small dish of salt to make a comforting bath soak to help the mind and body relax.

Grounded Tranquility Blend

You will need:

5 drops vetiver essential oil

3 drops cedarwood essential oil

3 drops juniper berry essential oil

Blend the oils together and mix into 1 tablespoon of your favorite carrier. Wear it as a scent to feel grounded. Mix the blend into a small dish of salt and add it to bathwater for a soak to relax and calm yourself.

Cheerful Rest Blend

5 drops chamomile essential oil

5 drops rose essential oil

3 drops vanilla essential oil

Burn this blend in a diffuser to fill a room with a relaxing scent. Blend oils together and mix them into 1 tablespoon of castile soap for a comforting bath to help the mind and body relax.

Blend to Ground and Soothe

You will need:

6 drops lavender essential oil

3 drops clary sage essential oil

3 drops ylang-ylang essential oil

2 drops bay essential oil

Blend the essential oils into 1 tablespoon of your favorite carrier oil and use it as massage oil to calm a racing heart. Massage the oil blend into the neck and shoulders to chase away a tension headache or ease muscle aches. Mix the oil blend into ¼ cup of salt and add it to bathwater to de-stress and unwind.

Relax and Smile

You will need:

3 drops lavender essential oil

2 drops frankincense essential oil

2 drops melissa essential oil

Blend the oils and burn in a diffuser to fill a room with a relaxing scent. Mix the oils into a small dish of salt for a comforting soak to help the mind and body relax. Add it to a footbath to treat aching feet and cheer sprit.

Get Some Rest Blend

You will need:

6 drops sandalwood essential oil

3 drops vetiver essential oil

2 drops neroli essential oil

2 drops coriander essential oil

2 drops ylang-ylang essential oil

Blend the essential oils together and diffuse to wind down. Mix the blend into coconut oil to make a salve to rub into pulse points for a bedtime ritual to get the mind ready for sleep.

Chapter 12

SELF-ESTEEM AND EMPOWERMENT

Self-esteem is a state of mind that affects how we feel about ourselves, what we are able to accomplish, and how others respond to us. According to the American Psychological Association, "A reasonably high degree of self-esteem is considered an important ingredient of mental health, whereas low self-esteem and feelings of worthlessness are common depressive symptoms."[29] When we build our self-esteem, we empower ourselves, build our resilience, and create positivity in our lives.

Nurturing a positive view of ourselves helps us see the world in a positive light. We are able to overcome obstacles and accomplish tasks we set our mind to. When we feel good about ourselves, we are on top of the world, we love ourselves, and the world loves us back. By taking charge of the way we think, holding on to our positive thoughts and dismissing the negative ones, we help cultivate a positive sense of self, build our happiness, and generally make our world a better place.[30]

. . . .

29. American Psychological Association, "Self-Esteem," APA Dictionary of Psychology, https://dictionary.apa .org/self-esteem.

30. Mayo Clinic Staff, "Self-Esteem: Take Steps to Feel Better about Yourself," Mayo Clinic, July, 6, 2022, https://www.mayoclinic.org/healthy-lifestyle/adult-health/in-depth/self-esteem/art-20045374.

> ──── Five Must-Have Herbs for Empowerment ────
> *Bay leaves, cinnamon, lemon verbena, rosemary, and witch hazel*
>
> Five Must-Have Essential Oils for Empowerment
> *Frankincense, lavender, peppermint, pine, and sweet orange*

Exercise
Set an Intention to Be Your Best

Intention-setting is a key magickal precept. When we set an intention, we state an outcome we are going to put energy toward achieving. Think of something you are going to work on accomplishing today. Say it aloud. It could be "Today I will be the best possible me that I can be," "I shine with the love of the Goddess," "I come to my place of power ready and willing to be a force of change," or "Today I hold kindness in my heart." Your intention might be about modifying a harmful behavior. Perhaps you intend to exercise more or to eat healthier, less, or mindfully.

Put this into practice. Before you start your morning, take a moment to ask yourself what you would like to manifest during the coming day. You may know before you begin this exercise. If you don't, set a piece of paper and pen in front of you, close your eyes and come to center. When you have reached a meditative state, move your attention to the area deep within your head between your ears and listen. If a positive message presents itself, embrace it. When you are ready, compose it as concisely as you are able. It could be something as simple as "Smile," "I am happy," or "Shine." You might want to embody gratitude, kindness, or love: "I resonate with the love of the goddess" or simply "I am love." You might write, "Success is mine!" or "I am victorious!" "My thoughts flow clear." "My words flow and are heard."

Fold the paper toward yourself and tuck it into your left pocket. As you go through your day, draw on the intention by pressing your right hand to where you have tucked the slip of paper, draw a breath, and intone the intention as you push energy through your body to empower it.

SPOTLIGHT INGREDIENT

Bay Leaves

I love bay leaves as a magickal kitchen ingredient. They hold energy to support victory, inspire self-confidence, and boost psychic abilities. You can drop them into a soup or sauce to infuse the brew with savory flavor. You can burn them as wish magick or to break curses. Bay leaf tea is a digestive aid drunk to calm indigestion and encourage a restful sleep. Bay leaves can also be infused into liquids, oils, and butters to build the complex flavor of custards, breads, and other sweets.

Bay Leaf Tea Cake

Bay infused butter adds elegance to this simple loaf cake. Serve this cake at any gathering to boost good mood and guard against negativity.

You will need:

8 Tablespoons butter

8 medium-size bay leaves

1⅔ cups flour

1 teaspoon baking powder

½ teaspoon salt

3 eggs

½ cup sour cream

1 cup sugar

½ teaspoon vanilla

powdered sugar to finish

Melt 6 tablespoons of the butter in a small saucepan. Take the pan off the heat and add 3 fresh or dried bay leaves. Set the pan aside to steep for at least 1 hour. Remove the bay leaves and reserve the infused butter.

Preheat your oven to 350 degrees Fahrenheit. Spray a 9-inch loaf pan with cooking spray and dust lightly with flour. Melt the remaining 2 tablespoons of butter in a saucepan. Take each remaining bay leaf and brush one side with the butter before placing in the bottom of the loaf pan, buttered side down. In a large bowl, stir together the flour, baking powder, and salt.

In a mixing bowl, mix together the eggs, sour cream, infused butter, sugar, and vanilla until smooth. Stir the flour mixture into the egg mixture until just combined, being careful to not over-mix.

Spoon the batter into the pan over the bay leaves. Bake 45 to 50 minutes, until a toothpick inserted in the center comes out clean.

Remove the cake from the oven and let it cool for 10 minutes. Run a knife around the edge of the pan, then turn the cake out onto a rack to cool completely. Dust the top with powdered sugar to finish. Peel off and discard the leaves as you serve it or instruct the person you are slicing it for to remove the leaves before taking a bite.

Hair Rinse to Restore a Positive Outlook

You will need:

1 part dried bay leaves

2 parts dried chamomile

Mix together the herbs and store in a clean, dry jar with a tight-fitting lid. Label the jar with the date and the name of the brew. If there is room, write your intention.

To use, bring 2 cups of water to a boil. Measure 3 tablespoons of the herbal mixture, and as you add it to the water, tell it what you would like it to do. Reduce the heat and simmer for 3 minutes, then turn off the heat and allow it to steep for 4 more minutes. Strain out the herbs and use the liquid as a hair rinse to refresh thought and lift outlook. Or add it to bathwater and soak in it to chase away worry and ease anxiety.

Psychic Enhancer Formula

You will need:

2 parts green tea

1 part dried bay leaf

1 part dried mugwort

⅓ cinnamon stick

Mix together the green tea, bay leaves, and mugwort and store in a clean, dry jar with a tight-fitting lid. Label the jar with the date and the name of the brew. If there is room, write your intention.

To use, heat water until it comes to a boil. Measure 1 tablespoon of herbal mixture into a tea strainer and tell it what you want it to do. Place the strainer in a mug. Pour 1 cup of hot water over the herb and add ⅓ piece of cinnamon stick. Cover to prevent steam from escaping. Let the infusion steep for up to 10 minutes. Remove the strainer. You can leave in the cinnamon stick if you'd like, and sweeten with honey. Sip the infusion to calm the psyche and open intuition. Or burn it as incense before ritual work to open your psychic channels.

Recipes for Self-Empowerment

Lemon Verbena Simple Syrup

Brew up an empowering simple syrup and use it to flavor drinks like iced tea, lemonade, and cocktails. Serve to lighten mood, stimulate energy, and vanquish nightmares.

You will need:

1 cup fresh lemon verbena leaves

1 cup water

1 cup sugar

Rinse the leaves and place them in a saucepan. Pour in the water and heat to a simmer. Stir in the sugar and cook for 3 more minutes. Strain the liquid into a jar. Take a spoonful whenever you need clarity. Use the syrup to flavor iced tea or lemonade and add energy for inspiration. Store the syrup by fixing the jar with a tight-fitting lid and keeping in the refrigerator for up to 2 weeks.

Lemon Infused Honey

You will need:

1 small jelly jar

1 organic lemon, washed and sliced as thinly as possible

½ cup honey, or enough to fill the jar

Fill a clean, dry jar with the lemon slices. Pour the honey over the top to completely fill the jar. Secure the jar with a tight-fitting lid and store in the refrigerator for 3 weeks. At this time the honey should be a jelly-like consistency. Add a spoonful to a mug of morning tea to encourage optimism. Take a spoonful to brighten your outlook and lift your mood.

Rosemary Infused Olive Oil

I always have a bottle of rosemary infused oil on hand to flavor foods. It is easy to make and adds a poshness to a meal when it is served as a dipping oil or drizzled over salads and pasta. The aromatic oil has a lovely scent, a savory flavor, and a versatile energy that can be used to deepen the memory of an occasion. It also makes a wonderful massage oil you can rub into your skin to heal and lift outlook. Mix a spoonful into a dish of salt and pour it into your evening bathwater to chase away worry and inspire good dreams, or use it as a blessing oil to clear and purify an object, to dress a ritual candle to attract good luck and love, or to empower abundance spells.

You will need:

¼ cup fresh rosemary leaves and flowers, stripped from their woody
   stems
olive oil

Put your dry, clean rosemary leaves and flowers into a small canning jar or a bottle with a tight-fitting lid. Top with oil and seal. Reinforce your intention as you roll the jar back and forth in your hands, making sure that the herbs are completely submerged in the oil. Label the jar, noting both the ingredients and the bottling date. Place it on a dimly lit shelf. Allow the oil to steep for 2 weeks. Be sure to check on it every few days and give it a gentle shake as you reinforce your intention. After 1 week, open your bottle and taste. Use it within 1 week or refrigerate it for up to 1 month.

Confidence-Boosting Massage Oil

You will need:
dried lemon verbena
olive oil or sweet almond oil

Fill a small canning jar with lemon verbena and cover with oil. Fill to the top, leaving no air pocket for mold to grow in. Seal the jar and shake to mix. Place it on a dimly lit shelf. Allow the oil to steep for 4 weeks. Be sure to check on it every few days and give it a gentle shake as you reinforce your intention. When it is ready, strain out the herbal matter and store the oil in a clean bottle. Label the bottle with the name, the date, and your intention. Massage the oil into the skin to boost attraction and improve self-image. Wear it to fortify resolve, break bad habits, and bring out inner beauty. Lemon verbena oil has a delicate, lovely scent and an enthusiastic energy that can breathe life back into that which has stalled or become stale. Add the oil blend to a small dish of salt and pour it under running bathwater for a soak that will change your luck, restore balance, or shift your perception to see potential in what has become dreary. Discard after 6 months.

Beauty-Enhancing Face Mask

You will need:

½ ripe banana

2 Tablespoons milk

In a small bowl, mash the banana into the milk to make a smooth paste. Settle comfortably into the bath or some other comfortable place and use your fingers to spread the mixture over your face, neck, and throat. Wear the face mask for 15 to 20 minutes to allow the mixture to hydrate and feed your skin. Rinse with warm water for beautiful glowing skin.

Uplifting Fizz Bath Bomb

I fell in love with bath bombs when my daughter gifted me a box. A nice bath bomb adds scent, sounds, and action as it dissolves, releasing its oils into the water. Good bath bombs are expensive. I discovered it's easy to make up batches of your favorite scent combinations for a fraction of the price.

In my experiments I tried all sorts of combinations. I discovered that recipes that don't use citric acid lack fizz. When the bomb hits the water, the citric acid mixes with the baking soda to form carbon dioxide bubbles. Citric acid is also a preservative and will keep your bomb fresh for months. Recipes that leave out the cornstarch fizz too fast. Cornstarch is a reducing agent and works to slow down the chemical reaction.

The following recipe makes 4 large bath bombs (2.56-inch diameter) or 8 mooncake-size bath bombs.

You will need:
spray bottle
bath bomb mold, mooncake stamp mold, or muffin tin
1 Tablespoon melted coconut oil
¼ cup witch hazel, plus 1 teaspoon, divided
1 cup baking soda
⅓ cup cornstarch
½ cup citric acid
½ cup Epsom salts
40–50 drops essential oil

Warm your coconut oil until it just melts. You don't want it to be hot when you add the essential oils. Measure ¼ cup witch hazel into a spray bottle and set aside. In a large bowl whisk together baking soda, cornstarch, citric acid, and Epsom salts. In a small bowl mix together the remaining 1 teaspoon of witch hazel, the coconut oil, and the essential oils. Slowly whisk the liquid mixture into the bowl of dry ingredients, 1 spoonful at a time, so as not to activate the dry ingredients. Whisk until it has a thick, even consistency. Lightly spritz the dry ingredients with the spray bottle until it all holds together without crumbling. Do not over-moisten. To do this, give the mix a couple of squirts from your spray bottle as you whisk, and then when its incorporated, do a squeeze test by squeezing a handful of the bath bomb mix to see if it will hold together. Only spritz enough to get the mixture to hold together. If you add too much liquid, the ingredients will activate and you'll ruin your batch.

Firmly press the mixture into the mold. Press both sides together, then remove the mold by gently tapping with a spoon. Set the bath bomb aside to dry on a tray covered with parchment paper. Repeat until all of the mixture has been used. Place the tray where it will not be disturbed, and let the bath bombs dry for a minimum of 24 hours before wrapping.

To store them, wrap individual bombs tightly in plastic wrap or stack them in an airtight container. Use within 6 months.

Some of my favorite essential oil combinations follow. Each blend should be made with equal parts.

- Bergamot and jasmine for a scent to encourage a positive outlook
- Bergamot and sweet orange for a scent to cheer and comfort
- Bergamot and lavender to enliven thought and restore energy
- Chamomile and lavender for a relaxing scent that encourages rest
- Frankincense and patchouli for scent that is grounding
- Grapefruit and ginger for a spicy scent to reawaken the senses
- Grapefruit and rose for a scent to inspire creative thought
- Lemongrass and marjoram for a scent to revive and restore
- Myrrh and sweet orange to cheer the spirit

Troubleshooting

I made this recipe five times before I got it to where I liked it. The first used 2 tablespoons oil, which made my skin feel too oily. I cut it to 1. I started with ½ cup of cornstarch, but the fizz action was too slow, so I reduced it to ⅓ cup. Also I only used 25 drops of essential oil, which gave the bomb a light scent. I upped it to 40 or 50. This is the max if you are making the large-size bath bombs, as any more may cause skin irritation.

Here are a few tips to get your recipe right:

- If your bath bombs crumble, your recipe was probably too dry. Spray your next batch a couple more times with witch hazel.
- If your bath bombs expand, there is probably too much moisture in your recipe. Spray less or reduce the amount of liquid. The weather can also affect your bath bomb results. Try making your batch on a day when it is not raining, or plug in a dehumidifier before you begin.
- You can add dry and liquid color to your batch. If using dry colors, mix them into your Epsom salts before you mix in the other dry ingredients. If using liquid color, add it to your bowl of oils and mix it in.

- While some oils like lavender are gentle, others such as thyme, cinnamon, and oregano are quite strong and can irritate skin or cause a reaction. Use less of these when making a batch and stop using them immediately if you experience any discomfort or irritation. For more information on essential oils, see pages 241–42.

Herbal Formulas for Empowerment

See page 18 for infusion brewing guidance.

Opportunities Open to Me Powder

You will need:

1 teaspoon allspice

1 teaspoon fennel seed

1 teaspoon nutmeg

Powder the herbs to use in your ritual work. Roll your oiled spell candles in them. Add a pinch to a burning candle, or brew up an infusion and add it to your bathwater and soak.

Help Me Quit Formula

Use this blend when you need to strengthen your resolve to quit a negative habit.

You will need:

1 part dried passionflower

1 part dried chamomile

1 part dried licorice root

1 part dried skullcap

Sip an infusion of these herbs to support your willpower when you're working to end a bad habit or addictive behavior.

Cognitive Support Formula

If you are having trouble with brain fog or forgetfulness, this pleasant-tasting brew can help sharpen thought. Sip a cup every morning for continuing cognitive support.

Note that ginkgo is a natural blood thinner and should be avoided if you are taking a blood-thinning medication.

You will need:

2 parts dried ginkgo leaf

2 parts dried holy basil

2 parts dried lemon balm

2 parts dried rosemary

Sip infusion of this blend to boost memory and support cognitive function.

Beauty Rinse Infusion

You will need:

1 part dried raspberry leaf

1 part dried witch hazel bark and leaves

1 part dried yarrow

Brew an infusion and use it to clear up minor skin eruptions. Place a clean cloth in the liquid and lay it over the infected area, or add the infusion to bathwater and soak to revitalize your skin and bolster beauty. Use it as a hair rinse to treat oily hair.

Essential Oil Formulas for Empowerment

Empowered and Positive Blend

You will need:

5 drops cinnamon essential oil

2 drops clove essential oil

5 drops jasmine essential oil

5 drops lavender essential oil

Blend essential oils into 1 tablespoon of a carrier oil and wear to increase positive attitude. Blend the oils into 1 cup of milk and add it to bathwater to improve self-image and expand positive feelings.

Awareness-Revitalizing Blend

You will need:

4 drops bergamot essential oil

4 drops lemongrass essential oil

2 drops clary sage essential oil

2 drops melissa essential oil

2 drops sweet orange essential oil

Mix the oils into 1 tablespoon of your favorite carrier and wear it as a scent to instill a positive outlook and chase away negative thoughts. Burn a blend of the oils in a tea light diffuser during meditation to focus thought and heighten feelings of spirituality.

Spiritual Empowerment Blend

You will need:

5 drops clary sage essential oil

5 drops ginger essential oil

5 drops melissa essential oil

5 drops rosemary essential oil

Blend the oils together and burn them in a tea light diffuser during meditation to focus thought and heighten feelings of spirituality. Or mix the oil blend into a small dish of salt and pour it into bathwater. Get in and soak to relax away nervous tension and open your chest to make breathing easier.

I Own the Power Blend

You will need:

10 drops rose essential oil

5 drops patchouli essential oil

Stir the essential oils into 1 tablespoon of your favorite carrier and wear it as a scent to support a positive outlook and lift mood. Burn the blend in a diffuser to eliminate feelings of insecurity.

Bright New Day Blend

You will need:

5 drops lavender essential oil

5 drops lemon essential oil

5 drops peppermint essential oil

Add the blend to a footbath to revive after a long day. Burn the blend in a diffuser to wake the mind. Mix the blend into 1 tablespoon of castile soap and add it to your bathwater. Soak in it to boost your sense of well-being, awaken your creativity, and enhance your immunity.

Make Me Smile Blend

You will need:

7 drops frankincense essential oil

5 drops lavender essential oil

5 drops pine essential oil

Blend the oils into 1 tablespoon of your favorite carrier and wear it as a scent to boost feel-good energy. Add the oil blend to 1 tablespoon of castile soap and pour it under running bathwater for an elevating bath to chase away the doldrums and brighten your mood.

Awakening Blend

You will need:

5 drops grapefruit essential oil

5 drops lemongrass essential oil

3 drops thyme essential oil

Blend the oils into 1 tablespoon of your favorite carrier and wear it to reenergize and fight fatigue. Mix the blend into 1 tablespoon of castile soap and add it to bathwater to vanquish feelings of apathy and lethargy.

Positive Empowerment Blend

You will need:
5 drops pine essential oil

3 drops peppermint essential oil

7 drops vetiver essential oil

Blend the oils into 1 tablespoon of your favorite carrier oil and wear it as a scent to ward off negativity and facilitate optimism. Add the oil blend to a small dish of salt and pour it under running bathwater for a magickal bath to boost well-being and renew your outlook. Burn the oil blend in a diffuser to wake your magickal power.

Good Luck Oil Blend

You will need:
5 drops cinnamon essential oil

5 drops patchouli essential oil

5 drops vanilla essential oil

Mix the oils into 1 tablespoon of your favorite carrier oil and rub into your hands whenever you need a dose of good luck.

Positive Power Blend

You will need:
7 drops frankincense essential oil

5 drops pine essential oil

3 drops clove essential oil

3 drops peppermint essential oil

Blend the oils and burn in a diffuser to banish negativity. Or blend them into 1 tablespoon of castile soap and add it to bathwater to chase away a negative outlook. Add the oil blend to a spray bottle of water and use it to spritz away annoyances.

Chapter 13

EMPOWERING YOUR RELATIONSHIPS

Our relationships are important. They are woven tightly into our identity and help us feel connected to our place in society. Our relationships add to our joy as they deepen our feelings of happiness and enrich the quality of our lives.[31] With all the negativity going on in the world today, it is easy to become distracted by the chaos and suffer feelings of isolation. You can avoid this by unplugging from the constant barrage of negative media and moving your focus to the good things right in front of you. Each of your relationships is a treasure. Devote your time, attention, and conversation to create shared experiences. It is through the unique experiences and interactions we share that we are able to create, nurture, and deepen our bonds.

Five Must-Have Herbs to Encourage Kindness
Basil, clove, catnip, lemon, and rose

Five Must-Have Essential Oils to Encourage Kindness
Clary sage, jasmine, melissa, rose, and ylang-ylang

· · · · · · · · · · · · · · · ·

31. Robert Puff, "How Relationships Enrich Our Lives," *Psychology Today*, March 19, 2021, https://www .psychologytoday.com/us/blog/meditation-modern-life/202103/how-relationships-enrich-our-lives.

Exercise
Cultivate Kindness

Life today is filled with stressors. Everyone is feeling them. The chaos is distracting, and as a result, our needs and the needs of those around us are often neglected. By mindfully shifting our attention, we can shift emphasis back to what is truly important. In his article for *Psychology Today*, author Isaac Lidsky writes, "In every moment, you choose who you want to be and how you want to live your life. It's your ultimate power, and your inescapable responsibility. You are the master of your reality—whether you realize it or not, whether you like it or not, whether you accept it or not."[32] You can become the change you wish to see in the world by choosing to mindfully practice kindness.

Start with an intention. Intentions are powerful. When we put the energy into forming an intention and state it aloud, we put energy toward transforming our reality as we reinforce the behavior we wish to cultivate. A kindness intention could be "I am kind. My words are kind. My actions are kind," or "I will respond today with kindness," or "My words and actions will inspire joy." State your kindness intention as you begin your day. Instead of reacting, make it a point to consciously respond with kindness. Take time to sit quietly and appreciate yourself, your life, and those you love. Praise yourself and others. Allow yourself to be happy, joyous, and successful. Appreciate the people you love. Make an effort to show how much you care. Be supportive. Hug them when you can. Reach out and hold that hand. The real superpower to master in this life is love. Love yourself. Love your friends and family members. Love your home, your community. When our lives are filled with love, with positive feel-good energy, we thrive.

You can take this further by striving to be a positive force in your community. Cancel out the hostility around by responding with kindness. Next time you are out and about, take a moment to observe how others are processing the moment. Make it a habit to consider how your thoughts and actions affect those around you. Acts of

. . . .

32. Isaac Lidsky, "Mastering Your Reality," *Psychology Today*, June 28, 2017, https://www.psychologytoday.com/us/blog/mastering-your-reality/201706/mastering-your-reality.

kindness are remembered. When you choose to do something kind for someone, it makes an impact. If someone looks sad, offer a word of encouragement. If someone is struggling with something, offer a helping hand. Performing an act of kindness is rewarding, as it stimulates the release of serotonin and oxytocin, two feel-good hormones that boost a positive mood and increase happiness.[33]

SPOTLIGHT INGREDIENT
Chocolate
Gratitude, happiness, health, longevity, love, luxury, and riches

Chocolate is an amazing, joyful food loaded with psychoactive feel-good chemicals that release dopamine in the pleasure centers of the brain to induce a sense of well-being. It also contains tryptophan, an amino acid that converts into serotonin, a neurotransmitter known to promote a sense of well-being and relaxation. Chocolate is loaded with antioxidants to fortify health, mood, and cognitive abilities.[34] Science is backing up what chocolate eaters have always known: eating chocolate makes you feel good.[35] Chocolate elevates mood, increases mental acuity, and decreases feelings of anxiety.[36] Eat some chocolate, share some chocolate, give some chocolate—because chocolate makes us happy, and when we are happy, other people enjoy being around us.

. . . .

33. Marianna Pogosyan, "Why Choose Kindness," *Psychology Today*, April 11, 2019, https://www.psychology today.com/us/blog/between-cultures/201904/why-choose-kindness.

34. R. Latif, "Chocolate/Cocoa and Human Health: A Review," *Netherlands Journal of Medicine* 71, no. 2 (March 2013): 63–68, https://pubmed.ncbi.nlm.nih.gov/23462053/.

35. Nidhi Joshi, "Eating Chocolates Can Boost Your Mental Health: Here's Why," Psychreg, July 10, 2020, https://www.psychreg.org/chocolates-brain-food/.

36. Emmy Tuenter, Kenn Foubert, and Luc Pieters, "Mood Components in Cocoa and Chocolate: The Mood Pyramid," *Planta Medica* 84, nos. 12–13 (August 2018): 839–44, doi:10.1055/a-0588-5534.

Decadent Hot Drinking Chocolate

This recipe makes 2 servings.

You will need:
8 ounces good dark chocolate, broken into small pieces
2 cups milk
pinch of salt
1 teaspoon vanilla extract or espresso powder

Break the chocolate into a bowl. In a small saucepan, mix together the milk and salt. Heat over medium-low heat, stirring continuously, until the milk just begins to simmer. Remove the pan from heat and stir in the vanilla. Pour the mixture over the chocolate and stir to melt. Pour the cocoa into mugs and serve for a delicious, uplifting treat. Top the hot chocolate with whipped cream and sip it with a loved one to increase feelings of contentment, or top it with a few marshmallows and serve to a child to brighten outlook.

Homemade Hot Cocoa

This recipe makes 2 servings.

You will need:
2 cups milk
5 teaspoons unsweetened cocoa powder
3 Tablespoons maple syrup
pinch of salt
2 Tablespoons chopped good dark chocolate
½ teaspoon vanilla extract
shaved dark chocolate to finish

In a small saucepan, heat the milk until just simmering. Remove from heat and stir in the cocoa powder, maple syrup, and salt. Add the chopped dark chocolate and vanilla and stir until smooth. Pour into mugs and top with shaved chocolate. Serve this cocoa to inspire affections or to sweeten someone's opinion of you. Drink a mug to comfort or to elevate mood.

Light and Gooey Flourless Chocolate Cake

You will need:

12 ounces chocolate chips or 3 bars (3–3.5 ounces) of your favorite chocolate

2 Tablespoons strong coffee or cognac

¼ cup butter, at room temperature

6 eggs, separated

2 teaspoons vanilla

½ cup sugar

Preheat your oven to 350 degrees Fahrenheit. Line the bottom of a 9-inch springform pan with parchment paper and set it aside. Boil water in a large saucepan. Place the chocolate chips in a heat-resistant bowl and set the bowl over the boiling water to melt the chocolate. If you are using bars, break the chocolate into bits as you place it in the bowl. Stir the chocolate as it begins to melt. Add the coffee and the butter and stir until mixture is smooth. Heat only until the chocolate is melted, taking care not to overcook. When the chocolate mixture is smooth, remove the pan from the heat. Mix the egg yolks and vanilla into the melted chocolate. Stir until smooth and set aside. In a separate bowl, whip the egg whites until foamy. Add the sugar and beat until shiny soft peaks form. Fold ⅓ of the whites into the chocolate mixture to lighten it. Gently fold another ⅓ of the whites into the batter. Then fold the remaining third into the chocolate mixture, retaining as much fluffiness as possible. Spoon the mixture into the springform pan and bake for 40 minutes. The outside should be crispy while the inside is gooey. Top with whipped cream or serve with vanilla ice cream. Serve this cake to inspire happiness. Eat to cheer.

Hazelnut and Almond Butter Truffles

For a sweet chocolaty treat to nourish the heart, mind, and soul, mix up a healthy no-guilt batch of truffles to lift mood and sweeten thoughts. These sweet treats use the loving energy of hazelnuts, almonds, and coconut to energize, stimulate, and clear the mind.

Makes about 26 balls.

You will need:

1 cup roasted hazelnuts

½ cup almond butter

½ cup unsweetened coconut

3 Tablespoons maple syrup

3 Tablespoons cocoa

3 Tablespoons coconut oil

2 teaspoons vanilla

½ teaspoon salt

¼ cup cocoa nibs

Process the hazelnuts in a food processor until they form a coarse meal. Add the remaining ingredients and blend until incorporated. Form the mixture into small balls that are roughly 1½ inches in diameter. Place the balls in the refrigerator to firm. Eat one when you feel down to cheer yourself up. Snack on one to inspire positivity. Pop one in your mouth before you venture out into the world to sharpen your thought and intuitions. Nibble on a truffle before meditation to facilitate higher thinking, the ability to ground, and an awareness of the natural energies all around.

Recipes for Relationships

Our food choices matter for our health and well-being. For physical beings, eating is necessary for life. We are driven to eat, just as we are driven to reproduce. While our food provides the nutrients and the energy we need to keep our bodies functioning, eating is also a wonderful sensory experience. It is one of the great pleasures of life. When you are presented with a food you enjoy, take the time to look at it and breathe in the smell of it. Hold a morsel in your mouth, taste it on your tongue, and feel the glorious texture of it as your teeth press through it. All these senses come together to envelope you in pleasure. Eating a good meal, alone or with someone you love, has the power to influence the way you feel about yourself or about them. It can expand your sense of well-being and can even transport the mind back in time. If you give it your full attention, eating becomes an amazing sensual experience.

Love-Booster Smoothie

Makes 2 servings.

You will need:

1 cup peach slices, fresh or frozen

5 Medjool dates, pitted

1 cup plain yogurt

Place the ingredients into a blender and process until smooth. Drink this smoothie cold to energize yourself, or serve it to inspire feelings of affection.

Overnight Rosemary Olive Bread

I like to use pitted kalamata to make this recipe, but you can use your favorite olives. Just make sure they have been pitted before adding them to the dough.

Baking bread, if done mindfully, is an act of self-care, and the comforting, luscious aroma that fills the house as it bakes lifts everyone's spirits. Wheat is known for its stable, supportive energy for abundance, while olives are a food of abundance, love, and fertility. Rosemary is associated with the sun and Leo. It holds energy to cleanse, heal, protect, and instill courage, but most of all rosemary is an herb of remembrance, eaten to encourage faithfulness and served to make a meal memorable.

You will need:

2¼ cups flour

¾ teaspoon salt

1½ teaspoons yeast

2 Tablespoons olive oil

½ cup pitted and chopped black olives

½ cup warm milk

water by the spoonful

½–1 teaspoon coarse salt

1 Tablespoon fresh rosemary leaves and flowers chopped into small bits

In a large mixing bowl whisk together flour, salt, and yeast. Mix in the oil and olives and add the milk. Knead, or if using a mixer, mix on low until no dry flour remains, about 5 minutes. You may need to add a sprinkle of water if flour remains in the bottom.

Transfer the dough to oiled bowl and cover with a sheet of plastic wrap that has been lightly coated with vegetable oil spray. Let the dough double in size, about 1 to 2 hours. When dough has risen, lift it from the bowl and work it with your hands by folding it over itself to create a disk. Fold the dough 7 more times. Program it with your intention as you work it, pressing it together and folding, and pressing it back into a disk again. Set the disk of dough back in the bowl and cover to rise again for 30 minutes. Wrap the dough tightly in oiled plastic wrap and refrigerate overnight (or up to 48 hours).

Take the dough out of the refrigerator 1½ to 2 hours before you are ready to bake it. Set the dough on a baking sheet without deflating. Gently stretch and press the dough to form a 9-inch round. Brush the dough with olive oil and sprinkle the chopped rosemary over the top. Add a sprinkling of coarse salt and press the salt and herbs into the dough. Cover loosely with the oiled plastic wrap and let the dough rest at room temperature until it has relaxed and is no longer cool to the touch, about 1 hour.

Heat your oven to 425 degrees Fahrenheit. When the oven is hot, bake the dough until it becomes fragrant and the top is golden brown, about 35 minutes.

Serve the bread with butter for a savory snack with energy to brighten the mood. Serve it with a side salad at a friendly luncheon to brighten the mood and make the meal memorable. Slice and toast it with cheddar cheese to make savory toasted cheese sandwiches with energy to instill affection.

Honey Thyme Goat Cheese Spread

You will need:

4 ounces goat cheese

2 ounces cream cheese, softened

½ teaspoon fresh thyme, chopped

1 Tablespoon honey

pinch of salt

In a medium bowl mix together goat cheese and cream cheese until smooth. Stir in the thyme, honey, and salt. Serve this spread with crackers for a tasty treat brimming with nurturing energy to foster affection. Spread it over a slice of pound cake and drizzle with honey for a posh dessert to sweeten and impress.

I'm Ready for Love Formula

Make a potion to inspire self-love or encourage romance by floating this flower mixture in your favorite champagne.

You will need:
1 part dried California poppies

1 part dried rose petals

1 part dried lavender buds

Mix together all the ingredients and store in a clean, dry jar with a tight-fitting lid. Label the jar with the date and the name of the brew. If there is room, write your intention.

To serve, measure ¼ teaspoon of flower mixture into a champagne flute. Top with champagne and sip to boost outlook and encourage happiness. Share it with a lover to heighten romance. You can also sprinkle the mixture evenly into an ice cube tray, fill it with water, and freeze. Serve the frozen cubes in iced tea to encourage affection and happiness.

Harmonious Home Simmer Pot

You will need:
1 apple, cut into slices

2 cinnamon sticks

1 Tablespoon cloves

1 teaspoon vanilla extract

Fill a small pot halfway with water and heat to a boil. Drop in the ingredients and turn the heat down to a slow simmer. Be sure to check on the pot every 20 minutes or so and add more water to maintain the water level. Simmer the brew to infuse the home with a delicious aroma to instill feelings of harmony and happiness.

Cozy Comfort Simmer Pot

You will need:

1 orange, cut into slices

2 cinnamon sticks

2 teaspoons vanilla extract

Fill a small pot halfway with water and heat to a boil. Drop in the ingredients and turn the heat down to a slow simmer. Be sure to check on the pot every 20 minutes or so and add more water to maintain water level. Simmer the brew to infuse the home with a luscious scent to instill feelings of comfort and cheer.

Home Safe Home Simmer Pot

You will need:

2 Tablespoons chamomile

1 Tablespoon allspice

1 Tablespoon cloves

1 Tablespoon nutmeg

2 cinnamon sticks

peel of 1 orange

Fill a small pot halfway with water and heat to a boil. Drop in the ingredients and turn the heat down to a slow simmer. Be sure to check on the pot every 20 minutes or so and add more water to maintain water level. Simmer the brew to infuse the home with feelings of love and peace.

Attraction Bath

You will need:

5 drops melissa essential oil

5 drops rose essential oil

3 drops jasmine essential oil

½ cup basic bath salts (see page 28)

Mix the oils into the basic bath salts. Fill the tub. Add the salt mixture to the running water. Get in and relax. Visualize the one you desire, and when you have a firm image on the screen of your mind, duck under the water. When you come up, smile and say,

See me. Hear me. Want me.
I shine. I shine.
I am a bright shining star.
I am love.

Repeat 9 times.

Enjoy this magickal soak whenever you need to boost your mojo or boost your sex appeal.

Herbal Formulas to Support Relationships

See page 18 for infusion brewing guidance.

Rose Friendship Tea

Aside from their nurturing qualities, roses are also aphrodisiacs associated with Taurus, the moon, and many goddesses, including Freyja, Hulda, and Aphrodite. Use their supportive energy to instill feelings of peace and love.

You will need:

2 parts dried lemon balm

1 part green tea

1 part dried lemon verbena

1 part dried linden flowers

1 part dried rose petals

Serve this tea at a friendly luncheon to inspire cheer and meld relationships. Serve it over ice on a hot day to lift moods and encourage a brighter outlook. Serve it to someone in need of comfort.

Sweet Spice Incense

You will need:

1 part dried clove

4 parts dried orange peel

2 parts dried thyme

Grind the ingredients together and burn the mix as an incense to encourage affection and strengthen relationships.

Harmonic Sensibility Blend

You will need:

1 part dried mint

1 part dried rose

1 part dried vervain

Add an infusion of these herbs to bathwater and soak to lift your outlook and encourage happiness. Burn the blend as an incense to instill a harmonic atmosphere. Use it to dress candles to empower spells for peace and harmony.

Essential Oil Formulas to Support Relationships

Love Potion

You will need:

6 drops lavender essential oil

4 drops cinnamon essential oil

2 drops clove essential oil

2 drops nutmeg essential oil

Blend the oils into your favorite carrier and wear it as a scent to maximize your mojo. Add oil blend to a footbath to restore energy and awaken the senses. Use it in a hair rinse to open communication channels. Or add it to a spray bottle of water for a bright and refreshing spritz to inspire creativity.

Blend to Wake Passions

You will need:

4 drops lemongrass essential oil

4 drops sandalwood essential oil

3 drops rosemary essential oil

Blend the oils into your favorite carrier and wear it as a scent to wake intuitive abilities and passion. Add the oil blend to a footbath to restore energy and awaken the senses. Use it in a hair rinse to open communication channels. Or add it to a spray bottle of water for a bright and refreshing spritz to inspire creativity.

I Am Love Blend

You will need:

5 drops yarrow essential oil

5 drops lavender essential oil

5 drops rose essential oil

3 drops basil essential oil

3 drops ginger essential oil

Blend the oils together and burn in an infuser to inspire feelings of love. Mix the oil blend into a spray bottle of water and use it to spritz a room to shift mood and inspire kindness. Or use the blend to anoint candles to empower a love spell.

Attraction Blend

You will need:

6 drops rose essential oil

3 drops basil essential oil

2 drops peppermint essential oil

Drop the oils onto a small cloth and tuck the cloth into clothing to be noticed. Or blend the oils into 1 Tablespoon of your favorite carrier and wear it as a scent to amplify your ability to charm. Rub the blend onto a candle and light it to instill a romantic ambiance.

Positive Blend to Beat Isolation

You will need:

5 drops jasmine essential oil

5 drops sandalwood essential oil

5 drops ylang-ylang essential oil

Blend the oils into 1 tablespoon of your favorite carrier and wear it as a scent for positive, feel-good energy. Wear the blend as a perfume to lift mood and encourage a sense of interconnectedness and belonging.

Harmony Now Blend

You will need:

5 drops frankincense essential oil

3 drops lavender essential oil

2 drops rose essential oil

Burn the blend in a diffuser to restore tranquility. Mix the blend into 1 tablespoon of castile soap and add it to running bathwater for a restorative bath to soothe away frustrations and anger.

Blend to Restore Self-Love

You will need:

3 drops frankincense essential oil

2 drops rose essential oil

2 drops ylang-ylang essential oil

Burn the blend in a diffuser to inspire kindness. Mix the blend into a small dish of salt and dump the mixture into running bathwater. Light a couple of candles and get into the water. Relax as you breathe in the scents and fix your attention on the immediate moment. Move your thoughts to everything positive you have to be thankful for. Luxuriate in the pleasure of the moment as you let your heart swell with gratitude. Thank the universe for your blessings. You might say something like "I am thankful for all that I have, all that I am, and all the potential I have to be." Soak to boost your self-image.

Chapter 14

BOOSTING YOUR IMMUNITY

The best way to supercharge your immunity is to eat nutrient-dense foods, exercise, and get a good amount of sleep. Missing out on any one of these can impact energy levels, mood, and eventually your health.

> ### Five Must-Have Herbs to Support Your Immune System
> *Echinacea, elderberry, garlic, ginger, and holy basil*
>
> ### Five Must-Have Essential Oils to Support Your Immune System
> *Bergamot, eucalyptus, lemon, oregano, and tea tree*

Exercise
Body Scan Meditation

Occasionally, I wake up feeling fragile. Sometimes it's obvious what's making me feel down. Other times it's a mystery. I've learned to scan my body to figure out just what is bothering me. Here's how:

Settle into the position most comfortable to you and close your eyes. Draw a deep, slow breath and focus on it, following as it enters your body. Follow it down into your lungs. Sit with your breath until your awareness expands. Then move your attention to your feet. Move your attention over your toes, across the arch of your foot, and up to your ankle. Notice any sensation of pain, tension, discomfort, or anything out of the ordinary.

If you notice any pain or unusual feelings, acknowledge them. Fix your attention on any trouble spot and breathe into it. If the area is tense, release and relax it. If you come across an area that aches or is injured, visualize healing energy wrapping around the spot, sinking in to heal it. When you have finished with this area, move your focus up to scan your legs. Repeat the process until you have scanned your entire body up to the top of your head.

Practice this meditation anytime you feel ill or stressed to uncover what it is that is bothering you.

SPOTLIGHT INGREDIENT
Sweet Potato
Beauty, comfort, health, and love

Sometimes there's nothing quite as comforting as a carb fix when you're feeling low. Instead of indulging in junk food, you'll feel a lot better if you satisfy your craving with healthy carbs like sweet potato.

Sweet potatoes are rich in magnesium, the mineral that helps you relax and de-stress by stimulating the brain's GABA(A) receptors.[37] They are also loaded with antioxidants to boost immunity, fight aging, and even protect you from cancers.[38]

---

37. T. Möykkynen et al., "Magnesium Potentiation of the Function of Native and Recombinant GABA(A) Receptors," *Neuroreport* 12, no. 10 (July 2001): 2175–79, doi:10.1097/00001756-200107200-00026.

38. James Colquhoun, "12 Reasons Why Sweet Potato Is So Good for You," Food Matters, October 22, 2015, https://www.foodmatters.com/article/12-reasons-why-sweet-potato-is-so-good-for-you.

Sweet Potato Pancakes

This recipe makes 8 pancakes.

You will need:

¼ cup flour, or gluten-free 1-to-1 flour replacement

½ teaspoon baking power

½ teaspoon cinnamon

½ teaspoon salt

2 medium sweet potatoes, shredded to make 6 cups

2 Tablespoons honey

2 eggs

olive oil for frying

In a mixing bowl, stir together the flour, baking powder, cinnamon, and salt. Add the sweet potato, honey, and eggs and stir to incorporate. Spray a pan with cooking spray and heat 1 teaspoon of oil over medium heat. Drop a scoop of batter onto the hot oil in the skillet and fry for several minutes to cook the sweet potato through. Flip and cook until both sides are golden brown. Repeat until all the batter has been fried. Add more oil to pan if needed.

Serve the pancakes with maple syrup and eat them for breakfast to fuel your body for the day. Serve with a sprinkling of powdered sugar for a sweet mid-morning treat. Eat them as a midday snack to fortify your mood and stabilize blood sugar, or top them with sour cream and serve them as a side at dinner.

Sweet Potato Burritos

This recipe makes 6 burritos.

You will need:

2 sweet potatoes

1 Tablespoon olive oil

1 cup chopped onion

2 cloves garlic, minced

½ cup water

1 teaspoon cumin

1 teaspoon paprika

1 teaspoon oregano

¼ teaspoon cayenne pepper

3 cups cooked black beans

salt and pepper to taste

6 warmed 10-inch flour tortillas

½ cup cilantro

1 avocado, destoned, peeled, and cut into chucks

sour cream

Heat the oven to 400 degrees Fahrenheit. Poke the sweet potatoes to give them a few steam vents and roast them until tender, about 45 minutes. In a medium sauté pan add the olive oil and heat over medium low. Add onion and cook until clear. Add the garlic and cook 1 more minute. Add the water, cumin, paprika, oregano, and cayenne and stir to mix. Add the black beans and season to taste with salt and pepper.

To assemble the burritos, lay out the warmed tortillas. Slice each sweet potato. Take a spoon and mash the flesh inside the peel. Divide the mashed potato between the tortillas, spreading down the center. Divide the bean mixture, spooning it over the sweet potato. Roll the burritos and top with avocado slices, sour cream, and cilantro. Serve for a nutrient-dense meal to foster good health and fuel the body. Eat a serving to power your day.

Sweet Potato with Maple Glazed Root Vegetables

This recipe makes 4 servings.

You will need:

1 Tablespoon butter

olive oil

1 onion, chopped

1 large sweet potato, peeled and cut into1-inch slices

1 turnip or rutabaga, trimmed and cut into 1-inch slices

2 parsnips, trimmed and cut into 1-inch slices

1 carrot, trimmed and cut into 1-inch slices

1 cup chicken broth

¼ cup maple syrup

1 Tablespoon fresh lemon juice

salt and pepper to taste

In a large pan with a tight-fitting lid, melt butter. Add 1 tablespoon olive oil and the onion and turn to coat. Cook until the onion is clear. Place the sweet potato and other roots in a bowl and drizzle lightly with olive oil. Stir to coat and add the vegetables to the onion in the pan. Stir to shift the onions off the bottom and cook until the slices begin to brown. Add the broth, maple syrup, and lemon juice. Bring to a boil, then reduce the heat to a slow simmer. Cover and cook 10 minutes. Uncover and cook over medium heat to reduce liquid for 7 to 9 minutes more. The roots should now be tender. Remove the pan from the heat and season the roots with salt and pepper to taste. Add this side to meals to increase nutritional value. Eat a serving to fortify health. Serve it to a loved one to deepen a sense of well-being.

Recipes to Boost Health

Your body is the vehicle you live in until the day you die. And just like an expensive sports car, your magick skeleton needs to be fueled with quality fuel for optimal performance. When you choose to eat whole foods, your body is supplied with the nutrients it needs, and food prep becomes a vehicle to restore wellness.

Hawthorn Wellness Infusion

A hot infusion made from hawthorn leaves and berries makes a pleasant-tasting winter drink with energy to fortify health, brighten the dark days, and restore the spirit. According to an article posted by the Icahn School of Medicine at Mount Sinai, "Hawthorn increases coronary artery blood flow, improves circulation, and lowers blood pressure."[39] This increase in circulation makes you feel relaxed. Some have compared the feeling to drinking alcohol but without being impaired.

You will need:

2 cups water

¼ cup dried hawthorn leaves

....

39. "Hawthorn," Icahn School of Medicine at Mount Sinai, accessed November 30, 2022, https://www.mount sinai.org/health-library/herb/hawthorn.

2 Tablespoons dried hawthorn berries
honey to sweeten

Heat the water until it comes to a boil. Take the leaves and hold your intention firmly in your mind as you crumble them into a medium-size bowl. This allows them to better release their oils. Add the berries and pour the hot water over the top. Cover to prevent the essential oils from escaping with the steam. Set aside for at least 4 hours. Strain out the herbal bits. Add a spoonful of honey to sweeten and sip a cup to elevate your mood and improve your outlook. Add ½ cup of this infusion to ½ cup of cranberry juice and drink it to fortify your health.

Lemon Ginger Tea

Soothe your digestive system with this sweet and tangy drink. This recipe makes 1 serving.

You will need:

2 cups water

1 lemon, cut into quarters

1-inch piece of fresh ginger, peeled and chopped

1 Tablespoon honey

Measure the water into a saucepan and heat to a boil. Add lemon and ginger and cover. Reduce heat to a simmer and cook for 10 minutes. Strain the liquid into a large mug and stir in honey to sweeten. Serve hot. Sip this tea to empower your immune system. Sip it to aid digestion and energize thought.

Ginger Turmeric Tea

This recipe makes 2 servings.

You will need:

3 cups water

1-inch piece of fresh ginger, peeled and chopped

1-inch piece of fresh turmeric, peeled and chopped

1 cinnamon stick

2 Tablespoons honey

lemon wedges

In a small saucepan, bring water to a boil. Add the spices and reduce the heat to a simmer. Cover and cook for 10 minutes. Strain the liquid into two mugs. Stir a tablespoon of honey into each. Serve with a side of lemon. Drink this tea to power up your immune system. Make a batch when you feel a cold coming on.

Tomato Holy Basil Soup

Soup is a nourishing meal cooked up to support the immune system when we are feeling challenged. Tomatoes are rich in vitamin C to lessen the severity of colds. Cook up a batch when you are in the need of some whole, healing food. This recipe makes 6 servings.

You will need:
1 Tablespoon butter or olive oil

1 onion, chopped

2 cloves garlic, minced

4 cups chopped tomatoes

1 cup fresh holy basil

1 teaspoon cumin

2 cups chicken or vegetable broth

salt and pepper

Heat butter or olive oil in a large saucepan. Add the onion and cook until the pieces begin to brown. Add the garlic and cook 1 more minute. Add the tomatoes, basil, and cumin and cook over medium heat for 3 to 5 minutes. Add broth and bring to a simmer. Reduce heat and simmer for 30 minutes, stirring occasionally. Transfer to blender and process until smooth. Season with salt and pepper to taste. Serve hot with a toasted cheese sandwich to nourish and comfort.

Golden Turmeric Paste

This is an amazing inflammation-fighting formula to reduce pain, ease depression, and improve memory. This recipe yields ¾ cup of paste.

You will need:
1½ cups water

½ cup ground turmeric

2 teaspoons ground black pepper

3 Tablespoons coconut oil

In a saucepan, heat the water and turmeric over low heat, stirring constantly. When the mixture thickens, add the black pepper and coconut oil. Stir to combine. Pour the mixture into a clean jar with a tight-fitting lid. Label the jar with the date and the name of the brew. Store it in the refrigerator for up to 2 weeks. Add a spoonful to a cup of tea or warm milk to help reduce aches and pains. Add a spoonful to a smoothie for an anti-inflammatory boost. Stir a spoonful into a measure of honey and spread it over toast for a feel-good, energy-boosting treat.

Witch Hazel Twig Astringent

Your skin is your largest organ. It protects your body by creating a flexible barrier to hold your blood in and keep pathogens out. Witch hazel extract is an old-fashioned natural astringent distilled from the bark and young stems of the witch hazel shrub. It is one of the few American medicinal plants still approved by the FDA to relieve minor skin irritations due to cuts, scrapes, and insect bites and relieve the pain and discomfort of varicose veins. Herbalists prescribe witch hazel as a remedy for herpes simplex virus. It is rich in tannins, which give it natural astringent and antiseptic properties. Herbalist Bevin Cohen writes that a witch hazel infusion brewed from the leaves can be used as a remedy to treat acne, sunburn, insect bites, and other skin irritations.[40]

Witch hazel has energy for beauty, and when used as a facial astringent, it will tone skin and heal the complexion. It also makes an excellent aftershave lotion, as it soothes razor burn.

You will need:

½ cup witch hazel extract

tea tree oil

Pour the witch hazel into a small jar and mix in 5 drops of tea tree oil. Use the mix as a first aid antiseptic solution to wash small cuts and wounds.

....

40. Bevin Cohen, *The Artisan Herbalist* (Gabriola Island: Canada, New Society Publishers, 2021), 69.

Milk, Honey, and Oat Mask

Sometimes rest and relaxation is the best medicine. Taking time for yourself to unwind and de-stress helps strengthen the immune system.

You will need:

3 teaspoons oats, ground to a meal

1 teaspoon milk

2 teaspoons honey

In a small bowl, mix the oats into the milk and honey to make a smooth paste. Settle comfortably into the bath or some other comfortable place and use your fingers to spread the mixture over your face, neck, and throat. Wear the facemask for 15 to 20 minutes to allow the mixture to heal and condition your skin. Rinse with warm water to even blotchy skin and help repair skin damage.

Herbal Formulas to Boost Health

See page 18 for infusion brewing guidance.

Charge My Battery Bath Salts

You will need:

3 bay leaves

1 teaspoon coriander

1 teaspoon ground nutmeg

½ cup sea salt

Grind the herbs together and add to the salt. Add ¼ cup of the salt mixture to running bathwater. Get in and soak to rinse away negative energy and charge your inner battery.

Health and Vigor Infusion

You will need:

4 teaspoons dried yarrow

2 teaspoons dried chamomile flowers

2 teaspoons dried echinacea flowers

2 teaspoons dried holy basil

Pour an infusion of these herbs into a mug and flavor with lemon juice or sweeten with honey if you don't care for the flavor. Sip it to restore vitality. Drink up to 3 cups a day to help the body overcome illness.

Yarrow Tea for Cold and Flu

You will need:

1 teaspoon dried yarrow leaves, stem, and flowers

1 cup water

pinch of cayenne pepper

honey

Pour an infusion of the yarrow and water into a mug and add a pinch of cayenne pepper to boost cold-fighting abilities. Stir in honey to taste. Drink up to 3 cups a day to open the chest, lessen a cough, and reduce nasal congestion.

Immunity Support Tea

If you are feeling run-down and think you might feel a cold coming on, this infusion contains a powerhouse of compounds to shore up your defensives. Brew a pot and sip it to lift your outlook, treat stomach disorders, fight infection, and reduce inflammation.

You will need:

1 part dried oregano

1 part dried rosemary

1 part dried thyme

Pour an infusion of these herbs into a mug and flavor with lemon juice or sweeten with honey if you don't care for the flavor. Sip it to boost your immune system when you feel under the weather or a cold coming on. Add it to bathwater and soak to ease muscle aches and treat minor skin irritations.

Infusion to Hasten Healing

You will need:

1 part dried lavender

1 part dried St. John's wort

1 part dried yarrow

Pour this infusion into a mug and sweeten with honey if you don't care for the flavor. Sip it to relieve anxiety and soothe a restless spirit. Add it to bathwater or to a foot soak to treat nerve pain and hasten wound healing.

Essential Oil Formulas to Boost Immunity

Immune-Boosting Blend

You will need:

7 drops lavender essential oil

3 drops eucalyptus essential oil

3 drops thyme essential oil

Blend the oils together and burn them in a diffuser to clear stagnant air in a sick-room. Or mix the oil blend into a small dish of salt and add it to a footbath to soothe aches and fortify health.

Blend to Power Health

You will need:

5 drops lavender essential oil

3 drops neroli essential oil

1 drop eucalyptus essential oil

1 drop oregano essential oil

1 drop rosemary essential oil

Blend the oils together and burn them in a diffuser to empower health. Add the blend to 1 tablespoon of castile soap and add it to bathwater for a luxurious soak to ease sore muscles and fortify health.

Blend to Soothe the Sick

You will need:

5 drops juniper essential oil

5 drops lavender essential oil

5 drops rose essential oil

Blend the oils together and burn them in a diffuser to soothe the mind and body when you feel malaise. Add the oil blend to a small dish of salt and add the mixture to bathwater for a comforting soak when you feel fragile.

Cold-Busting Blend

You will need:

2 drops lemon essential oil

1 drop clove essential oil

1 drop peppermint essential oil

1 drop tea tree oil

Mix the oils into a small dish of salt and add it to a footbath to fortify feel-good energy. Add it to bathwater and soak to fight off a cold.

Healing Floral Blend

You will need:

4 drops rose essential oil

4 drops ylang-ylang essential oil

2 drops vanilla essential oil

Add these oils to jojoba and wear it as a scent to encourage acceptance and move thoughts forward. Mix the oils into 1 tablespoon of castile soap and add it to bathwater for a healing bath to soothe grief and anger and calm the spirit.

Chapter 15

MAGICKAL PROTECTION

Sometimes the bad you are feeling originates outside yourself. If you begin to experience feelings of exhaustion or an unexplained illness, you might have been hexed. If you find yourself suddenly caught in a cycle of bad luck or the victim of jealousy, you might have been hexed. If you experience an attack of vicious words or spiteful deeds, you might have been hexed. When you come face to face with negativity, it's time to brew up some magickal protection.

Five Must-Have Herbs to Protect Yourself
Garlic, peppercorns, sage, St. John's wort, and vervain

Five Must-Have Essential Oils to Protect Yourself
Cedarwood, cypress, juniper berry, myrrh, and pine

Invoking Protection

A psychic shield is an energetic construct made of universal energy. It is an energy shield or bubble constructed around your body to act as a barrier and keep you safe from negative energy, energy vampires, and marauding energy forms. You can call it into place before journeying, scrying, communicating with spirits, or working ritual or whenever you fall under attack and are in need of some psychic protection.

Draw a breath and come to center. Visualize a bright light glowing above you. This light is the infinite energy of the universe. See it glowing softly as it streams down to surround you. Visualize the energy encompassing you, encasing you in a protective field. The energy surrounds you like a shell that extends all the way through the ground.

Build the shield with your mind. It can be a bubble. It can glow brightly or power up to turn reflective and send the negative vibes right back to the sender. If the attack continues, you might need to hold focus to reinforce it and keep it strong. Visualize energy pouring into it, filling the space, to create an energetic barrier between your aura and the outside world.

Call your shield up into place as a barrier whenever you are being harassed, when you feel someone draining your energy, or when you become immersed in negativity. The more you work with the visualization, the quicker you will be able to manifest it and the stronger it will be.

If you are more comfortable working with earth energy, you might draw your shield energy up from the ground and extend it up above your head. Use a trigger word to prompt the visualization and snap your shield in place. A practiced trigger word helps the mind work quickly through a series of exercises to build the visualization. Your trigger word can be anything that fuels the process. Make up your own or try these:

Shield: To protect or hide

Clear: To clear the area around you of all negativity

Cancel: To dispel negative energy or anxiety

Reflect: To send negative energy back

Soothe: To calm ruffled feathers or soothe a reaction

Love: To heal or turn anger into acceptance

SPOTLIGHT INGREDIENT
Salt

Salt is an age-old protective aid strewn across thresholds, cast over the shoulder, and added to baths. The humble mineral is both a purifier and a protector that will cleanse and banish negative energy from a person, place, or object. Sprinkle salt across the floor of any room to clear negative energy. Strew it over a threshold or windowsill to keep out pesky energy. Add salt to washwater and wipe down the surfaces to clean an area of negativity after an argument. Add salt to bathwater and immerse your body to balance emotions and rinse away the negative.

Bath of Protection

This formula uses the energy of basil and hyssop to counter any malevolence directed toward you.

You will need:
7 drops basil essential oil
½ cup salt
1 handful basil leaves
1 handful hyssop leaves and flowers
1 red or white candle
matches or a lighter

Mix the basil oil into the salt and pour the mix under the running bathwater. Toss in the fresh basil and hyssop and light the candle. (If you would rather, you can make an infusion with the herb and add the liquid.) Get in and relax. Splash the water over yourself. Dunk your head, and when you come up, say,

> *With these words spoken,*
> *the hex is broken.*
> *By the power of water, basil, hyssop, and salt,*
> *the assault is repelled.*
> *By the power of water, basil, hyssop, and salt,*
> *the trouble sent is now quelled.*

By the power of three times three,
ill will is negated.
I am free.

Unhexing Bath

This spell works great when you've experienced a run of bad luck and suspect that someone's jealousy has hexed you.

You will need:
olive oil
frankincense essential oil
eucalyptus essential oil
juniper essential oil
1 black candle
½ cup salt
matches or a lighter

Pour a dime-size amount of olive oil into your hand. Add 1 drop of each essential oil to the olive oil and use it to dress the candle. Add 5 drops of frankincense, 2 drops of eucalyptus, and 2 drops juniper oil to the salt. Fill the bathtub. Pour the salt mixture under the running water. Light the candle and get into the tub. To change your luck and nullify the ill wishes, duck under the water three times and as you surface say,

By these words spoken,
ill luck is broken.

Duck under again and say,

By the power of three times three,
I banish all negativity.

Repeat until you have completed the phrase 9 times. If you wish to rid yourself of a hex or the evil eye, say,

By water and salt,
your ill will is cleared.

I have nothing to fear,
   for the ill you sent to me
   is now returned by the power of three.
   It is yours to bear as you now reap what you have sown.

Release the energy to run down the drain with the water.

Bath to End Unwanted Attentions

Sometimes we attract the attention of someone or something that we do not want. Tell someone you trust about the situation if you feel you are in danger. Sometimes just talking about it helps defuse the situation. Sometimes you need reinforcements. Work some bath magick to thwart the unwanted attention.

You will need:
1 black or white candle
olive oil
½ teaspoon caraway seeds
½ teaspoon cloves
mesh bag
1 handful chamomile flowers
1 handful blackberry leaves
frankincense oil
½ cup salt
matches or a lighter
5 dried vervain leaves
firesafe dish

Anoint the candle with olive oil. Grind the caraway and cloves together and roll the candle in the powder. Set the candle where it can easily be reached from the tub. Stuff a mesh bag with equal parts chamomile flowers and blackberry leaves. Fill the tub and toss in the mesh bag. Add 9 drops of frankincense oil to the salt and dump it under the running water. Light the candle. Get in the tub and soak. Gaze at the candle and breathe out all the negative emotions you are feeling. Submerge to rinse away all the residual emotions.

When you emerge, take a vervain leaf and hold it to the flame. As it burns, say,

You are not welcome here.
Not now, not ever.

Drop the leaf into the firesafe dish and light another.

I banish you
from my life.

Drop the leaf into the firesafe dish and light another.

I banish you
from my thoughts.

Drop the leaf into the firesafe dish and light another.

I banish you
from my future.

Drop the leaf into the firesafe dish and light another.

I banish you
now and forever.

When you are ready to get out, release the energy to run down the drain with the water.

Recipes for Protection

Banishing Oil

Combat the negative with a batch of banishing oil. Banishing oil is good to have on hand because you never know when you might need it.

You will need:
1 handful pine needles
sprig of rosemary
3 cloves of garlic, crushed

1 teaspoon crushed black peppercorns

pinch of cayenne

small canning jar with a tight-fitting lid

olive oil, to fill

Ask the herbs if they will lend their protection powers to your formula as you gather them. If you are using fresh herbs, you should fresh-wilt them to decrease their moisture content. To do this, lay the herbs out on your counter in a single layer and cover with a dishtowel. Leave them to wilt overnight.

To make your oil, place the pine needles, rosemary, garlic, peppercorns, and cayenne into a small clean jar. Pour oil over them, making sure they are completely covered. Fill the jar to the top with the oil. Seal the jar and shake to make sure there are no trapped air bubbles. Set it on a shelf in a dark cupboard for at least 3 days; allow a week if you aren't pressed for time. Visit the jar daily and give it a shake as you reinforce your intention. When the oil is ready, strain out the herbs. Pour the oil into a clean jar with a tight-fitting lid and label. Store the jar in a cool, dry place. Watch out for any signs of spoilage and discard the oil if you see any.

Use the banishing oil to ward your home. Dip your finger in and trace the oil over the threshold to repel negativity. Draw a protective symbol with it on your door. Trace it across a windowsill that faces an aggravating neighbor to repel their unwanted attentions. Use the oil to empower a banishing ritual. Use the oil to anoint ritual candles. Or write what you would like to banish on a paper, anoint it with banishing oil, and fold the page away from you. Light the folded page and drop it into a firesafe dish.

If you need some instant protection, make a batch of banishing oil with essential oils, as in the following two recipes.

Banishing Oil 2

You will need:

12 drops pine essential oil

9 drops peppermint essential oil

9 drops rosemary essential oil

Banishing Oil 3

You will need:

12 drops cypress essential oil

9 drops cedarwood essential oil

9 drops clove essential oil

Spell: Make a Protection Mojo Bag

You will need:

candle

matches

small muslin or cotton bag

1 agrimony stalk or a handful of dried bits

1 small burdock root

bit of dried rue

small hagstone, a piece of jet, or hematite

Light the candle and settle down comfortably where you can see it. Arrange your supplies in front of you and draw a breath as you let your thoughts clear. Breathe and sit with the moment until your awareness has sharpened and fixed in the moment. Take the bag in your nondominant hand and select one of the items. Name it. Tell it what you want it to do, and then blow across it to activate its energy and stuff it into the pouch. Do this for the agrimony, burdock, rue, and stone until the pouch is full. Wear the pouch for protection or tuck it into something you wish to protect.

The following are some other protective herbs you might carry:

- Burdock to end bad thoughts and feelings
- Pennyroyal to block the negativity of others
- Rosemary to dispel negative energy
- Rue to ward your energy from jealousy
- St. John's wort to guard against spiritual attack
- Vervain to banish a negative outlook, harmful habits, or hurtful people from your life

Vervain Aspersion Infusion

Aside from being a mood elevator, vervain is also an herb of protection. Brew up an infusion and use it as a spritzer to banish negative energy. Pour it into your bathwater and soak to rid yourself a negative outlook.

You will need:
1 handful fresh or dried vervain

Bring 2 cups of water to a boil. Turn off the heat and add the vervain. Cover the pan to prevent steam from escaping. Let the infusion steep for up to 10 minutes. Strain out the herbal matter and let the liquid cool. Pour the infusion into a spray bottle and use it as a spritzer to lift vibration. Spritz the air above you and be present as the mist falls around you to refresh thought and stimulate a positive outlook. Spritz the room to clear away negativity or to cleanse a ritual space. Use it in work to banish harmful habits and hurtful people from your life. Add the infusion to your bathwater and soak to banish anxiety and worry.

Protective Garlic Paste

You will need:
2 heads garlic, cloves separated, peeled, and minced
olive oil

Scrape the garlic into a small caning jar. Top with olive oil to fill the jar and seal with a tight-fitting lid. Place the jar in the refrigerator and let the garlic infuse the oil for 1 week. Scrape the mixture into a small blender or food processor and whiz to make a paste. Store the mixture in a jar in the refrigerator. It should keep for several months.

Add a spoon to salad dressing when you need to protect your words. Spread it on a crusty piece of bread and eat it to preserve your personal space, or toss it with pasta to protect health and ward your body. Rub the paste on the soles of your shoes to keep the negative energy from following you home. Rub it on the front step of your home to keep a troublemaker away.

Spell: Clear Your Home of Bad Luck

You will need:

1 part rosemary

1 part mint

1 part thyme

Sprinkle the mixture across the floors as you say,

Herbs of luck, with this brew,
I charm this place,
Your power true.
Banish ill and in its place
good fortune flows through this space.

Leave the strew in place overnight. Sweep it up the next morning and discard it by dumping it on the other side of your property line.

Herbal Formulas for Protection

See page 18 for infusion brewing guidance.

Psychic Protection

You will need:

1 part dried rosemary

1 part dried St. John's wort

1 part dried yarrow

Add this blend to a dish of salt and pour it into your bathwater to grant psychic protection. Mix the oil blend with your favorite carrier and wear it as a psychic shield.

Bay and Garlic Protection Powder

You will need:

1 part dried bay leaves

1 part garlic skins

Grind the garlic skins and bay leaves together. Anoint your candles with oil and roll them in the powder to empower banishing spells. Burn the powder on a charcoal disk as a protective incense to rid yourself or your house of negativity.

Energy-Clearing Incense Powder

You will need:

1 part dried rue

1 part dried vervain

1 part dried sage

Grind the dried ingredients together and burn a pinch on a charcoal disk to clear away stagnant or negative energy and raise the vibration of a room.

Wash Away the Negative

You will need:

1 part basil

1 part hyssop

1 part pine needles

Brew an infusion with these herbs and add it to your washwater. Use it to wash your countertops and floors to get rid of negative energy and instigate positive energy flow.

Barrier of Protection

You will need:

2 parts frankincense

2 parts myrrh

1 part clove

Grind the herbs together and burn them as incense to protect a space. Burn the blend to transform fear into peace.

Essential Oil Formulas for Protection

Mood-Protecting Blend

You will need:

5 drops cypress essential oil

5 drops myrrh essential oil

Mix myrrh oil into cypress oil and use the blend to banish negativity and sorrow. Burn in a diffuser to repel sadness. Mix the blend into 1 tablespoon of castile soap and add it to bathwater to banish negativity. Add the blend to washwater and use it to clear away frustration and restore harmony.

Protect Your Space Blend

You will need:

6 drops clary sage essential oil

2 drops bay essential oil

2 drops lavender essential oil

Mix the oils together and burn them in a diffuser or trace them over a threshold to keep negative energy out. Add the oil blend to a small dish of salt and dump it into bathwater for a protective soak to rinse away negativity and lift vibration.

Drive Away the Negative Blend

You will need:

6 drops sandalwood essential oil

2 drops cinnamon essential oil

2 drops clove essential oil

Blend the oils into 1 tablespoon of your favorite carrier and wear it as a scent to lift a bad mood. Add it to a dish of salt and pour it under running bathwater for a soak to banish aggravation. Burn it in a diffuser to ward a room.

Curse Removal Blend

You will need:

7 drops sandalwood essential oil

5 drops lavender essential oil

5 drops rose essential oil

3 drops bay oil essential oil

3 drops vetiver essential oil

Mix the oils together and burn them in a diffuser to break a hex or trace them over a threshold to keep out negative energy. Add the oil blend to a small dish of salt and dump it into bathwater for an energy-clearing soak to dispel negativity or break a curse.

Hex-Breaking Blend

You will need:

5 drops patchouli essential oil

5 drops myrrh essential oil

5 drops sandalwood essential oil

Blend the oils together and burn them in a diffuser to banish a bad mood. Add the oil blend to a small dish of salt. Add it to bathwater and immerse yourself to get rid of bad luck. Dunk completely under the water several times when you suspect you may have been hexed.

Blend to Banish Negativity

You will need:

5 drops lemon essential oil

4 drops oregano essential oil

3 drops juniper berry essential oil

Blend the oils into 1 tablespoon of your favorite carrier and wear it as a scent to bust a bad mood. Add to a dish of salt and pour under running bathwater for a soak to banish aggravation. Dab the blend on a mirror and place it between you and the troublemaker to send the ill will back. Use the blend to fight negativity and break jinxes.

Part 3

Apothecary
for Wellness

Chapter 16

PLANT ALLIES TO EMPOWER WELLNESS

During a discussion about Yule and food magick, a listener asked if the pandemic and the changes in the world had affected my practice. As I thought how to answer, I realized that not only had my practice shifted from bold rituals for prosperity and abundance to smaller, more frequent rituals for comfort and solace, but I had embraced the adaptogens and nervines growing in my environment and made them the foundation of most of my remedies, potions, and formulas. The next day I began composing these plant profiles. These are the allies that have become prominent in my practice. Many are either adaptogens that help us deal with stress and restore balance or nervines that calm anxiousness and support the nervous system. Each has the potential to become a powerful ally to help you be healthy, happy, and magickal.

Bay

Botanical Name: *Laurus nobilis*

Parts Used: Leaf

Magickal Properties: Glory, luck, psychic vision, protection, strength, victory, vitality, wisdom, and wishes

Healing Benefits: While the bay is not a nervine, its uplifting, protective
energy can be used to protect your state of mind and increase your sense
of well-being.

Warning: Do not confuse the bay tree, *Laurus nobilis*, with the mountain
laurel, *Kalmia latifolia*, which is poisonous.

I have a potted bay that has traveled with me through several address changes. In
Arizona it lived in the garden. In LA it lived in a pot on my balcony. Now that we are
in Northern Oregon, it lives in my greenhouse. I've read that it is hardy to zone 8b,
but with the erratic extreme cold we have been experiencing here these last couple
of years, I am afraid to plant it outside and risk damaging it.

Bay trees are slow growing and only need to be repotted into a larger pot every
couple of years. When I bought mine, it was a small sapling. Twelve years have
passed and now it is five feet tall and three feet wide. The tree would be larger, but
because I continually harvest the leaves and new growth, it has stayed a manageable
size to move in and out of my greenhouse. I use the leaves fresh and dry in formulas
to empower intention and add a pleasant and savory flavor to soups, sauces, and
beans.

A Brief History

The bay tree is native to the Mediterranean, where it was symbolic of victory and
wisdom. The athletes and scholars of ancient Greece were honored with laurel
crowns and wreaths to celebrate their triumphs.[41] In fact the name *Laurus* is from
Latin meaning "to praise" or "to honor," while *nobilis* means "renowned."[42] Its aromatic leaves have been used as medicine and to flavor food for thousands of years.[43]
It was one of the herbs burned to cleanse and purify. Bay leaves were used in Roman
baths to scent the air and grant relief from aching muscles.[44] Andrew Chevallier

. . . .

41. Emma Callery, *The Complete Book of Herbs: A Practical Guide to Cultivating, Drying, and Cooking with More Than 50 Herbs* (Philadelphia, PA: Courage Books, 1994), 85.

42. Lorraine Harrison, *Latin for Gardeners: Over 3,000 Plant Names Explained and Explored* (Chicago: University of Chicago Press, 2012), 120.

43. Saima Batool et al., "Bay Leaf," *Medicinal Plants of South Asia* (2020): 63–74, doi:10.1016/B978-0-08-102659 -5.00005-7.

44. Margaret Picton, *The Book of Magical Herbs: Herbal History, Mystery, and Folklore* (London: Quarto, 2000), 19.

writes in his *Encyclopedia of Herbal Medicine* that in ancient Rome "an infusion of leaves was taken for its warming and tonic effect on the stomach and bladder, and a plaster made from the leaves was used to relieve wasp and bee stings."[45]

How to Use

The bay tree has a history steeped in lore. It was worn for protection, carried as a lucky charm, and used to enhance psychic abilities. According to the Roman poet Ovid, the bay tree was once a nymph named Daphne who escaped Apollo's advances by having Gaia transform her into the laurel tree.[46] Historically, the bay was held as a tree of protection. In her article in *Fine Gardening* magazine, Susan Belsinger writes, "Sorcerers and poisoners could not harm the person who carried bay. It was believed that lightning would not strike where bay was planted. The Caesars appropriated bay as their special protector against accidents and conspiracies. Though not notably successful, its efficacy in this field was maintained even in sixteenth- and seventeenth-century England. Witches and devils were supposedly rendered helpless by it."[47] In ancient Greece and Rome it was a common practice to keep a potted bay beside the front door to keep out malicious sprits.[48] If you'd like to try this but you don't have a potted bay to set beside your door, you can make a protective incense by crumbling three dry bay leaves with dried basil, cloves, garlic skins, and rosemary. Burn the incense on a charcoal disk to drive away malevolent energies.

The bay also is known for its ability to increase psychic abilities. Greek priestesses in the temples of Apollo chewed bay leaves and burned them to fumigate themselves so that they could receive visions.[49] Today the camphoraceous scent is inhaled to inspire creative thought and encourage psychic sight. Simply hold a dry bay leaf over a firesafe dish and hold a lit match to it. When it begins to burn, breathe in the

. . . .

45. Andrew Chevallier, *Encyclopedia of Herbal Medicine* (New York: DK Publishing, 2016), 227.

46. Ovid, *Metamorphoses*, the Ovid Project, University of Vermont, accessed January 13, 2022, book 1, https://www.uvm.edu/~hag/ovid/garth/garthb1p11.html.

47. Susan Belsinger, "Bay (*Laurus noblis*): From Legend and Lore to Fragrance and Flavor," *Fine Gardening*, accessed December 1, 2022, https://www.finegardening.com/article/bay-laurus-nobilis-from-legend-and-lore-to-fragrance-and-flavor.

48. Jack Staub, *The Illustrated Book of Edible Plants* (Layton, UT: Gibbs Smith, 2016), 19.

49. Jennifer Peace Rhind, *Fragrance and Wellbeing: Plant Aromatics and Their Influence on the Psyche* (London: Singing Dragon, 2014), 82.

aroma and take note of what follows. The scented smoke has a calm awakening effect to open the mind, stimulate psychic powers, and inspire creative thought.

In *Plant Lore, Legends, and Lyrics,* Richard Folkard details a ritual to achieve prophetic dreams:

> Rise between three and four o'clock in the morning of your birthday, with cautious secresy, so as to be observed by no one, and pluck a sprig of Laurel; convey it to your chamber, and hold it over some lighted brimstone for five minutes, which you must carefully note by a watch or dial; wrap it in a white linen cloth or napkin, together with your own name written on paper, and that of your lover (or if there is more than one, write all the names down), write also the day of the week, the date of the year, and the age of the moon; then haste and bury it in the ground, where you are sure it will not be disturbed for three days and three nights; then take it up, and place the parcel under your pillow for three nights, and your dreams will be truly prophetic as to your destiny.[50]

A modern bay spell is to write a wish on a dry bay leaf and burn it to release your desire to the universe.

The bay tree's aromatic leaves contain 1,8-cineole, also known as eucalyptol, the same compound found in eucalyptus leaves and cardamom.[51] Today we know it has analgesic, antifungal, antibacterial, antiviral, anti-inflammatory, and immune-stimulant properties to accelerate wound healing.[52] Brew a bay leaf infusion and pour into bathwater to relieve muscle aches. Soak feet in a bay leaf infusion to revive a weary spirit. Bay leaf tea can be useful in the treatment of migraines.[53] It also contains enzymes that aid digestion.[54] Drop a few leaves into soup to increase nutrient absorption.[55] Or tie a bay leaf with sprigs of fresh parsley, rosemary, and thyme to

. . . .

50. Richard Folkard, *Plant Lore, Legends, and Lyrics* (London: Sampson Low, Marston, Searle, and Rivington, 1884), 102.

51. Andy Brunning, "Chemical Compounds in Herbs & Spices," *Compound Interest* (blog), March 13, 2014, https://www.compoundchem.com/2014/03/13/chemical-compounds-in-herbs-spices/.

52. Batool et al., "Bay Leaf," 63–74, https://www.ncbi.nlm.nih.gov/pmc/articles/PMC7152419/.

53. "The Benefits of Drinking Bay Leaf Tea," Flushing Hospital, April 1, 2015, https://www.flushinghospital.org/newsletter/the-benefits-of-drinking-bay-leaf-tea/.

54. "The Benefits of Drinking Bay Leaf Tea," Flushing Hospital.

55. Chevallier, *Encyclopedia of Herbal Medicine*, 227.

make the classic French *bouquet garni*. Drop the bundle into the cooking pot to add complexity to the flavor of soups.

California Poppy

Botanical Name: *Eschscholzia californica*

Parts Used: Aerial parts

Magickal Properties: Cheer, dreams, intuition, love, and sleep

Healing Benefits: The California poppy has a gentle, calming energy used to lift outlook, ease anxiety, promote a better night's sleep, and just overall make life more manageable. It is known for its sedative action and ability to relieve pain due to tension. The California poppy is an edible plant. It is eaten and brewed into tension-taming infusions to calm nervousness and soothe headaches. If taken before bed, it can help you get a restful sleep.

Warning: None.

I love this cheerful little flower. It is a wild volunteer, popping up year after year in my wildflower beds. In the summer California poppies provide a source of pollen for bees, bumblebees, and butterflies and a supply of food, medicine, and magick for me. I add California poppies to my flower teas and eat them in salads and sandwiches for an uplifting, feel-good energy to lift mood and encourage a positive outlook.

A Brief History

The California poppy is a New World wildflower. Like its cousin the opium poppy, the California poppy contains sedative alkaloids, but because it does not contain morphine, it is nonaddictive. California poppies were used by Native Americans as sedatives, hypnotics, and analgesics.[56] According to Reader's Digest's guide *Magic and Medicine of Plants*, "The local Indians used the plant as a painkiller, especially for toothache; as a remedy for insomnia and headache; and as a poultice for sores and ulcers."[57] The Chumash and Yuki used the plant as a sedative and crushed it to make

....

56. Aviva Romm, *Botanical Medicine for Women's Health* (St. Louis, MO: Elsevier, 2010), 493.

57. Reader's Digest, *Magic and Medicine of Plants* (New York: Reader's Digest, 1986), 128.

a compress for pain relief to treat toothache, headache, and insomnia.[58] In 1816 a naturalist aboard a Russian exploration ship named the species *Eschscholzia* after the ship's surgeon, who was his friend.[59] Andrew Chevallier writes in *Encyclopedia of Herbal Medicine*, "Early settlers used California poppy for sleep problems, especially in children, and for whooping cough."[60] In the late 1800s a liquid extract made from California poppies was sold as a relaxant and pain medication for children as a substitute for opium.[61]

How to Use

The bright blossoms are also known as "cup of sunlight," and they hold a cheerful yet sedative energy to calm nerves and banish worry. According to the herbalist and medical professional authors of *Mental Wellness*, "Its profoundly calming, almost hypnotic, effects are ideal for those who get easily overexcited and distracted, then have trouble settling back down to everyday life."[62] In *The Woman's Book of Healing Herbs*, herbalist Christopher Hobbs shares in an interview, "California poppy is the best antianxiety herb I've found, and it works quickly, often within three hours."[63] A study found that California poppy makes life seem a little better, a little more manageable, to patients.[64] Make your own happy poppy tea by mixing the dried flowers with chamomile and lemon balm. Drink a mug to lift your outlook or pour the infusion into bathwater and soak to brighten your mood. All aerial parts of the California poppy, including the seeds, are edible. The Association for the Advancement of Restorative Medicine lists California poppy as a safe, nonaddictive substance for

. . . .

58. Lanny Kaufer, *Medicinal Herbs of California* (Guilford, CT: Falcon Guides, 2021), 192.

59. Julie Kierstead Nelson, "California Poppy (*Eschscholzia californica*)," US Forest Service, accessed March 21, 2022, https://www.fs.fed.us/wildflowers/plant-of-the-week/eschscholzia_californica.shtml.

60. Chevallier, *Encyclopedia of Herbal Medicine*, 207.

61. Kaufer, *Medicinal Herbs of California*, 192.

62. Pat Thomas et al., *Mental Wellness: A Holistic Approach to Mental Health and Healing* (New York: DK Publishing, 2021), 50.

63. Sari Harrar and Sara Altshul O'Donnell, *The Woman's Book of Healing Herbs* (Emmaus, PA: Rodale Press, 2000), 436.

64. Kathy Abascal and Eric Yarnell, "Nervine Herbs for Treating Anxiety," *Alternative and Complementary Therapies* 10, no. 6 (December 2004): 309–15, doi:10.1089/act.2004.10.309.

"managing pain, anxiety, and insomnia."[65] Brew up a calming tea by mixing California poppy with passionflower and skullcap. Sip it to unwind. Drink a cup an hour before bedtime to promote a good night's sleep and encourage pleasant dreams. Unlike opium-producing varieties, California poppy does not cause a high and instead produces a mild analgesic effect to calm the psyche, help overcome fears, and normalize social functions.[66] Drink a glass of California poppy tea before a social encounter to reduce anxiety.

Catnip

Botanical Name: *Nepeta cataria*

Parts Used: Aerial parts

Magickal Properties: Beauty, familiar magick, friendship, joy, and love

Healing Benefits: Catnip acts as a mild nervine to calm the nerves and induce sleep. Its gentle sedative properties calm anxiety and help relax and restore digestive health.

Warning: Do not smoke or ingest catnip while pregnant or breastfeeding. It is not suitable for children and should not be consumed in excess.

Catnip is a fast-growing perennial wildflower that spreads by sending runners through the soil, which is why I grow mine in a garden box. It is an attractive plant, and when it flowers, the bees and butterflies appreciate it even more than my cat. Its flavor is not as nice as some of the other mints, but it adds a relaxing quality to a glass of iced tea. Pair it with peppermint or lemon balm to make it more palatable. It is important to note that if catnip is taken in high doses, it may cause vomiting and headaches. Nepetalactone, the compound that acts as a sedative, can also be used as an insecticide and an herbicide.[67]

....

65. "California Poppy (*Eschscholzia californica*)," Association for the Advancement of Restorative Medicine, accessed February 2, 2022, https://restorativemedicine.org/library/monographs/california-poppy/.

66. Abascal and Yarnell, "Nervine Herbs for Treating Anxiety," 309–15.

67. Foster and Duke, *A Field Guide to Medicinal Plants*, 70.

A Brief History

Catnip was used for centuries as a potherb and a medicine.[68] The fresh leaves have a green, woodsy flavor and can be added to salads and made into sauces. In the Middle Ages catnip was one of the medicinal herbs grown by monks and brewed into a tea that was drunk as a relaxant and general tonic.[69] Catnip was listed in an herbal from 1735 as a remedy for indigestion and upset stomach.[70] The leaves were chewed to treat toothaches.[71] And late-nineteenth-century herbalist Jethro Kloss praised catnip, saying that it would save parents many sleepless nights if only they had it on their shelf.[72] In France catnip was a kitchen herb, and in England it was infused into a tea to treat nervous headaches, colds, and fevers and to aid sleep.[73]

Catnip traveled with the settlers to the New World, where its use was adopted to treat cold symptoms and other ailments.[74] Today, catnip tea is consumed for its calming effects. It is said to promote relaxation and reduce tension.[75]

How to Use

Catnip is associated with Bast and Sekhmet, and while it is most known for the euphoria it triggers in cats, it has a relaxing effect on humans when eaten or taken as tea.[76] Simply brew an infusion from the aerial parts and sip.

In her book *Nature's Remedies,* Jean Willoughby writes, "Catnip has a gentle, soothing effect on the body and can be combined with chamomile to make a relaxing tea. … It is also an effective treatment for colds, upset stomachs, and the irritability

. . . .

68. Steven Foster and Rebecca L. Johnson, *Desk Reference to Nature's Medicine* (Washington, DC: National Geographic, 2006), 88.

69. Foster and Johnson, *Desk Reference to Nature's Medicine*, 88.

70. Cohen, *The Artisan Herbalist*, 79.

71. Reader's Digest, *Magic and Medicine of Plants*, 134.

72. Rosemary Gladstar, *Rosemary Gladstar's Herbal Recipes for Vibrant Health* (North Adams, MA: Storey Publishing, 2008), 170.

73. Grieve, *A Modern Herbal,* vol. 1, 174.

74. Foster and Johnson, *Desk Reference to Nature's Medicine*, 88.

75. Emily Cronkleton, "What Are the Risks and Benefits of Catnip Tea?" Medical News Today, September 29, 2021, https://www.medicalnewstoday.com/articles/catnip-tea.

76. Foster and Johnson, *Desk Reference to Nature's Medicine*, 88.

and tension that may accompany theses ailments."[77] Brew catnip with lavender and marjoram to lift spirits and foster joy.

Catnip is associated with Libra and Venus and is used in beauty, love, and fertility charms. Use catnip to embolden love and anchor friendship. Drop a fresh sprig into a glass of iced tea and serve it at a friendly luncheon to deepen relationships. Tuck a few leaves into your left pocket when you are meeting someone new to enhance charm. Brew a catnip infusion and add it to your bathwater to boost attraction and charm. Hang a sprig of catnip over a threshold to attract positive energy, or sprinkle it across your bed to attract a new lover. Stuff a sachet with dried catnip and dried rose petals to a make love charm. Tuck it into your left pocket to attract a love that is true. Burn dried catnip with dragon's blood to repel a negative influence.

Chamomile

Botanical Names: *Chamaemelum nobile* (Roman chamomile) and *Matricaria chamomilla* (German chamomile)

Parts Used: Flowering tops

Magickal Properties: Abundance, communication, healing, peace, rest, and water elemental

Healing Benefits: A gentle sedative used to promote relaxation and reduce anxiety, chamomile is especially beneficial for those who feel the effects of anxiety in their stomachs, as it helps calm the signals between the nervous system and the gut, soothing the stomach, relaxing the body, and reducing the stress response.[78]

Warning: May be an allergen, especially if you are allergic to ragweed.

I grow both German and Roman chamomile. Roman chamomile is a creeping perennial often used as a ground cover. German chamomile is a tall annual. Both species produce aromatic white daisylike flowers with yellow centers in the spring and summer. Though Roman chamomile isn't as floriferous as the German variety, its flowers exude a stronger apple-like scent. Both species are lovely additions to any

. . . .

77. Willoughby, *Nature's Remedies*, 62.

78. Thomas et al., *Mental Wellness*, 57.

garden and both are plant doctors, as they have natural antibacterial and antifungal properties that cause neighboring plants to be healthier just by growing nearby.

A Brief History

Although Roman and German chamomile are two plants belonging to different species, both are Old World medicine plants used to treat are same ailments. Chamomile has been used down through the ages to calm and sedate.[79] Researchers found evidence Neanderthals were self-medicating with both chamomile and yarrow 50,600 years ago.[80] Chamomile was popular with the Greeks, Romans, and Egyptians, who used it for a range of conditions.[81] In ancient Egypt, chamomile was a sacred medicine associated with the sun and a medicine to ease fever and chills.[82] The Greeks used chamomile to treat both fevers and female disorders, while the Anglo-Saxons incorporated it into a charm to repel illness.[83] Chamomile was a popular strewing herb and was boiled with orange peels to scent washwater.[84] Today we know that chamomile is a carminative with the power to ease gas and bloating, and it has antispasmodic qualities to relieve muscle tension. You can brew an infusion of equal parts chamomile and blackberry leaves to calm a trouble stomach.

How to Use

Chamomile is by far the most popular of the herbal teas. It contains apigenin, a natural compound that when ingested produces a calming effect to ease anxiety and cause drowsiness.[85] Sipping a cup of chamomile tea is an age-old practice to quell

· · · · · · · · · · · · · · · ·

79. Picton, *The Book of Magical Herbs*, 48.

80. Zach Zorich, "Neanderthal Medicine Chest," *Archaeology*, January/February 2013, https://www.archaeology.org/issues/61-1301/features/top-10/266-top-10-2012-neanderthal-medicine.

81. Willoughby, *Nature's Remedies*, 145.

82. Nancy J. Hajeski, *Nature's Best Remedies* (Washington, DC: National Geographic, 2019), 112; Foster and Johnson, *Desk Reference to Nature's Medicine*, 94.

83. Hajeski, *Nature's Best Remedies*, 112.

84. Picton, *The Book of Magical Herbs*, 49.

85. Kelly Burch, "Yes, Chamomile Tea Does Make You Sleepy—Here's How It Can Help You Fall Asleep," *Insider*, June 29, 2020, https://www.insider.com/does-chamomile-tea-make-you-sleepy.

worry and gain a restful sleep. Medieval herbals recommended chamomile as a remedy for pain and weariness.[86] An old Elizabethan herb song directs,

> *Plant me a garden to heal the heart,*
> *Balm for joy, and sweet violet,*
> *Cowslips, pansies, and chamomile*
> *To ease the pain I want to forget.*[87]

Drink a cup before bedtime to unwind. Pour a chamomile infusion into bathwater and soak to calm the nervous system and relax the body.

Chamomile is also a skin healer. Saturate a washcloth with a chamomile infusion and use it to clean your face to reduce blemishes. Use the washcloth as a compress to treat rashes, chicken pox, and eczema, or drape the wet cloth over your eyes to remedy puffy, tired eyes. Brew an infusion of chamomile, lavender, and sage. Add it to bathwater and soak to boost attraction powers.

Chamomile also has energy for protection. Drink a mug of chamomile tea to ward your state of mind before a confrontation. Add catnip to ease a nervous stomach. Pour a chamomile infusion into your bath and soak to remove negative energy. Brew it with basil to remove a hex.

Hawthorn

Botanical Name: *Crataegus* spp.; *C. monogyna* and *C. laevigata* plants can be used interchangeably.[88]

Parts Used: Leaf, flower, and fruit

Magickal Properties: Cleansing, cheer, faery magick, healing, protection, and wishes

Healing Benefits: Hawthorn increases circulation and has a mild sedative effect. It is used to protect heart health, calm restlessness, and help the mind deal with trauma and overwhelming emotions. Hawthorn is also used to remedy insomnia and relieve tension.

. . . .

86. Foster, *National Geographic Desk Reference to Nature's Medicine*, 94.

87. Picton, *The Book of Magical Herbs*, 49.

88. Thomas et al., *Mental Wellness*, 48.

Warning: Consult with an experienced practitioner before using hawthorn
if you are taking heart medications such as digitalis or beta blockers. Do
not use if you have diastolic congestive heart failure.

Hawthorn is a species of deciduous shrubs and small trees. English hawthorn (*Crataegus monogyna*), also known as common hawthorn, single-seed hawthorn, one-seed hawthorn, thornapple, Maythorn, May-tree, and Mayblossom, is a small, thorny European tree that was bred into dwarf varieties and planted throughout Oregon as an ornamental. As a result, the small, adaptable tree has now naturalized and can be found growing wild on both the east and west coasts of the United States.

Even though it is an attractive tree with abundant white flowers in the spring and bright red fruit in the fall, its name *Crataegus* is from the Greek *kratios*, or "strength," and *akis*, "sharp tips."[89] I have several small hawthorn trees in my yard. They have become allies with a gentle, uplifting energy to cheer and soothe. By observing their habits, I discovered they are a wildlife favorite. Hummingbirds, bees, and many other insects feed on the nectar-rich blossoms, and in the fall, the red berries feed small mammals and a range of birds from chickadees to waxwings. After some research and a period of experimentation, hawthorn has become one of the main ingredients in many of my formulas, for both medicine and magick.

A Brief History

The hawthorn is an attractive tree. It was once known as Maythorn, as it flowers abundantly at the end of April. When it was in fashion to go out "a-Maying," or go out on the morning of the first of May to collect flowers to wear and decorate the home and the street, gatherers would return with boughs of hawthorn covered in Mayblossoms.[90] The small blossoms exude a sweet honey scent even as the small lobed leaves hide the sharp thorns running along the branches. In China, hawthorn was used as medicine for high blood pressure and arteriosclerosis as far back as the fifth century.[91]

· · · · · · · · · · · · · · · · ·

89. Ross Bayton, *The Gardener's Botanical* (Princeton, NJ: Princeton University Press, 2020), 98.

90. Folkard, *Plant Lore, Legends, and Lyrics,* 58.

91. Foster and Johnson, *Desk Reference to Nature's Medicine,* 204.

How to Use

In the Middle Ages, hawthorn was given to treat many ailments.[92] It has been used for centuries as a heart tonic.[93] The leaves, flowers, and fruit are used to treat matters of the heart, including reducing blood pressure, treating melancholy, and helping heal the brokenhearted. Herbalist Holly Bellebuono writes that hawthorn tones the heart "by increasing coronary and myocardial circulation through a dilation of the coronary arteries. This dilation naturally lowers blood pressure and allows greater circulation throughout the body."[94] Hawthorn also produces a calming effect, especially when it is paired with a nervine such as California poppy.[95] Brew a relaxing tea with equal parts of hawthorn leaves and California poppy flowers. Sip it anytime life becomes overwhelming.

Hawthorn has become my go-to remedy to support a positive outlook or lift a darkened mood. The leaves, flowers, and berries have mild sedative properties that make the hawthorn helpful in treating nervous conditions. The young leaves, fresh flowers, and ripe fruit are all edible. The leaves can be harvested when they are young and added to salads. A hawthorn leaf infusion makes a wonderful hot or iced tea and creates a relaxing bath to soothe away worry and encourage acceptance when added to bathwater. Combine it with yarrow to ease a broken heart.

Hawthorn flowers should be harvested as they bloom. Float the flowers in a glass of iced tea for afternoon cheer, or add them to a glass of champagne and serve for a festive, feel-good drink. The hawthorn is a wishing tree. Pluck a flower on the first of May and make a wish upon it. Pop the flower in your mouth and swallow it to help manifest your desire.

The fruit, or haws, should be picked when they are ripe and grow sweeter after the first frost. They can be made into jellies, sauces, and wines.

The hawthorn held power over storms at sea and lightning. It was a guardian of wells and a lucky talisman to fishermen.[96] To the ancient Greeks and Romans

....

92. Chevallier, *Encyclopedia of Herbal Medicine*, 87.

93. Rosalee de la Forêt, *Alchemy of Herbs* (Carlsbad, CA: Hay House, 2017), 211.

94. Holly Bellebuono, *An Herbalist's Guide to Formulary* (Woodbury, MN: Llewellyn Publications, 2017), 79.

95. Abascal and Yarnell, "Nervine Herbs for Treating Anxiety," 309–15.

96. Diane Morgan, *The Charmed Garden: Sacred and Enchanting Plants for the Magically Inclined Herbalists* (Scotland, UK: Findhorn Press, 2004), 120.

the hawthorn symbolized hope, and they used the flowers in bridal bouquets and strewed the leaves and flower to repel demons.[97] Plant a hawthorn tree in your yard to stand guard and protect the house against lightning, wind, and evil spirits. Tie a thorn with red ribbon to create a protective amulet. Wrap a photo of a loved one in a cloth and tuck it into the branches for the hawthorn to hold and protect.

The hawthorn gets its name from the Old English word for hedge or enclosure, as hawthorns or "haws" were planted along land boundaries to mark the borders.[98] It became known as a liminal tree associated with faeries. In *The Religion of the Ancient Celts*, J. A. Macculloch writes, "In Ireland and the Isle of Man the thorn is thought to be the resort of fairies, and they, like the woodland fairies or 'wood men' are probably representatives of the older tree spirits and gods of groves and forests."[99] It was held that a trio of trees made up of an oak, ash, and thorn, or the faery triad, acted as a gateway to the faery realms.[100] Thread hawthorn, oak, and ash leaves together on a string and wear them into the woods to interact with nature spirits.

Holy Basil

Botanical Name: *Ocimum tenuiflorum*, syn. *O. sanctum*

Parts Used: Aerial parts

Magickal Properties: Balancing, beauty, happiness, healing, love, peace, and protection

Healing Benefits: Holy basil is a calming nervine and an adaptogenic herb known for its ability to encourage a positive outlook, soothe the nervous system, and help manage the stress response. It is helpful in the treatment of generalized anxiety disorder.[101]

Warning: May lower sperm count.

. . . .

97. Nancy Burke, *The Modern Herbal Primer* (Dublin: Yankee Publishing, 2000), 115.

98. Online Etymology Dictionary, s.v. "haw (n.)," by Douglas Harper, accessed March 4, 2022, https://www.etymonline.com/word/haw?ref=etymonline_crossreference#etymonline_v_6223.

99. J. A. Macculloch, *The Religion of the Ancient Celts* (New York: Charles Scribner's Sons, 1911), 203.

100. DJ Conway, *By Oak, Ash, & Thorn* (St. Paul, MN: Llewellyn Publications, 2004), 187.

101. D. Bhattacharyya et al., "Controlled Programmed Trial of *Ocimum sanctum* Leaf on Generalized Anxiety Disorders," *Nepal Medical College Journal* 10, no. 3 (September 2010): 176–79, https://pubmed.ncbi.nlm.nih.gov/19253862.

There are several varieties of holy basil, *Ocimum tenuiflorum*; green leaf holy basil is the kind I grow and use. Green leaf holy basil is a mint, a cousin of sweet basil. It is an erect, multistemmed plant with purple stems, green leaves, and white or purple blossoms. In Ayurvedic medicine, green leaf holy basil is known as *Rama tulsi*. Though it is a milder-tasting variety of holy basil, green leaf does contain eugenol, which gives it a spicy bite and a pungent, herbaceous clove-like scent.

A Brief History

Holy basil is native to India, where it is known as tulsi. Called the protector of life, the herb, and even the soil in which it grows, is held to be sacred.[102] Holy basil is grown in houses, gardens, and near temples all over India, and it has been used in Ayurvedic medicine for centuries. The aromatic leaves exude a pleasant clove-like fragrance.

Holy basil is a sacred herb associated with Vishnu, Krishna, and Lakshmi.[103] Richard Folkard wrote in 1884 that holy basil was venerated in India,

> where it is daily watered and worshipped by all the members of the household. Perhaps, also, it was on account of its virtues in disinfecting and vivifying malarious air that it first became inseparable from Hindu houses in India as the protecting spirit or Lar of the family. The pious Hindus invoke the divine herb for the protection of every part of the body, for life and for death, and in every action of life; but above all in its capacity of ensuring children to those who desire to have them.[104]

How to Use

Holy basil is an Ayurvedic herb also known as the "elixir of life." In their book *Adaptogens*, David Winston and Steven Maimes write that holy basil has been one of India's most important herbs, honored for more than three thousand years, "as a rasayana, an herb that nourishes a person's growth to perfect health and promotes long life."[105] Holy basil is also a traditional *shen* tonic used for thousands of years in

. . . .

102. Rachel Landon, *Superherbs* (London: Piatkus, 2017), 131.

103. Folkard, *Plant Lore, Legends, and Lyrics*, 244.

104. Folkard, *Plant Lore, Legends, and Lyrics*, 244.

105. Winston and Maimes, *Adaptogens: Herbs for Strength, Stamina, and Stress Relief* (Rochester, VT: Healing Arts Press, 2007), 168.

Chinese medicine to quiet the mind and calm the nervous system.[106] It works on the body as a nerve tonic to calm mood, reduce the stress response, and encourage a positive outlook.

Holy basil helps protect us from environmental stresses. As a natural adaptogen, it helps the mind and body cope during times of change. In t *Adaptogens* herbalists Winston and Maimes write, "Adaptogens are remarkable natural substances that help the body adapt to stress, support normal metabolic functions, and help restore balance. They increase the body's resistance to physical, biological, emotional and environmental stressors. … They are unique from other substances in their ability to restore the balance of endocrine hormones, modulate the immune system, and allow the body to maintain homeostasis."[107] According to Healthline, adaptogens "work to counteract the effects of stress in the body," doing so "at a molecular level by regulating a stable balance in the hypothalamic, pituitary, and adrenal glands." Additionally, "they increase mental work capacity, enhance attention, and prevent stress and fatigue."[108] A 2010 study in *Pharmacognosy Reviews* found that the combination of active phytochemicals in holy basil helps the body balance processes in times of stress, which acted as a "significant preventive and curative potential with respect to the stress-related degenerative diseases endemic to industrialized societies."[109] Brew a cup of holy basil tea and drink to balance emotions. Drink holy basil tea hot with milk in the morning to fortify resolve and face the day. Sweeten it with honey to brighten your outlook.

Holy basil is a Hindu wedding herb and a funeral herb and is used to make traditional water given to the dying.[110] Today we know that holy basil is an adaptogen with properties to lift mental fog, improve cognitive function, and ease mild depression. It contains properties to deepen concentration and aid learning. In her book *Nature's Remedies*, Willoughby writes that holy basil "is thought to work in part by

. . . .

106. Rachel Landon, *Superherbs* (London: Piatkus, 2017), 133.

107. Winston and Maimes, *Adaptogens*, 17.

108. Chaunie Brusie, "Adaptogenic Herbs: List, Effectiveness, and Health Benefits," Healthline, June 29, 2017, https://www.healthline.com/health/adaptogenic-herbs.

109. Priyabrata Pattanayak et al., "*Ocimum sanctum* Linn. A Reservoir Plant for Therapeutic Applications: An Overview," *Pharmacognosy Reviews* 4, no. 7 (2010): 95–105, doi:10.4103/0973-7847.65323.

110. Melissa Petruzzello, "Holy Basil," *Encyclopaedia Britannica*, accessed March 21, 2022, https://www.britannica.com/plant/holy-basil.

increasing circulation to the brain. This may help improve overall brain function, in turn reducing cloudy thinking and enhancing mental clarity."[111] The plant "is recognized both as a calming nervine that soothes the mind and as an adaptogenic herb with a normalizing effect on the body."[112] Whiz holy basil with spinach and coconut water to make a power drink to carry you through a challenging day. Mix ¼ cup holy basil into 1 cup of ricotta cheese and bake it into a galette or a pasta dish to add to its comforting powers.

Hops

Botanical Name: *Humulus lupulus*

Parts Used: Strobiles, or cone-like flowers

Magickal Properties: Banishing worries, calming, healing, prosperity, and sleep

Healing Benefits: Hops is a nervine with calmative properties to calm the nervous system. The soothing scent promotes drowsiness.

Warning: May cause dermatitis. This herb should not be used during pregnancy. Do not use if you suffer from depression.

Hops is a species of flowering plant in the Cannabaceae family, which also includes cannabis, and like its cousin, hop flower cones, or strobiles, are a strong sedative.[113] They are used to remedy anxiety, stress, and insomnia. I inherited a yearly crop of Cascade hops when I bought my Oregon home. Every spring, the dormant vines wake and quickly grow up to cover the deck in a lush wall of green. A hops vine can grow to be twenty feet tall in a growing season. Hops plants produce a flower that is a cone-like leafy bract. In late August to early September the cones are harvested. To tell if they are ready to harvest, give them and shake. If you hear a rattle, they are ready.

. . . .

111. Willoughby, *Nature's Remedies*, 67.

112. Willoughby, *Nature's Remedies*, 67.

113. Andrew Chevallier, *Herbal Remedies Handbook* (New York: DK Publishing, 2018), 146.

A Brief History

The hop is a bitter herb used to stimulate digestion. It is paired with chamomile to treat irritable bowel syndrome.[114] The hop flower has a bitter, piney-citrusy flavor and has been used as far back as the fourteenth century to add a bitter taste to beer.[115] The Romans ate the young hops shoots in spring as a potherb.[116] In Italy hops were considered a vegetable and eaten like asparagus.[117]

Hops have been used to remedy a wide range of conditions, from rheumatism, fevers, and hysteria to dispelling worms.[118] The history of hops as a sedative and a sleep aid goes back to the ninth century and the Arabian physician Mesue, who used hops to induce sleep.[119] King George III used a pillow stuffed with hops as a sleep aid.[120] Hops are also a remedy for insomnia, excitability, and stress. Hops were prescribed to remedy "a quarrelsome nature."[121] In the New World hops were used to relieve pain and treat fevers. The Algonquin and Mohegan used the cones to remedy nervousness, while the Fox and Cherokee used them to make a sedative.[122]

How to Use

The hop is an edible plant. The young leaves can be blanched and eaten like spinach. The shoots can be cooked up into a dish that tastes similar to fiddlehead ferns. The flowers, or strobiles, are valued for their relaxing effects on the nervous system. They have a long history of being added to beer to give it a bitter hoppy flavor. Hops are recognized as a nervine relaxant for treating insomnia.[123] The flowers contain

. . . .

114. Chevallier, *Herbal Remedies Handbook*, 146.

115. Ben McFarland, *World's Best Beers: One Thousand Craft Brews from Cask to Glass* (New York: Sterling, 2009), 12.

116. Maud Grieve, *A Modern Herbal*, vol. 1 (New York: Dover Publications, 1971), 411.

117. Julie Bruton-Seal and Matthew Seal, *Backyard Medicine: Harvest and Make Your Own Herbal Remedies* (New York, NY: Skyhorse Publishing, 2009), 72.

118. Foster and Johnson, *Desk Reference to Nature's Medicine*, 212.

119. Kenneth T. Farrell, *Spices, Condiments, and Seasonings* (Gaithersburg, MD: Aspen Publishing, 1999), 106.

120. Bruton-Seal and Matthew Seal, *Backyard Medicine*, 72.

121. Ernest Small, *North American Cornucopia* (Boca Raton, FL: Taylor & Francis, 2014), 382.

122. Anthony J. Cichoke, *Secrets of Native American Herbal Remedies* (New York: Avery Books, 2001), 49.

123. Vincent Minichiello, "Botanical Medicines to Support Healthy Sleep and Rest," VA Office of Patient Centered Care and Cultural Transformation (2018), 3, https://www.va.gov/WHOLEHEALTHLIBRARY/docs/Botanical-Medicines-to-Support-Healthy-Sleep-and-Rest.pdf.

volatile oils, resins, and pollens that have gentle sedative properties to relax the body without any harmful side effects. For a tea that naturally promotes relaxation, pour 1 cup boiling water over 1 teaspoon of hop flowers. Cover and steep for 5 minutes. Strain the liquid into a mug and stir in a spoonful of honey to curb the bitterness. Drink it to aid relaxation, induce sleep, or enhance dreams. Stuff a small pillow with dried hop flowers and tuck it under your pillow so the scent will lull you to sleep. Add rosemary and thyme for a sleep talisman to keep nightmares at bay.

Hops are associated with Jupiter, Mars, and the element air. They hold positive energy to inspire relaxation and happiness and are used to usher luck and prosperity into the home. In parts of Eastern Europe hops are thrown at newlyweds to instill fertility instead of rice.[124] It is an old English custom to hang a sprig of hops in the kitchen to ensure a plenty. Add hop flowers to potpourris to raise the vibration of a room. Add flowers to healing rituals and sachets and incense to instill peace.

Lavender

Botanical Name: *Lavandula angustifolia*

Parts Used: Flowers

Magickal Properties: Calm, cheer, clarity, communication, healing, love, peace, protection, sleep, and transformations

Healing Benefits: Lavender is an uplifting nervine. It is used to relieve tension headaches, calm anxiety, and remedy sadness and depression.

Warning: None.

Lavender is a lovely fragrant garden flower. I grow two varieties, Munstead and Spanish lavender, in swathes along the edge of my flowerbeds. Both varieties are hardy in my grow zone and bloom each year, feeding bees, hoverflies, and butterflies. The lavender border is planted with California poppies, and the luscious orange complements the graceful lavender flower spikes, making it a favorite place to visit. Lavender is one of the first herbs I began working with as a young witch. Its ease to grow and dry gave me a good supply to experiment with. Lavender is still a favorite ingredient of mine to use in teas; flavor kombucha; decorate icing; bake into cakes,

....
124. Arrowsmith, *Essential Herbal Wisdom*, 406.

cookies, and breads; and add to incenses, candle dressings, bath salts, and other magickal formulas.

A Brief History

Lavender is an herb of antiquity. It was a strewing herb, an insect repellent, an insomnia remedy, and a remedy to lift outlook, reduce anxiety, and calm irritability. The ancient Romans, Egyptians, and Phoenicians used lavender as perfume and as an embalming herb.[125] It was grown in the famed gardens of Thebes, and it is said that Tutankhamen was buried with so much lavender that it still scented the air when his chamber was opened.[126] Gardener Jack Staub writes, "Lavender was prized both for its calming and aphrodisiacal effects, having been broadly employed to dispel headaches while, at the same time, being strewn about Cleopatra's chambers to entice both Julius Caesar and Mark Antony."[127]

Lavender was also a healing balm. Elizabeth I drank daily cups of lavender tea to remedy migraines.[128] Seventeenth-century English botanist John Parkinson wrote that lavender was "of especiall good use for all the griefes and paines of the head and braine."[129] In her book *A Modern Herbal*, Maud Grieve writes, "In France, it is a regular thing for most households to keep a bottle of Essence of Lavender as a domestic remedy against bruises, bites and trivial aches and pains, both external and internal."[130] The tradition of "to lay up in lavender" means to take care of or put away.[131] And it was once held that if you carried a sprig of lavender with you, it would enable you to see ghosts.[132]

· · · · · · · · · · · · · · · · ·

125. Michelle Schoffro Cook, *Be Your Own Herbalist* (Novato, CA: New World Library, 2016), 106.

126. Picton, *The Book of Magical Herbs*, 91.

127. Staub, *The Illustrated Book of Edible Plants*, 90.

128. Picton, *The Book of Magical Herbs*, 94.

129. John Parkinson, *Theatrum Botanicvm* (London: Thomas Cotes, 1640), 74.

130. Maud Grieve, *A Modern Herbal*, vol. 2 (New York: Dover Publications, 1971), 472–73.

131. Ebenezer Cobham Brewer, *Dictionary of Phrase and Fable* (London: Cassell and Company Limited, 1895), 734.

132. Laura C. Martin, *Garden Flower Folklore* (Guilford, CT: Globe Pequot Press, 2009), 169.

How to Use

Lavender is associated with the planet Mercury, Gemini, Virgo, and the element air. The scent of lavender holds energy to clear the mind and open awareness. In Victorian England sprigs of lavender were sold on the street as tussie-mussies that were carried to cover unwanted odors and keep fevers away.[133] Today we know that breathing in the scent helps calm the spirit and encourage clear thinking. Fill your shirt pocket with dried lavender to chase away anxiety. Crush the herb through your shirt and breathe the scent deeply to clear thought.

Lavender is an ingredient in many healing formulas. It can both calm the mind and lift mood and energy. It was made into waters, gargles, and teas to remedy laryngitis, treat skin complaints, and balance emotions.[134] According to a 2013 study, drinking two cups of a lavender infusion daily is an effective treatment for some forms of depression.[135]

Lavender is also an herb of love. Use the buds in love formulas. Use lavender in spells to attract and protect relationships or to promote harmony in the home. Combine lavender flowers with bachelor's button, basil, and rosemary and brew them into an infusion. Add it to your washwater and use it to wipe down countertops and floors to promote peace. Add the infusion to your bathwater to encourage a harmonious mindset. Use lavender to enhance divination and dreamwork. Burn it as an incense to facilitate communication.

Lemon Balm

Botanical Name: *Melissa officinalis*

Parts Used: All aerial parts

Magickal Properties: Friendship, happiness, healing, love, peace, and success

. . . .

133. Callery, *The Complete Book of Herbs*, 87.

134. Picton, *The Book of Magical Herbs*, 95.

135. Masoud Nikfarjam et al., "The Effects of *Lavandula angustifolia* Mill. Infusion on Depression in Patients Using Citalopram: A Comparison Study," *Iranian Red Crescent Medical Journal* 15, no. 8 (August 2013): 734–39, doi:10.5812/ircmj.4173.

Healing Benefits: Lemon balm has soothing, anti-inflammatory, and antibacterial properties. It supports cognitive function and is known as heart's delight because of its ability to instill inner calm.[136]

Warning: This herb should not be used during pregnancy.

Lemon balm is an attractive and very helpful plant. It is easy to use, as it has a pleasant lemony flavor. The pollinators love its small flowers. But beware—if you plant it once, you will most likely have it forever. I planted one lemon balm plant five years ago, and now each spring it comes up all across my yard. Yesterday I noticed it had come up in the dahlia beds and the onion box and that it had sporadically mounded throughout the lawn.

A Brief History

Lemon balm is native to Southern Europe, but because of its popularity as a medicinal herb, it has naturalized across the world.[137] Hajeski writes in *Nature's Best Remedies*, "Since before the Middle Ages, traditional healers have relied on lemon balm to reduce anxiety, increase appetite, ease pain, and support thyroid, liver, and digestive health."[138] And lemon balm does seem to be a panacea, as modern science has found it contains powerful antioxidants that protect the brain, skin, and body from damaging free radicals, which in turn supports health, memory, mental alertness, complexion, and mood.[139] Lemon balm was used to make Carmelite water, or *Eau de Mélisse*, a restorative water that dates back to the 1300s.[140] Culpeper wrote that lemon balm was one of the best heart and nerve herbs.[141] Grieve tells us that lemon balm tea was drunk daily for longevity.[142] John Evelyn held that balm is "sovereign for the Brain, strengthening the Memory, and powerfully chasing away Melancholy."[143]

. . . .

136. Thomas et al., *Mental Wellness*, 95.

137. Cohen, *The Artisan Herbalist*, 93.

138. Hajeski, *Nature's Best Remedies*, 129.

139. Hajeski, *Nature's Best Remedies*, 129.

140. Rosalee de la Forêt, "Herbal Carmelite Water Recipe with Lemon Balm," Mountain Rose Herbs, September 12, 2018, https://blog.mountainroseherbs.com/herbal-carmelite-water-recipe.

141. Nicholas Culpeper, *Culpeper's Complete Herbal* (Manchester, UK: J. Gleave and Son, 1826), 14.

142. Grieve, *A Modern Herbal*, vol. 1, 77.

143. John Evelyn, *Acetaria: A Discourse on Sallets* (London: B Tooke, 1699), 10.

How to Use

Lemon balm tea has a pleasant scent and flavor. It is a natural nervine that has been used for thousands of years to lift the spirit and calm anxiety. In Germany lemon balm is prescribed to treat insomnia and nervous conditions.[144] And indeed human studies indicate lemon balm significantly reduces anxiety and depression without serious side effects.[145] The leaves can be used fresh or dried to brew a gentle, calming infusion taken to ease a nervous stomach, encourage mental clarity, and comfort the overwhelmed.[146]

Lemon balm is a versatile herb. Not only is it a cheerful aid to treat anxiety, insomnia, and sadness, but the pleasant flavor makes it easy to use for all sorts of remedies. Chew a leaf and spit it onto an insect bite to soothe the discomfort or dab it onto a cold sore to hasten healing time. Add the chopped leaves to salads or use them to dress a sandwich to increase a sense of well-being. Or brew up a simple syrup and use it to sweeten your favorite beverages.

Lemon balm is associated with Diana, Jupiter, the moon, and the element water. It holds energy for love and attraction. Legend says a fourteenth-century Hungarian queen restored her youthful appearance with the use of a lemon balm serum known as the Queen of Hungary's Water.[147] Have a hot date? Fill a bath sachet with lemon balm leaves and rose petals. Toss the sachet into the bath and soak. When you get out, pour a drop of jasmine, rose, or vanilla essential oil into your palm and rub it into your skin, and you will be ready to woo. Use lemon balm in formulas for love and friendship spells. Anoint a pink candle with oil and roll it in crumbled bits of dried lemon balm to inspire compassion and kindness. Burn it as incense to encourage patience. Stuff a sachet with dried lemon balm and hang it to inspire affection. Tuck a sprig of lemon balm into your left pocket to be lucky in love.

. . . .

144. Foster and Johnson, *Desk Reference to Nature's Medicine*, 227.

145. Javid Ghazizadeh et al., "The Effects of Lemon Balm (*Melissa officinalis* L.) on Depression and Anxiety in Clinical Trials: A Systematic Review and Meta-Analysis," *Phytotherapy Research* 35, no. 12 (December 2021): 6690–705, doi:10.1002/ptr.7252.

146. Willoughby, *Nature's Remedies*; 70.

147. Irene, "Queen of Hungary's Water," Mountain Rose Herbs, May 5, 2012, https://blog.mountainroseherbs.com/queen-hungarys-water.

Lemon Verbena

Botanical Name: *Aloysia citrodora*, syn. *A. triphylla*

Parts Used: All aerial parts

Magickal Properties: Attraction, beauty, dreams, luck, mental clarity, and purification

Healing Benefits: Lemon verbena has sedative properties to soothe and lift mood. It boosts a sense of well-being by supporting a positive outlook and stimulating creativity. The leaves are brewed into an infusion with an uplifting energy to energize the mind, body, and spirit. It also calms the digestive system and reduces bloating.

Warning: May be toxic to horses, dogs, and cats.

Lemon verbena, also called lemon beebrush, is a flowering plant with fragrant citrus-scented leaves.[148] It is a sun-loving plant native to South America. I would have retired growing this plant when I left the Southwest except for the fact that I enjoy it so much. It has a brilliant fragrance and a bright lemony flavor without being bitter. Unfortunately, lemon verbena is frost tender, which means I have to bring it inside to overwinter. I grow it in pots and move them into the greenhouse when temperatures begin to drop. Inside, I set the pots in the brightest spot and cut back on watering.

A Brief History

In Mexico lemon verbena tea is known as *té de cedrón*. Spanish explorers imported the herb to Europe where it became a favorite. They named it *Aloysia* in honor of the king's wife, Maria Luisa of Parma.[149] By 1784 it had traveled to England, where it was used to enliven meat dishes and desserts and was brewed into an infusion named *Louisa*.[150] To the Greeks it became known as *luiza*.[151] The French developed

. . . .

148. Nancy J. Hajeski, *National Geographic Complete Guide to Herbs and Spices: Remedies, Seasonings, and Ingredients to Improve Your Health and Enhance Your Life* (Washington, DC: National Geographic, 2016), 138.

149. Ross Bayton, *The Gardener's Botanical* (Princeton, NJ: Princeton University Press, 2020), 37.

150. Hajeski, *National Geographic Complete Guide to Herbs and Spices*, 138.

151. Nancy Gaifyllia, "Greek Lemon Verbena Herbal Tea (Luiza)," last modified June 21, 2019, Spruce Eats, https://www.thespruceeats.com/louisa-greek-lemon-verbena-herbal-tea-1706006.

an affinity for lemon verbena and made it into a calming tonic they named *verveine*.[152] Chevallier writes in his *Herbal Remedies Handbook* that lemon verbena "has a mild tonic effect on the nervous system, which lifts the spirits and helps counter depression.[153]

How to Use

Lemon verbena is associated with Mars and is used in dreamwork and attraction spells. It is also added to other formulas to get the energy moving. Lemon verbena contains anti-inflammatory compounds and antioxidants that help protect the body against inflammation, oxidative stress, and cell damage.[154] Fresh or dried lemon verbena brews up into a pleasant-tasting, feel-good infusion. Sip a cup to brighten outlook. Add it to bathwater and soak to boost allure. Use the infusion as a hair rinse to inspire creative thought. Empower yourself with a confidence-boosting massage oil. Fill a jar with lemon verbena and cover with sweet almond oil. Seal with a tight-fitting lid and set aside to macerate for two weeks. Strain out the herb. Massage the oil into the skin to boost attraction and improve self-image. Wear it to fortify resolve, break bad habits, and bring out inner beauty.

Lemon verbena holds an enthusiastic energy that can breathe life back into that which has stalled or become stale. Stuff the herb into a sachet and toss it into bathwater for a soak that will change your luck, restore balance, or shift perception to see potential in what has become ordinary. Burn the dried herb to clear away obstacles.

In the kitchen you can add lemon verbena to anything you want to add a lemony flavor to. Its uplifting fragrance and lovely lemony flavor can be used to brighten everything from salads to desserts. Simply drop a sprig in a glass of iced tea to encourage happy, friendly affections. Make a simple syrup and use it to flavor drinks and foods and add positive, uplifting energy. Chop the leaves and add them to salad dressings or puree with oil and add to salsas and soups.

. . . .

152. Andi Clevely, Katherine Richmond, Sallie Morris, and Lesley Mackley, *Cooking with Herbs and Spices* (Leicester, UK: Anness Publishing, 1997), 101.

153. Chevallier, *Herbal Remedies Handbook*, 157.

154. Jillian Kubala, "5 Potential Health Benefits of Lemon Verbena," *Healthline*, October 18, 2021, https://www.healthline.com/nutrition/lemon-verbena-uses.

Mimosa

Botanical Name: *Albizia julibrissin*

Parts Used: Bark and flowers

Magickal Properties: Calming, cheerful, ease trauma, emotional balance, finding joy, hex breaking, love, and peace

Healing Benefits: Mimosa is a gentle, mood-elevating adaptogen used to treat insomnia and brain fog and to ease feelings of anxiety, sadness, depression, and lack of enthusiasm. It has sedative, analgesic, and nerve-relaxant properties that work to elevate mood.

Warning: Avoid using if pregnant.

I have a massive mimosa tree in the center of my front yard. It is a beautiful tree that brims with positive, life-affirming energy. The mimosa is known as the "collective happiness tree," and it truly is. Mine is the only one in the neighborhood and people often stop to look at it and sometimes even ask if they can gather some blossoms.

It is so majestic when it flowers. Bees, butterflies, and hummingbirds are attracted to the abundant acacia-like, faery-duster flowers that bloom from June through September. In the fall, the seedpods provide food for birds and squirrels. The life up among the branches is fascinating to watch. I have a lounge chair underneath so that I can lie back and gaze up into the branches.

The mimosa is an ornamental flowering tree, and even though it is very messy, it is my favorite tree in the yard. I was naturally drawn to collect its small fragrant flowers to brew a mimosa flower and hawthorn leaf infusion that I sipped by day and added to my bath in the evening, a practice supported by Jean Willoughby in her book *Nature's Remedies*: "When consumed in combination, hawthorn and mimosa form a powerful remedy for easing emotions such as sadness and grief."[155]

. . . .

155. Willoughby, *Nature's Remedies*, 64.

A Brief History

Mimosa trees are from Asia.[156] They are named after an Italian naturalist, Filippo degli Albizzi, who introduced the mimosa to Italy.[157] The mimosa tree is also known as the silk tree. In June a profusion of fragrant rose-colored flowers opens to create a bright and fragrant umbrella of blossoms. Mimosa bark and flowers are a traditional Chinese medicine to ease depression, calm anxiety, and quickly induce cheer.[158] A University of Arkansas profile of the plant shares that in 1745 a French Jesuit missionary named Pierre Nicolas d'Incarville introduced the mimosa to Western gardens, and Thomas Jefferson is known to have a mimosa tree in his Monticello garden.[159] For a while the mimosa was a symbol of the South, but recently several states have added the tree to their invasive species lists.

How to Use

The mimosa is known as the tree of happiness. In Italy, it represents love, and instead of red roses, a lover may give a bouquet of mimosa flowers.[160] In Chinese medicine, mimosa blossoms are known as *he huan hua*. It is a medicine used to ease irritability, anger, and depression and a remedy for bad dreams.[161] Both the bark and the flowers are used to make infusions and tinctures to improve mood, elevate outlook, and reduce brain fog. Gather a handful of fresh flowers and brew an infusion. Let it cool and pour it over ice for a refreshing drink to boost outlook and restore a good mood.

Mimosa energy encourages kindness. Float the flowers in a flute of champagne and drink to inspire self-love, for a cheering drink to encourage celebration, or to inspire romance.

The mimosa encourages us to release anger and embrace acceptance. In his book *Herbal Therapeutics*, David Winston writes, "Mimosa bark is the most effective mood

. . . .

156. William Willard Ashe, *Shade Trees for North Carolina* (Raleigh, NC: North Carolina Geological and Economic Survey, 1908), 58.

157. *"Albizia julibrissin,"* North Carolina State University Extension, accessed April 2, 2022, https://plants.ces.ncsu.edu/plants/albizia-julibrissin/.

158. Maria Noel Groves, *Grow Your Own Herbal Remedies* (North Adams, MA: Storey Publishing, 2019), 285.

159. Gerald Klingaman, "Plant of the Week: Mimosa," University of Arkansas Division of Agriculture, July 23, 2004, https://www.uaex.uada.edu/yard-garden/resource-library/plant-week/mimosa.aspx.

160. Sara-Chana Silverstein, *Moodtopia* (New York: Da Capo Press, 2018), 76.

161. Winston and Maimes, *Adaptogens*, 254.

elevator I have ever utilized, helping to relieve grief, chronic emotional pain, and sadness." Brew an infusion from a handful of mimosa flowers and a spoonful of green tea. Sweeten it with honey and drink it to fortify the spirit and encourage a positive outlook.

Motherwort

Botanical Name: *Leonurus cardiaca*

Parts Used: All aerial parts

Magickal Properties: Calm, love, luck, peace, protection, and warding

Healing Benefits: Motherwort is a nervine with antispasmodic priorities. It is used to treat anxiety, depression, and stress. Motherwort is an herb that strengthens the heart. It was a traditional woman's herb to support contractions and induce calmness for birthing mothers.[162] Today it can be found in formulas to instill peace, calmness, acceptance, and courage.

Warning: This herb is a uterine stimulant and should not be used during pregnancy. This herb should not be used for extended lengths, as it may have addictive qualities.

Motherwort is a bushy, attractive perennial herb with a pungent scent. This member of the in the mint family is also known as lion's ear, lion's tail, and throwwort. Its name *Leonurus* refers to the shape of the leaves resembling a lion's tail.[163] Motherwort's nervine qualities work as a calming herb.[164] It is very helpful in shifting feelings of anxiety into peaceful acceptance, but because it is so bitter, it is usually combined with other herbs, such as hawthorn, lemon balm, passionflower, or skullcap, to craft a remedy to treat nervous tension and anxiety.

I love working with motherwort. For someone who is often dealing with digestive issues, motherwort offers soothing bitterness to heal digestive problems. Motherwort works by stimulating the parasympathetic nerves in the gastrointestinal tract that ask us to relax and rest rather than flee or fight. Instead of being nervous and

. . . .

162. Anna Kruger, *The Pocket Guide to Herbs* (London: Parkgate Books, 1992), 119.

163. Bayton, *The Gardener's Botanical*, 182.

164. Abascal and Yarnell, "Nervine Herbs for Treating Anxiety," 309–15.

restless, motherwort helps us be calm and cool as it remedies a bitter stomach, eases headaches, and even helps relieve insomnia.[165]

A Brief History

It is not known if motherwort is native to Europe or Asia, but because of its value as a medicine herb, it now can be found growing wild across the world. As long as two thousand years ago motherwort was a medicine pregnant women used to gain relief from stress and restlessness.[166] Today we know it is a uterine stimulant and should be avoided during pregnancy.

Motherwort has been shown to have sedative and antispasmodic properties.[167] Europeans and some Native American tribes both brewed a motherwort infusion to calm nervous tension.[168] Burke reports that motherwort is "one of the best" treatments for issues related to menstruation and menopause "when anxiety is an underlying problem."[169] In his *Herbal Remedies Handbook*, Andrew Chevallier writes that motherwort is an undervalued remedy to "calm those with a nervous disposition, while strengthening cardiovascular and digestive function."[170]

How to Use

Drink a mug of sweetened motherwort tea to shore up good health.

Motherwort lightens mood and promotes peace. To the Greeks and Romans motherwort was an herb to lighten mood and cure a whole host of emotional problems.[171] Grieve wrote, "It is good against hysterical complaints, and especially for palpitations of the heart when they arise from hysteric causes, and that when made into a syrup, it will allay inward tremors, faintings, etc."[172] Culpepper wrote, "Venus owns

· · · · · · · · · · · · · · · ·

165. Ryn Midura, "Motherwort: Herb of the Week," CommonWealth Holistic Herbalism, accessed April 1, 2022, https://commonwealthherbs.com/motherwort-herb-of-the-week/.

166. Nancy Burke, *The Modern Herbal Primer* (Dublin: Yankee Publishing, 2000), 81.

167. Jean M. Bokelmann, "Motherwort (*Leonurus cardiaca*): Above-Ground Parts," in *Medicinal Herbs in Primary Care: An Evidence-Guided Reference for Healthcare Providers* (Philadelphia, PA: Elsevier, 2022), 511–14.

168. Willoughby, *Nature's Remedies*, 86.

169. Burke, *The Modern Herbal Primer*, 81.

170. Chevallier, *Herbal Remedies Handbook*, 156.

171. Harra and Altshul O'Donnell, *The Woman's Book of Healing Herbs*, 67.

172. Grieve, *A Modern Herbal*, vol. 2, 555–56.

the herb and it is under Leo. There is no better herb to drive melancholy vapours from the heart, to strengthen it, and make a merry, cheerful, blithe soul."[173] Brew an infusion with motherwort and lemon balm. Sweeten it with honey and drink to lift mood and elevate outlook.

In *Moodtopia*, master herbalist Sara-Chana Silverstein writes that motherwort is an ideal herb for difficult times, as it is a fast-acting mood stabilizer that works within as little as twenty minutes of ingesting. Motherwort is "a nervine for women who feel gloomy (it's used for hormonal grumpiness or just grumpiness without the hormonal edge), a lack of libido, feeling stuck, agitation, and anger." She continues, "Motherwort is wonderful for taking that 'edge' off your more negative emotions and is helpful if you suddenly feel that 'black cloud' descending…My motto: Motherwort—don't leave home without it."[174] Pour a sweetened motherwort infusion over ice and drink to encourage a good mood. Carry the infusion in a thermos and drink it when you need fortification.

Motherwort holds protective energy that can act as a ward to guard against bad luck, jealousy, malicious intent, and negative influences. In spellwork it is used to repel curses and break hexes. A Hindu story advocates adding an infusion of motherwort to laundry, especially when washing garments like socks and underwear, to bring peace and harmony to the home.[175] Add a motherwort infusion to your washwater and use it to clean up after an argument to rid a room of negativity.

In *The Complete Illustrated Encyclopedia of Magical Plants*, Susan Gregg writes that motherwort "brings out your ability to nurture yourself," as it helps you release judgment and false beliefs while encouraging acceptance.[176] Add a motherwort infusion to your bathwater and soak to rinse away troubled thoughts and restore peace of mind.

. . . .

173. Culpeper, *Culpeper's Complete Herbal*, 99.

174. Silverstein, *Moodtopia*, 77.

175. "Motherwort," Mountain Rose Herbs, accessed January 13, 2022, https://mountainroseherbs.com /motherwort.

176. Susan Gregg, *The Complete Illustrated Encyclopedia of Magical Plants* (Beverly, MA: Fair Winds Press, 2014), 123.

Passionflower

Botanical Name: *Passiflora incarnata*

Parts Used: The whole plant and fruit

Magickal Properties: Beauty, calmness, friendship, harmony, and sleep

Healing Benefits: A nervine and sedative with antispasmodic properties used for insomnia, excessive worry, pain, stress, sciatica, spasms, fevers, and stomachaches. A study found passionflower as effective in relieving anxiety as the tranquilizer oxazepam.[177]

Warning: May produce a hypnotic or narcotic effect in sensitive individuals. Avoid if pregnant or breastfeeding. Do not combine with prescription sedatives. Discontinue use if you experience oversedation.

There are many varieties of passionflowers, or passion vines. It is a genus consisting of about 550 species, with *Passiflora edulis*, the producer of the exotic food passionfruit, being the most well-known member of this group. *P. incarnata*, also known as maypop and apricot vine, is a common garden vine with nervine and slight sedative properties. It is an attractive vine with gorgeous flowers. Don't be fooled by its tropical appearance. *P. incarnata* is a hardy, drought-tolerant evergreen, the hardiest of all the passifloras. I planted a cutting that I rooted two years ago, and today my front fence is covered by the sprawling vine.

A Brief History

Passionflower is a New World plant. To some native peoples it was a medicine plant made into a poultice to treat injuries.[178] The Incas brewed an infusion from the leaves and flowers to make a tonic.[179] In his *Secrets of Native American Herbal Remedies*, Cichoke tells us the Housma used passionflower as a blood tonic, while the

. . . .

177. Shahin Akhondzadeh et al., "Passionflower in the Treatment of Generalized Anxiety: A Pilot Double-Blind Randomized Controlled Trial with Oxazepam," *Journal of Clinical Pharmacy and Therapeutics* 26, no. 5 (October 2001): 363–67, doi:10.1046/j.1365-2710.2001.00367.x.

178. Reader's Digest, *Magic and Medicine of Plants*, 266.

179. Hajeski, *Nature's Best Remedies*, 136.

Cherokee brewed an infusion to treat liver problems and used the plant to treat earaches, boils, and wounds.[180]

When Spanish explorers invaded in the sixteenth century, they observed the calming properties of the plant and carried it back to Europe, where it became a part of folk healing there.[181] Today passionflower has been found to help with neuropsychiatric disorders with no adverse effects. In the majority of studies, participants reported reduced anxiety levels.[182] The dried fruit and flower tops are ingredients in many sedatives.[183]

How to Use

The passionflower is associated with Neptune, Venus, and the moon. It contains sedative and antispasmodic properties and holds a harmonious energy to calm, relax, and soothe. Combine passionflower with catnip, hop flowers, lemon balm, or mimosa flowers to create a wonderful evening tonic to encourage a restless mind to relax and wind down.

Passionflower leaves and flowers contain tranquilizing chemicals to help remedy insomnia, depression, sadness, nervousness, and grief. These chemicals promote relaxation by inhibiting certain actions and nerve impulses of the nervous system. In the *The Woman's Book of Healing Herbs,* Sari Harrar and Sara Altshul O'Donnell write, "Herbalists say that it is one of the best tranquilizing herbs for insomnia, making it a good sleep inducer when nighttime rest is disturbed by anxiety or during menopause."[184] Drink a passionflower infusion before bed to quiet the mind and end an annoying thought loop. Add hops and lemon balm to banish troubling thoughts.

Serve passionflower tea during reconciliations to ease annoyance and encourage an amicable attitude. Serve an infusion to stem jealousy. Add the infusion to your bathwater and soak to release anger or fear. Add the dried leaves and flowers to formulas to bring peace or instill harmony. Stuff dried passionflower leaves into

. . . .

180. Cichoke, *Secrets of Native American Herbal Remedies*, 61.

181. "Passionflower," National Center for Complementary and Integrative Health, last modified August 2020, https://www.nccih.nih.gov/health/passionflower.

182. Katarzyna Janda et al., "*Passiflora incarnata* in Neuropsychiatric Disorders—A Systematic Review," *Nutrients* 12, no. 12 (2020): 3894, doi:10.3390/nu12123894.

183. Reader's Digest, *Magic and Medicine of Plants*, 266.

184. Harrar and Altshul O'Donnell, *Woman's Book of Healing Herbs*, 71.

dream pillows to end troubled dreams. Use passionflowers in charms to encourage friendship.

Rose

Botanical Name: *Rosa* spp.

Parts Used: Flowers and hips

Magickal Properties: Acceptance, attraction, divination, dreams, feminine power, healing, happiness, love, protection, secrecy, and wish magick

Healing Benefits: Roses have mild sedative, antiseptic, anti-inflammatory, and antispasmodic properties. Rose energy is calming and uplifting. It supports us as we move through grief and find our way back to openheartedness. The scent of rose lifts outlook and encourages the ability to love.

Warning: None.

The rose is one of the world's most beloved flowers. There seems to be a rose for everyone, from the elegant long-stemmed tea roses to the thorny wild ramblers. *Rosa* is one of the largest plant genera with more than 150 different species and new hybrids being introduced each year.

My house came with a range of mature roses. There is a bed of tea roses in the front, a red rose rambler climbing the house, and a massive rambler with small pinkish-white flowers that drapes over the back fence. There is even a wild rose in the side yard that is covered in the prickliest thrones I have ever seen. It produces an abundance of sweetly scented, simple pink flowers that become swollen red hips.

A Brief History

Roses grow all across the temperate regions of the Northern Hemisphere. There are even several varieties of wild roses native to the Pacific Northwest. The rose is one of the oldest-known perennial shrubs, most likely cultivated as early as 3000 BCE in Asia and northeastern Africa.[185] It was a beloved flower of the Persians, Greeks, and

. . . .

185. Ernst Lehner and Johanna Lehner, *Folklore and Symbolism of Flowers, Plants and Trees* (New York, NY: Tudor Publishing Company, 1960), 76.

Romans, who called it the "queen of flowers."[186] It is said that Nero spent more than the equivalent of 30,000 British pounds on roses for a single evening, according to an 1839 article, and Cleopatra laid a floor of roses in her banquet hall that was one and a half feet deep.[187] Such extravagances led to the rose becoming a symbol of indulgence and excess so that early Christians denounced its use.[188]

Roses were more than just a beautiful flower. They also provided medicine and oil for early perfumes. Burke tells us that as long as 2,000 years ago the Chinese, Egyptians, Greeks, Persians, and Romans used roses to treat "aliments—from coughs and kidney disorders to fatigue and infections."[189] In Persia, rose water became a favored food ingredient and a source of perfume, while across the world rose essence became an important ingredient in perfumes, soaps, shampoos, and other personal care products.

How to Use

Roses are wound healers with properties that work to heal our body, mind, and spirit. They have been used to remedy depression since the Middle Ages.[190] Rose energy is cooling and comforting especially when we are feeling vulnerable. In her book *Moodtopia*, Silverstein calls the rose, "An uplifting nervine for women with sadness, stuck feelings, agitation, depression, grief, and gloominess."[191] Rose petal tea is a lovely infusion taken as a nerve tonic and used externally to ease headaches and skin irritations.

The rose holds a nurturing energy and offers feelings of security and safety that help us mitigate troubling times. Use roses in love, luck, grief, and healing rituals. Herbalist Holly Bellebuono tells us that roses "provide a lasting and visceral feeling of release from states of debilitating grief," and they hold a special place in therapy for bereavement.[192] Use rose petal tea in rituals to relieve grief and emotional

· · · · · · · · · · · · · · · · ·

186. Maggie Oster, *Flowering Herbs* (New York: Longmeadow Press, 1991), 81.

187. Randle Wilbraham Falconer, *The Ancient History of the Rose* ([London]: [Longman, Orme, Brown, Green, and Longmans], 1839), 10.

188. Martin, *Garden Flower Folklore*, 195.

189. Burke, *The Modern Herbal Primer*, 121.

190. Chevallier, *Encyclopedia of Herbal Medicine*, 263.

191. Silverstein, *Moodtopia*, 76.

192. Bellebuono, *An Herbalist's Guide to Formulary*, 94.

pain. Brew an infusion of fresh rose petals to help you accept difficult issues without feeling victimized.

Roses are flowers of love used to empower love magicks and quicken results. Their scent encourages both acceptance and affection. Fill a vase with roses to instill feelings of love and happiness. Dry rose petals to use in love and attraction magicks. Anoint a candle with olive oil and roll it in crushed petal bits to empower a love spell. Or make a batch of lightly scented rosewater by placing 2 packed cups of clean, fresh rose petals in a bowl and pouring 2 cups of boiling water over the top of them. Cover and let the liquid steep until it is room temperature. Then strain, bottle, and refrigerate it. Use the liquid in love spells. Add it to enchant a glass of champagne for a romantic encounter. Measure 3 teaspoons of rosewater into a champagne flute glass, add 1 teaspoon of sugar and swirl to dissolve. Fill with champagne and serve with a smile. Add a cup of rosewater to a bath to heal a wounded spirit. Use rosewater to anoint the body to boost confidence and appeal. Mix rosewater with saffron to make a magickal ink with power to supercharge any love charm.

Rosemary

Botanical Name: *Salvia rosmarinus*

Parts Used: Leaves and flowers

Magickal Properties: Beauty, communication, friendship, love, protection, purification, remembrance, and rest

Healing Benefits: Rosemary is a nervine with antibacterial, antidepressant, antifungal, and antispasmodic properties. It supports the liver and digestive system and helps rid the body of toxins. The scent of rosemary is known to lift mood. It is used to help relieve headaches, reduce stress, and ease depression and is now being used to treat Alzheimer's, epilepsy, and Parkinson's disease.[193]

Warning: Avoid using if you are pregnant or trying to conceive.

. . . .

193. Mahboobeh Ghasemzadeh Rahbardar and Hossein Hosseinzadeh, "Therapeutic Effects of Rosemary (*Rosmarinus officinalis* L.) and Its Active Constituents on Nervous System Disorders," *Iranian Journal of Basic Medical Sciences* 23, no. 9 (September 2020): 1100–12, doi:10.22038/ijbms.2020.45269.10541.

Rosemary was one of my very first herbal allies. It grew abundantly where I grew up and could be found growing in yards and planters all over my neighborhood. I learned from my father how to use it to flavor breads, rolls, soups, sauces, and chicken dishes, and later I discovered its power as a medicine herb.

A simple infusion of rosemary became my go-to brew whenever I need a gentle antiseptic, a health tonic, or a cognitive booster. I drink it to fortify health, clear away mental fog, and enhance both memory and mental clarity. I pour it into my bathwater and soak whenever I need to shrug off fatigue and help clear away the stress of the day, and I combine it with basil to curtail the onset of a urinary tract infection.

A Brief History

Rosemary is one of the Mediterranean herbs. Its history as a medicine, a strewing herb, and as a culinary herb goes back 2,000 years.[194] It was sacred to the Egyptians, Greeks, and Romans, who valued it as medicine and for its scent and flavor.[195] The Romans adorned their household altars with rosemary and hung sprigs as a charm against evil.[196] The Greeks wore crowns made of rosemary. They believed it improved cognitive function and memory.[197] Around the fourteenth century rosemary appeared in England. English herbalist John Gerard wrote rosemary "comforteth the harte, and maketh it merie," and Philippa of Hainault, wife of Edward III, is known to have grown rosemary in her garden.[198]

How to Use

Rosemary is a guardian of health and a restorer. In her book *Essential Herbal Wisdom*, organic gardener Nancy Arrowsmith writes that rosemary was used "to drive old age from the doorstep and Death from the door." Patients were "wrapped in warm woolen sheets smoked with rosemary, elderly people were given smelling-boxes made of rosemary wood to preserve their vanishing youth, and rosemary leaves

....

194. Burke, *The Modern Herbal Primer*, 123.

195. Hajeski, *Nature's Best Remedies*, 140.

196. Folkard, *Plant Lore, Legends, and Lyrics*, 526; Clevely et al., *Cooking with Herbs and Spices*, 113.

197. Picton, *The Book of Magical Herbs*, 73.

198. John Gerard, *The Herball: or the Generall Historie of Plantes* (London: John Norton, 1597), 1111; Penelope Ody, *The Complete Medicinal Herbal* (London: Dorling Kindersley, 1993), 92.

were placed under beds to prevent nightmares."[199] In the Middle Ages rosemary was carried to avert the evil eye.[200] It was customary to keep a sprig of rosemary on the lintel to keep "uncanny" people from entering the British home.[201] Mourners carried rosemary to repel graveyard spirits.[202] Burn a sprig of rosemary with juniper to purify a room. Fill a muslin bag with rosemary, thyme, and hop flowers, and hang to keep nightmares away.

Rosemary stimulates the mind, circulation, and the digestive system. It can be used to fight infection or brewed into a simple infusion to decrease inflammation. Sip a rosemary infusion to bolster your health when you begin to feel run-down. Pour a rosemary infusion into bathwater and soak to revive a weary spirit. Add the infusion to a spray bottle of water and use it as a spritzer to revitalize after an exhausting ordeal. Add rosemary to a meal when you want it to be remembered. Drop a few sprigs of rosemary into a bottle of red wine. Seal and let the bottle sit for three days. Strain out the herb and take a tablespoon whenever you need to ward off a migraine. Add rosemary to a glass of white wine, cover with a towel, and let it sit out overnight. Remove the herb and use the liquid as a facial rinse to tighten skin and make it glow.

The scent of rosemary eases headaches, calms the psyche, and increases feelings of well-being. Silverstein writes in *Moodtopia*, "It's known as an antidepressant and a soothing tonic for the nerves, which makes it excellent for people who deal with anxiety and depression."[203] Pick a sprig, rub it between your fingers, lift it to your nose, and breathe in the scent to calm racing thoughts. Place a sprig of rosemary in your pocket when you have to deal with a troublesome person. Crush the herb and breathe in the scent to keep your wits and find the right words.

. . . .

199. Arrowsmith, *Essential Herbal Wisdom*, 217.

200. Victoria Zak, *The Magic Teaspoon: Transform Your Meals with the Power of Healing Herbs and Spices* (New York: Berkley Books, 2006), 68.

201. Arrowsmith, *Essential Herbal Wisdom*, 219.

202. Burke, *The Modern Herbal Primer*, 123.

203. Silverstein, *Moodtopia*, 80.

Skullcap

Botanical Name: *Scutellaria lateriflora*

Parts Used: All aerial parts

Magickal Properties: Fidelity, love, peace, and rest

Healing Benefits: Skullcap is a nervine with sedative effects and antispasmodic action. It works as a tonic for the nervous system, taken to calm the nerves and grant resilience. Skullcap is used to reduce anxiety, ease nervous tension, and alleviate sadness, anger, and fear. It is an ingredient in many nonprescription medications for anxiety and sleep problems.[204]

Warning: This herb should not be used during pregnancy. Large doses may cause dizziness and confusion.

Skullcap is an attractive bluish-violet flower that blooms from May through September. It is native to North America but now grows in gardens across the world. Skullcap prefers cool, moist areas and thrives in woodland gardens. The first year I tried growing skullcap, I planted it in an area that was too warm and bright, and the plants did not live through the hot summer months. The next year I planted skullcap in my woodland garden, an area that has partial sun exposure and a drip hose that keeps the soil evenly moist, and it flourished. I snip off the flowering tops to make a lovely infusion that improves my mood without lowering my energy levels or affecting my cognitive abilities.[205]

A Brief History

Skullcap is a member of the mint family. It gets its name from its small, helmet-shaped flowers. It is also known as Quaker bonnet, mad-dog, and madweed, as it was once a treatment for rabies.[206] Skullcap is a New World healing herb that grows across the United States and Canada. It was used by native peoples to treat menstrual

....

204. Chevallier, *Herbal Remedies Handbook*, 206.

205. Christine Brock et al., "American Skullcap (*Scutellaria lateriflora*): A Randomised, Double-Blind Placebo-Controlled Crossover Study of Its Effects on Mood in Healthy Volunteers," *Phytotherapy Research* 28, no. 5 (May 2014): 692–98, doi:10.1002/ptr.5044.

206. Kruger, *The Pocket Guide to Herbs*, 160.

disorders, nervousness, insomnia, digestive issues, and kidney problems.[207] The Cherokee used skullcap as a women's herb to bring on menstruation and ease breast pain.[208] The Iroquois powdered the root to treat smallpox and clear the throat.[209] Skullcap traveled to Europe, where it was cultivated and adopted by European herbalists. By the twentieth century, it became a respected nerve tonic.[210]

How to Use

Skullcap has a long history as a nervous system tonic and restorative, and its use is being revived as modern studies examine its usefulness.[211] It has a gentle, calming, sedative action that, when taken internally, soothes anxiety and lifts mood without decreasing energy. Brew a simple infusion of skullcap and sip to relax. Choose skullcap after a taxing event to grant fortitude and comfort without making you tired. Drink as a tonic to soothe the psyche and restore peace of mind.

In an article for the Botanical Institute, nutritionist Tara Bassi writes that skullcap is used to treat "nervous disorders due to anxiety, tension, or stress; headaches; migraines; panic attacks; restlessness; sleep disorders; premenstrual tension and period pain; and to assist withdrawal from benzodiazepines."[212] Use skullcap to restore strength to the overwhelmed. Combine it with hawthorn, lemon balm, passionflower, or wild lettuce for a helpful formula to remedy stress and reduce anxiety.

Skullcap is a nurturing herb. Brew an infusion of skullcap tea and drink it when you need some calming comfort. Use its gentle strength to bolster your resolve and keep your thoughts clear. Pour it into bathwater and soak to gain strength to break a habit, ease withdrawal symptoms, or gain the ability to be present in the moment. Drink a cup before bed to gain a peaceful rest and reduce nightmares. Add hops to increase the effects.

. . . .

207. Cichoke, *Secrets of Native American Herbal Remedies*, 70.

208. Chevallier, *Encyclopedia of Herbal Medicine*, 135.

209. Foster and Johnson, *Desk Reference to Nature's Medicine*, 330.

210. Harrar and Altshul O'Donnell, *Woman's Book of Healing Herbs*, 76.

211. Christine Brock et al., "American Skullcap (*Scutellaria lateriflora*): An Ancient Remedy for Today's Anxiety?" *British Journal of Wellbeing* 1, no. 4 (July 2010): 25–30, doi:10.12968/bjow.2010.1.4.49168.

212. Tara Bassi, "American Skullcap: 5 Key Benefits, Dosage, & Safety," the Botanical Institute, February 3, 2022, https://botanicalinstitute.org/american-skullcap/.

Skullcap is associated with Mercury, the moon, Neptune, Pluto, Saturn, and Venus. It is an herb of love used to bind oaths and consecrate vows. Sew dried skullcap leaves into the hem of your lover's coat to encourage fidelity and remain unaffected by another's charms. Tuck a few leaves into your left pocket when you need energy to avoid straying.

St. John's Wort

Botanical Name: *Hypericum perforatum*

Parts Used: Flowering tops

Magickal Properties: Abundance, happiness, health, love, luck, protection, and strength

Healing Benefits: St. John's wort is a popular nervine used to support emotional well-being and reduce agitation, moodiness, and depression.

Warning: May cause photosensitivity. May decrease blood level of prescriptions medications, including birth control pills, protease inhibitors, warfarin, and digoxin.

I grow St. John's wort in its own raised bed to contain it. It thrives here and grows robustly up to three feet tall, sprawling out to fill its space. Around midsummer, St. John's wort produces a bright yellow flower that becomes black, strongly scented seeds. The flowering ends are harvested to make formulas to support emotional well-being, repel negativity, and attract abundance. In several states, such as Washington, St. John's wort has been classified as a noxious weed out of concern for livestock, as it causes animals to become highly sensitive to sunlight.[213]

A Brief History

St. John's wort is native to Europe and Western Asia, but as it was so revered as a medicine plant, it traveled with settlers and now grows across the world. St. John's wort has been used as a medicine herb since recorded history. The early healers Dioscorides, Galen, Pliny, and Paracelsus all included St. John's wort in their

....

213. Kris Zouhar, *"Hypericum perforatum,"* Fire Effects Information System, US Department of Agriculture, 2004, https://www.fs.fed.us/database/feis/plants/forb/hypper/all.html.

herbals.[214] In ancient Greece, St. John's wort was a remedy for anxiety and used to improve outlook.[215] During the Middle Ages, St. John's wort was a first aid herb used to treat sword cuts.[216] In the 1660s English doctors used it to treat melancholia and insanity.[217]

How to Use

St. John's wort has astringent, antibacterial, and sedative properties. It is used topically to treat skin conditions and drunk as tea and taken as supplements (one of the most popular is SAM-e) to ease anxiety, treat mild depression, and help manage obsessive-compulsive conditions and ADHD. In fact a German study found St. John's wort to be as effective at relieving moderate depression as the prescription antidepressant imipramine (trade name Tofranil).[218] Brew an infusion and sip it to lift your outlook or revive a weary spirit. Use it as a foot soak to relax and renew.

St. John's wort is an herb of protection used to drive away evil and end enchantments. In fact, it gets its name *Hypericum* from the Greek words *hyper* and *eikon*, meaning "above" and "icon," as it was often hung over religious icons toward a room of wicked spirits.[219] There were all sorts of rituals around harvesting St. John's wort to maintain its magickal powers. Folkard writes that St. John's wort had "immense power against evil spirits" when it was "gathered with great ceremony on the eve of St. John's Day, the 24th of June, to be hung up in windows as a preservative against evil spirits, phantoms, spectres, storms, and thunder; whence it derived its ancient name of *Fuga Dæmonum* (Devil's Flight)."[220] Herbalist Nancy Arrowsmith tells us that old manuscripts advise that for the herb to be at full potency, one should go out without being seen and without speaking to anyone and then address the plant and

....

214. Arrowsmith, *Essential Herbal Wisdom*, 272.

215. Bevin Cohen, *The Artisan Herbalist*, 65.

216. Kruger, *The Pocket Guide to Herbs*, 154.

217. Arrowsmith, *Essential Herbal Wisdom*, 272.

218. Helmut Woelk, "Comparison of St John's Wort and Imipramine for Treating Depression: Randomised Controlled Trial," *British Medical Journal* 321, no. 7260 (September 2000): 536–39, doi:10.1136 /bmj.321.7260.536; Eric A. Apaydin et al., "A Systematic Review of St. John's Wort for Major Depressive Disorder," *Systematic Reviews* 5, no. 1 (September 2016): 148, doi:10.1186/s13643-016-0325-2.

219. Bayton, *The Gardener's Botanical*, 159.

220. Folkard, *Plant Lore, Legends, and Lyrics*, 52 and 536.

thank it. Then tell it how it will be used before you pick it.[221] Sprigs of St. John's Day were fashioned into crosses and placed on windowsills, over thresholds, and in the corner of the home, the barn, and the field to protect the house, the family, and the family's crops and animals from falling under an evil influence.[222] Carry a sprig of St. John's wort to ward against faery mischief or avoid falling under the enchantment of another. Tuck a sprig into your pocket when traveling or hiking to avoid losing your way.

St. John's wort is associated with the sun, Leo, the element fire, and midsummer festivals. Magickally, it holds a protective energy to heal, repel negativity, and attract abundance. The flowers can be picked and hung to protect the home from lightning, fire, and malicious spirits.

Vervain

Botanical Name: *Verbena officinalis*

Parts Used: All aerial parts

Magickal Properties: Communication, health, love, money, peace, protection, purification, sleep, and wish granting

Healing Benefits: Vervain is a nervine that supports the nervous system to relax the nerves, lift mood, and calm mental agitation. Its anxiolytic and sedative properties are used to treat insomnia, depression, and anxiety.[223]

Warning: This herb may cause addiction and miscarriage. This herb should not be used by children. Avoid if pregnant or breastfeeding.

Vervain is a modest little wildflower that grows in pastures and along roadsides across North America. It is native to Europe but was brought to the New World by settlers and now has naturalized across the continent.[224] In the garden, vervain is a spindly plant with jagged leaves and clusters of small lilac or white flowers. It fills in

. . . .

221. Arrowsmith, *Essential Herbal Wisdom*, 269.

222. Arrowsmith, *Essential Herbal Wisdom*, 276.

223. Abdul Waheed Khan, Arif-Ullah Khan, and Touqeer Ahmed, "Anticonvulsant, Anxiolytic, and Sedative Activities of *Verbena officinalis*," *Frontiers in Pharmacology* 7, no. 499 (December 2016): n.p., doi:10.3389/fphar.2016.00499.

224. Reader's Digest, *Magic and Medicine of Plants*, 323.

well where other plants won't grow and is a good candidate for meadow and butterfly gardens, as the flowers are nectar rich and provide food for bees, butterflies, and moths.

A Brief History

Down through history, vervain was used as a healing restorative to calm restlessness, soothe irritability, ease anxiety, and treat madness.[225] Herbalist John Parkinson (1567–1650) prescribed vervain to relieve "all the inward paines and torments of the body."[226] Vervain works as a beneficial restorative to help a patient regain their health after a chronic or long-term illness.[227] In Medieval times fresh vervain was worn as a necklace to inspire good luck.[228]

Lore tells that vervain sprang from the tears of Isis after her husband, Osiris, was murdered.[229] The name *Verbena* is from the Latin for "sacred bough" and alludes to a history as a religious herb carried in processions.[230] The Romans and Druids both used vervain as a ritual herb and gathered it with ceremony.[231] To the Anglo-Saxons, vervain was a ceremonial herb of magick that was collected on moonless nights, and in its place an offering of honeycomb was left.[232]

How to Use

I hold anxiety in my belly and as a result am plagued with digestive troubles. Vervain is my go-to cure. It is a bitter herb that lifts mood as it relaxes a troubled stomach. Herbal author Anna Kruger shares that modern herbalists use vervain to treat headaches and nausea, as it "has a strengthening effect on the nervous system."[233] Ody writes that vervain is an "effective nerve tonic, liver stimulant, urinary cleanser, and

. . . .

225. Julie Bruton-Seal and Matthew Seal, *The Herbalist's Bible* (New York: Skyhorse Publishing, 2014), 219.

226. Bruton-Seal and Seal, *The Herbalist's Bible*, 219.

227. Bruton-Seal and Seal, *Backyard Medicine*, 170.

228. Kruger, *The Pocket Guide to Herbs*, 177.

229. Burke, *The Modern Herbal Primer*, 101.

230. Bayton, *The Gardener's Botanical*, 304.

231. Graeme Tobyn, Alison Denham, and Midge Whitelegg, *The Western Herbal Tradition* (Philadelphia, PA: Jessica Kingsley Publishers, 2016), 327.

232. Burke, *The Modern Herbal Primer*, 102.

233. Kruger, *The Pocket Guide to Herbs*, 177.

fever remedy."[234] Brew up a simple infusion of vervain and sweeten it with honey to relieve anxiety, improve stomach health, and treat insomnia.

Vervain was also a popular antimagick herb used to purify places and guard against hexes and negative energy.[235] Edible gardening lecturer Jack Staub writes in *The Illustrated Book of Edible Plants*, "In medieval times, amulets of verbena root were habitually worn about the neck to ward off pestilence and witchcraft, and verbena leaves and flowers were employed in countless incantations, evil-dispelling ointments, and erstwhile love potions by aspiring sorcerers."[236] Herbalist Penelope Ody tells us that "its association with magic and ritual was still popular in the 17th century."[237]

Vervain was also an herb of love used in love potions and is associated with Virgo, Libra, Gemini, Jupiter, Venus, Cerridwen, Diana, Midsummer, and the underworld. Folkard writes that sorcerers used vervain to enchant and that "by smearing the body over with the juice of this plant, the person would obtain whatever he set his heart upon, and be able to reconcile the most inveterate enemies, make friends with whom he pleased, and gain the affections, and cure the disease of whom he listed."[238]

Violet

Botanical Names: *Viola odorata, V. sororia, V. tricolor, V. papilionacea*

Parts Used: All aerial parts

Magickal Properties: Cheer, console, love, rain, and magick

Healing Benefits: The violet is a soothing nervine with slightly sedative properties that can be made into an infusion to grant calm clarity without drowsiness. It is used to heal the heart, sweeten attitude, and reduce anger and grief.

Warning: None.

. . . .

234. Ody, *The Complete Medicinal Herbal*, 112.

235. Pam Shade, "The Supernatural Side of Plants," Cornell Botanic Gardens, October 27, 2020, https://cornellbotanicgardens.org/the-supernatural-side-of-plants/.

236. Jack Staub, *The Illustrated Book of Edible Plants* (Layton, UT: Gibbs Smith, 2017), 99.

237. Ody, *The Complete Medicinal Herbal*,112.

238. Folkard, *Plant Lore, Legends, and Lyrics*, 573.

I love violets. I love how they pop up alongside the muscari and wild cyclamen. Violets grow in the most surprising places because ants like the seeds and carry them around.[239] I know some people think they are a scourge and spend time and money trying to eradicate them from their lawns, but I love their sweet, cheerful faces. When I spot one, I can't help but smile.

Oregon has a lot of wild violets, with *Viola odorata* and *V. sororia* being the most common. With their cheerful flowers and heart-shaped leaves, they are lovely to look at. They are also edible, as are most violets, and make wonderful ground covers.

A Brief History

The violet is an early spring flower also known as heartsease, pansy, Johnny-jump-up, and viola. It is an Old World medicine plant used to treat a range of ills from heartbreak to constipation.[240] The Romans used violets to treat hangovers and headaches.[241] Grieve notes that the Athenians used violets as a heart tonic and a remedy to cool anger and treat insomnia. The ancient Britons used violets to heighten beauty, while Anglo-Saxons used them to treat wounds.[242] Violets were used as a gentle medicine to strengthen voices and treat children's colds and coughs.[243] Historical herbalists Nicholas Culpeper and John Parkinson both prescribed a decoction of violet leaves and flowers to ease headache pain due to insomnia.[244] In the sixteenth century violet syrup was used as a laxative and a remedy to treat epilepsy, pleurisy, and jaundice.[245] Today a tea brewed from dried leaves and flowers is taken to treat everything from anxiety to constipation.[246] Modern research has shown the flower

. . . .

239. Arrowsmith, *Essential Herbal Wisdom*, 518.

240. Gabrielle Hatfield, *Hatfield's Herbal: The Curious Stories of Britain's Wild Plants* (London, UK: Penguin Books, 2009), 336.

241. Bruton-Seal, *The Herbalist's Bible*, 219.

242. Maud Grieve, *A Modern Herbal*, vol. 2, 835.

243. Arrowsmith, *Essential Herbal Wisdom*, 521.

244. Culpeper, *Culpeper's Complete Herbal*, 191; Bruton-Seal and Seal, *The Herbalist's Bible*, 222.

245. Reader's Digest, *Magic and Medicine of Plants*, 316.

246. Burke, *The Modern Herbal Primer*, 98.

has an anti-inflammatory and purifying action to remedy skin conditions and treat coughs and bronchitis and has potential for inhibiting cancers.[247]

How to Use

Violets hold a cheerful, positive energy. The flowers are edible and can be used fresh and added to salads or candied and used to decorate baked goods. The leaves are also edible, with *V. odorata* having the sweetest flavor. Freeze fresh flowers in ice cube trays and use them to chill beverages. Serve the drinks to lift the spirits of someone suffering. Crumble dried violet leaves and roll candles in the bits to empower spells for happiness.

The name "heartsease" comes from the plant's use in medieval love potions.[248] The violet's power to induce love plays a role in the plot of Shakespeare's *A Midsummer Night's Dream*, when characters smear the "juice" of *V. tricolor* on the eyelids of those they want to fall in love.[249] To the Scottish the violet was an herb of beauty. They made a face wash by infusing violets in milk to improve beauty and charm.[250] Soak a cloth in a warm infusion of violet leaves and flowers and drape over the face to heighten beauty. Add an infusion to bathwater and soak to enhance charm.

Violets are associated with Eros, Cupid, Jove, Pluto, Saturn, and Venus, and even though they are known as flowers of beauty and love, their curative powers also earned them the power of protection. During the Middle Ages, violets were used as protective talismans to guard against wicked spirits.[251] In Transylvania babies were washed in a violet bath to protect against illness and keep them safe from evil.[252]

· · · · · · · · · · · · · · · · ·

247. Chevallier, *Encyclopedia of Herbal Medicine*, 282; Mohaddese Mahboubi and Leila Mohammad Taghizadeh Kashanib, "A Narrative Study about the Role of *Viola odorata* as Traditional Medicinal Plant in Management of Respiratory Problems," *Advances in Integrative Medicine* 5, no. 3 (December 2018): 112–18, https://doi.org/10.1016/j.aimed.2017.12.003; Shirin Zeinoddini, Mohammad Nabiuni, and Hanieh Jalali, "The Synergistic Cytotoxic Effects of Doxorubicin and *Viola odorata* Extract on Human Breast Cancer Cell Line T47-D," *Journal of Cancer Research and Therapeutics* 15, no, 5. (2019):1073–79, doi:10.4103/jcrt.JCRT_990_17.

248. DK, *Home Herbal: Cook, Brew and Blend Your Own Herbs* (New York: DK Publishing, 2011), 130.

249. William Shakespeare, *A Midsummer Night's Dream*, Folger Shakespeare Library, accessed April 15, 2022, 2.1.257–67, https://shakespeare.folger.edu/shakespeares-works/a-midsummer-nights-dream/.

250. Bruton-Seal and Seal, *Backyard Medicine for All*, 193.

251. Burke, *The Modern Herbal Primer*, 98.

252. Arrowsmith, *Essential Herbal Wisdom*, 526.

Witch Hazel

Botanical Name: *Hamamelis virginiana*

Parts Used: Bark and young twigs

Magickal Properties: Balance, beauty, communication, dowsing, protection, and psychic sight

Healing Benefits: A natural astringent used to soothe and heal skin irritations and soothe away troubles.

Warning: This herb should not be used during pregnancy or while breast-feeding. Do not ingest.

Witch hazel belongs to a genus of hardy, deciduous shrubs and small trees also known as winterbloom. With its yellow, stringy, winter-blooming flowers, witch hazel is a striking plant in the winter garden. Even though it is a new friend to me, I grew up using witch hazel extract as an after-wash face astringent to keep my oily skin clear. It was only after I moved to Oregon that I met the lovely plant it was sourced from.

A Brief History

Witch hazel is native to North America where its anti-inflammatory and sedating actions and natural astringency made it a useful medicine plant.[253] The leaves, twigs, and flowers contain tannins to stanch blood flow and reduce swelling and bruising.[254] According to the *Desk Reference to Nature's Medicine*, "The Cherokee, Chippewa, Iroquois, Mohegan, and Potawatomi tribes used the leaves and bark in many ways. They brewed a tea to relieve mouth and throat irritations, reduce fever, and relieve menstrual cramps."[255] Witch hazel was used in steam baths and made into compresses and infusions to treat burns, bites, and rashes. The settlers adopted its use and introduced it to Europe.[256] It was so effective that by 1860, witch hazel

. . . .

253. Burke, *The Modern Herbal Primer*, 130.

254. Robin Rose Bennett, *This Gift of Healing Herbs: Plant Medicines and Home Remedies for a Vibrantly Healthy Life* (Berkley, CA: North Atlantic Books, 2014), 482.

255. Foster and Johnson, *Desk Reference to Nature's Medicine*, 372.

256. Chevallier, *Encyclopedia of Herbal Medicine*, 102.

was recognized for its curative properties and included in the *Pharmacopoeia* of the United States.[257]

How to Use

Witch hazel is not a nervine and never should be taken internally, but instead it holds protective qualities. Brew an infusion of witch hazel leaves and add it to bathwater to banish troubling emotions or break a hex. Add the infusion to washwater to deter negative energy to guard outlook and banish negative energy.

Witch hazel wood holds energy to heal and comfort. Break twigs into pieces and soak them in water overnight. Strain and add the water to bath magick to ease depression and comfort the grieving. Add the water to a footbath to revive the spirit after a difficult day.

Witch hazel also holds energy to improve psychic abilities. Rinse your forehead with a cloth that has been soaked in witch hazel water to heighten psychic powers. Wash hands with the water before divination to gain a deeper understanding. Forked witch hazel sticks made popular divining rods to find lost things.[258] In the past in rural North Carolina it was a common practice to hang green branches of witch hazel above thresholds to keep evil out.[259]

Yarrow

Botanical Name: *Achillea millefolium*

Parts Used: All aerial parts

Magickal Properties: Banishing, courage, exorcism, healing, love, protection, and psychic powers

Healing Benefits: A healing, uplifting herb used to treat liver deficiencies and chase away melancholy.

. . . .

257. Foster and Johnson, *Desk Reference to Nature's Medicine*, 372.

258. Kruger, *The Pocket Guide to Herbs*, 185.

259. Betsy Green Moyer and Ken Moore, eds., *Paul Green's Plant Book: An Alphabet of Flower Folklore* (Chapel Hill, NC: Botanical Garden Foundation, 2005), 85.

Warning: Extended use can cause photosensitivity and skin rashes. Do not take if you are pregnant or trying to conceive. May be toxic if taken over an extended time.

My lawn is full of yarrow. It self-seeded throughout the backyard well before I moved here. It would truly be a bane if I ever wished to eradicate it. But I like how it looks in the lawn. I appreciate its attractive lacy leaves and lovely white flowers. The nectar-rich flowers feed pollinators, while its seeds provide food for birds.

A Brief History

Long ago yarrow was a medicine herb and an herb of magick. It was reputed to heal so many aliments that it was known as "allheal."[260] Dried yarrow was found among the herbs in a Neanderthal grave, dating its use back 60,0000 years.[261] Yarrow was used to treat fever, influenza, measles, and chickenpox. Yarrow tea was drunk hot and poured into baths to open pores, encourage sweating, reduce fever, and relax a patient.[262] In England yarrow became known as "Englishman's quinine" because of its use in treating malaria.[263]

Yarrow was both a woman's herb and a battle herb known as soldier's wound-wort and knight's milfoil. The ancient Greeks named it *Achillea* after the hero Achilles, who lore holds was taught by the wise centaur Chiron to press the plant to a wound to stop bleeding.[264] During the Trojan War, Achilles is said to have used yarrow to treat his wounded soldiers.[265] Yarrow's antiseptic, anti-inflammatory, and astringent properties make it a valuable first aid herb to avoid infection, ease pain, reduce fevers, and staunch bleeding.[266] It was a common practice in the English countryside to stick a yarrow leaf into a nostril to stop a nosebleed.[267] The Scottish

. . . .

260. Reader's Digest, *Magic and Medicine of Plants*, 350.

261. Foster and Johnson, *Desk Reference to Nature's Medicine*, 176.

262. Bruton-Seal and Seal, *Backyard Medicine*, 194.

263. Bruton-Seal and Seal, *Backyard Medicine*, 194.

264. Folkard, *Plant Lore, Legends, and Lyrics*, 589.

265. Cook, *Be Your Own Herbalist*, 200; Homer, *Iliad*, trans. Stephen Mitchell (New York: Simon & Schuster, 2011), book 11, lines 779–81.

266. Jack Sanders, *The Secrets of Wildflowers* (Guilford, CT: Lyons Press, 2003).

267. Kruger, *The Pocket Guide to Herbs*, 189.

made a yarrow ointment to treat wounds and brewed an infusion called milfoil tea to treat melancholy.[268] The Norse chewed yarrow for toothache relief and used it to treat rheumatism.[269] While in the New World, the Cheyenne, Menominee, Lakota, Assiniboin, Gros Ventre, and Okanagan used yarrow to treat colds and accelerate wound healing.[270]

How to Use

When taken as tea, yarrow is an age-old tonic used to remedy a melancholy outlook, treat mild depression, relieve a headache, and even break a fever.[271] It is a bitter herb. Brew yarrow with lemon balm to make an uplifting infusion to lift your mood. Add the infusion to bathwater and soak to ease troubled thoughts. Brew an infusion of yarrow, thyme, and rose petals. Add it to bathwater and soak to heal past hurts and quell frustration.

Yarrow works as a diuretic and, when taken as a tea, increases the urge to urinate, flushing the body.[272] Its antispasmodic properties make it a helpful woman's herb. It is used to reduce cramps and regulate menstrual flow.[273] Yarrow tea's decongestant properties make it an effective treatment for colds, while yarrow compresses are used to ease the pain of hemorrhoids.[274]

Magickally, yarrow is a healing herb, a protective herb, and an herb of love. It is associated with Venus, Mars, and Libra and has a history rich in lore. Wish upon the first yarrow flower of the season to gain a favor. Burn dried yarrow to instill harmony. Grow yarrow down walkways to keep negative influences, unwanted guests, and pests away. Hang a sprig of yarrow over a doorway to keep negativity away.

Yarrow is excellent for eliminating negativity from a person, place, or thing. Carry a sprig of yarrow into a confrontation to help keep the conversation light. Yarrow is a helpful workplace herb and can be employed to drive away annoyances.

. . . .

268. Grieve, *A Modern Herbal*, vol. 2, 864.

269. Grieve, *A Modern Herbal*, vol. 2, 864.

270. Cichoke, *Secrets of Native American Herbal Remedies*, 80.

271. Danny Pharr, "Winter Solstice-Sown Herbs," in *Llewellyn's 2010 Herbal Almanac* (Woodbury, MN: Llewellyn Publications, 2009), 49.

272. Bellebuono, *An Herbalist's Guide to Formulary*, 81.

273. Cook, *Be Your Own Herbalist*, 201.

274. Hajeski, *National Geographic Complete Guide to Herbs and Spices*, 164.

Keep a dried bouquet of yarrow flowers on your desk to keep frustration at bay. Add yarrow to a vase of flowers for any family gathering to keep feelings positive.

Yarrow was a traditional wedding flower used to ensure a seven-year love, and a dream of picking yarrow meant good news was coming.[275] Yarrow was also used in divination. In China, yarrow stalks were used to foretell coming events, while in the British Isles, druids used yarrow stems to predict the weather.[276] In England yarrow was plucked from a grave to use in dream divination. A man would find a yarrow plant growing upon a woman's grave, or vice versa, pluck it, and then silently return home. Speaking would break the spell. Once the person returned home, the yarrow was placed under the pillow to encourage dreams of their future spouse.[277]

. . . .

275. Picton, *The Book of Magical Herbs*, 21–23.

276. Foster and Johnson, *Desk Reference to Nature's Medicine*, 176.

277. Folkard, *Plant Lore, Legends, and Lyrics*, 588.

ESSENTIAL OILS TO SUPPORT WELLNESS

While the plants that grow in my yard hold a special place in my practice, I know it isn't possible to grow every ingredient we need. We will, in fact, never meet some of the items most important to our daily practice except in the versions we buy at the market. Two prime examples are coffee and tea, the magickal elixirs most of us deem necessary to start our day. Cinnamon and vanilla are two other ingredients that I use regularly but have never met in person. For ingredients that grow on the other side of the world, I often utilize the plant's essential oil to access its healing powers and empower my magickal formulas.

Essential oils are natural aromatic compounds found in the seeds, bark, stems, roots, and flowers that have been extracted, usually by distillation, and are much more concentrated than the oil in the plant itself. A good essential oil is often expensive. As you begin to explore essential oils, you will find cheaper offerings labeled "fragrance oil" or "perfume oil." Try to avoid these, as they often are synthetic and therefore will not contribute the same energy that the true oils will give your magickal workings.

Choose just a few to begin and get to know them. Start with formulas that use three or fewer oils. Keep your batch size small until you know whether or not you like it and will use the blend. When you are working with a number of essential oils, never use the same dropper or you may contaminate your oils and ruin their scent. If you experience any sort of negative reaction, discontinue using immediately.

Safety Tips and Precautions

While many plants provide a gentle medicine for us to use, essential oils are much stronger. Essential oils are concentrated, and though they have many therapeutic uses, they can be dangerous too. Some negative side effects include chemical burns, allergic reactions, photosensitivity, and respiratory issues. Some essential oils should not be used by children, pregnant women, or nursing mothers. Dermatologist Cynthia Bailey warns, "There is definitely credible science behind certain benefits for certain essential oils. But you have to choose wisely, and you cannot use them indiscriminately." Regarding overuse, she notes, "Once you become sensitized, you will forever be allergic to it."[278]

Diffusing essential oils may seem like a safe practice, but in reality it can lead to some health problems, especially for children and pets. When diffused, some common essential oils have been known to cause breathing problems, fatigue, vomiting, and difficulty walking.

As you begin to work with essential oils, be aware of how you interact with each one. Avoid any oil that causes a negative reaction. Keep a journal and take note of your experiences. Which oil calls to you? Grapefruit oil is my personal power oil. It has a nurturing, uplifting energy that renews, restores, lifts, enlivens, and invigorates. Its scent inspires creativity. To use it, simply fill a small spray bottle with water and add 9 drops of grapefruit essential oil for a spritzer that will lift your mood and reenergize your mind. Add the oil to bathwater to soothe stress, remedy fatigue, and ease depression. Burn it in a diffuser to grant resilience in adversity or defuse a negative situation.

. . . .

278. Lisa Marshall, "Essential Oils: Natural Doesn't Mean Risk-Free," WebMD, August 8, 2017, https://www .webmd.com/skin-problems-and-treatments/news/20170809/essential-oils-natural-doesnt-mean-risk-free.

Basil Essential Oil

Botanical Name: *Ocimum basilicum*

Magickal Properties: Cheer, creativity, exorcism, happiness, harmony, love, luck, protection, and wealth

Emotional Response: Calmly stimulating. Basil essential oil reduces anxiety and fights mental fatigue as it alleviates nervous disorders, increases concentration, and enhances memory.

Healing Benefits: Antibacterial, antidepressant, antispasmodic, carminative, nervine properties. Its uplifting energy lifts and clears the mind as it calms anxiety and increases well-being. It is used to ease headaches, improve appetite, calm the stomach, and treat intestinal gas, diarrhea, constipation, and nasal congestion.

Warning: This oil should not be used for extensive periods, as it is potentially toxic over time. Avoid if pregnant or breastfeeding. Do not use if you have a history of seizures. Should not be used by children.

Blends Well With: Citrusy, spicy, or floral essential oils such as bergamot, cedarwood, clary sage, ginger, grapefruit, lavender, lemon, lemongrass, neroli, peppermint, rosemary, and sweet orange

Basil oil is extracted through steam distillation of the flowering herb. Even if you think the pungent scent smells a little funky, its versatile, uplifting energy makes it a good stock oil to have on hand. The scent of basil oil is uplifting. It is used to ease headaches and nasal congestion, lift mood, clear the mind, and inspire creative thought. In Europe basil oil is used to treat melancholy.[279] For the spellcaster, the versatile energy of basil can be used to empower a diverse array of intentions. Use it in formulas to soothe emotions, ease anxiety, and end quarreling. Use basil oil to banish negativity and cheer the soul. Dab some on and wear when you need to instill harmony into a situation. Add a few drops of basil oil to washwater to clean up after a confrontation and restore peace.

Basil is an herb of Samhain. The scent stimulates the senses and enhances spirit communication. Basil oil is an ingredient in flying ointments and can be used to

....

279. Roberta Wilson, *Aromatherapy: Essential Oils for Vibrant Health and Beauty* (New York: Avery, 2002), 50.

summon dragons and basilisks. Basil oil also holds energy for protection and can be used to break hexes and counter the evil eye. Add basil oil to water in an infuser and mist the air to protect a space from negativity.

Basil is also an herb of prosperity and can be used to empower rituals to attract money. But most of all, basil is an herb of love, a favorite of Lakshmi, Hindu goddess of marriage and good fortune, and the oil is used in love magick. Use basil oil in your bath whenever you need to invoke the essence of a love goddess. Mix basil with lavender and rose oil to empower an attraction bath. Or anoint a candle with basil oil and burn it to promote a happy family life.

Bay Laurel Essential Oil

Botanical Name: *Laurus nobilis*

Magickal Properties: Glory, luck, psychic vision, protection, strength, victory, vitality, wisdom, and wishes

Emotional Response: This warm and uplifting oil relaxes the mind and helps relieve pain.

Healing Benefits: Analgesic, antibacterial, antiseptic, antispasmodic, and expectorant properties. Bay oil has antibacterial, antifungal, and antiviral properties and is used as an external treatment for some bacteria and fungus infections. It is useful during cold and flu season.

Warning: May cause skin irritation. Not suitable for children.

Blends Well With: Bergamot, clary sage, cypress, frankincense, ginger, juniper berry, lavender, patchouli, pine, rosemary, sweet orange, and ylang-ylang

Bay oil is another good oil to keep on hand. It is distilled from the leaves of the evergreen tree *Laurus nobilis*. Bay oil is antiseptic. It was mixed with olive oil to make Aleppo soap, an ancient soap made in Syria.[280]

Bay essential oil has a mild analgesic action to ease aches and pains and relieve tension headaches. Magickally, it holds a bold victorious energy that can be used to

. . . .

280. Cathy Hanson, "Aleppo Soap," *Historical Research Update*, December 19, 2016, https://www.historical researchupdate.com/news/aleppo-soap/.

purify, increase vitality, encourage psychic development, and even break curses. Its uplifting energy stimulates creative thought. Fill a spray bottle with water and add 9 drops of bay oil and spritz to awaken creativity. (Just be careful not to get it near your eyes.) Anoint a candle with bay oil and burn it to clear away confusion or grant clarity. Mix bay oil with olive oil and wear it when you need athletic endurance. Rub the blend into your hands, lift it to your nose, and breathe in the scent to stay clear of distractions.

Burn bay oil to stimulate energy flow and draw opportunity. Blend with lemon and pine oil to make a road-opener oil. Mix bay oil with nutmeg oil and heat the blend in a tea light oil burner to remove barriers. Blend bay oil with lavender, rose, sandalwood, and verbena to break a hex.

Bergamot Essential Oil

Botanical Name: *Citrus ×aurantium* ssp. *bergamia*

Magickal Properties: Abundance, communication, destiny, joy, luck, money, opportunity, prosperity, and success

Emotional Response: Soothing, balancing. Bergamot boosts self-confidence, elevates mood, and enhances well-being.

Healing Benefits: Analgesic, antibacterial, antidepressant, antispasmodic, antiseptic, and sedative properties. Its natural healing properties are used to heal skin irritations, fade scars, and treat herpes.

Warning: May make skin more sensitive to sunlight. Avoid if you are pregnant or breastfeeding. Not recommended for young children.

Blends Well With: Citrusy, spicy, or floral essential oils such as basil, cardamom, chamomile, clary sage, clove, coriander, cypress, frankincense, ginger, grapefruit, jasmine, juniper berry, lavender, lemon, lemongrass, melissa, myrrh, neroli, nutmeg, patchouli, pine, rose, rosemary, sandalwood, sweet orange, vanilla, vetiver, and ylang-ylang

Bergamot oil comes from the aromatic peel of the green fruit from a European citrus tree. The fragrant oil is extracted from the rind and is used to make colognes, perfumes, and scented soaps. Bergamot oil holds positive, uplifting energy to elevate mood, clear the mind, and lift the spirit. Mix with sweet almond oil and wear it to lighten mood and sharpen thoughts. Use bergamot oil during meditation to work toward your destiny and connect to the higher self. Bergamot oil energy is soothing and can be used to calm anger. Use it in harmony spells to ease resentments. Mix a few drops into a dish of salt or a spoonful of castile soap and add it to bathwater to ease depression.

Bergamot is associated with Mercury, the sun, and the element air and is best known for its attraction powers. Use bergamot oil to empower fast money magick, boost prosperity spells, or accelerate a victory. Mix bergamot oil with sesame oil to usher in opportunities. Make a good luck talisman with 3 bay leaves tucked into a small white or orange bag. Add a cotton ball with 9 drops of bergamot oil. Carry the talisman in your left pocket to draw good luck to you throughout the day.

In Hoodoo, bergamot has power to compel and is used in work to dominate another. Wear it as a scent to enhance your personal power, bolster magnetism, and inspire others to admire you.

Cardamom Essential Oil

Botanical Name: *Elettaria cardamomum*

Magickal Properties: Clarity, creativity, enthusiasm, love, and lust

Emotional Response: Revitalizing, stimulating, encouraging self-acceptance, and helping alleviate stress and release trauma.

Healing Benefits: Antiseptic, antispasmodic, carminative, and nervine properties. This nervine combats fatigue, relieves abdominal discomfort, and alleviates headaches while lifting outlook.

Warning: Not recommended for young children. May cause skin irritation.

Blends Well With: Bay, bergamot, cedarwood, cinnamon, clary sage, clove, coriander, ginger, grapefruit, jasmine, lemon, lemongrass, melissa, neroli, patchouli, sandalwood, sweet orange, vetiver, and ylang-ylang

Cardamom oil is distilled from the fruit of the cardamom plant. The oil has an earthy-woody, slightly spicy scent that boosts energy and mood. Cardamom is used in Ayurvedic medicine. The seeds contain detoxifying enzymes that promote digestion. The Greeks and Romans used cardamom for perfumes.[281] The Vikings introduced it to Northern Europe, where it became a favorite spice.[282]

Cardamom oil has an uplifting scent that grants clarity and inspires creative thought. Burn it in a tea light warmer to enhance mental performance. Blend cardamom oil with lemon oil and dab the oil blend on a crystal, stone, or statue to open the mind to possibilities. Blend cardamom oil with sweet orange oil into melted coconut oil to make a salve to warm the heart and a encourage a positive outlook. Blend cardamom oil with cedarwood oil to renew energy or combat fatigue. Blend cardamom oil with cinnamon, frankincense, and lavender oil to improve mood and diminish aggravations.

Cardamom oil is associated with Venus. It has an enthusiastic energy that is used for both commanding and compelling. Burn it in a diffuser to stir feelings of passion and encourage romance. Use cardamom oil to empower love spells. Cardamom oil will act as a catalyst to encourage the action of other herbs. Blend cardamom oil with sweet orange, and ylang-ylang. Mix it into coconut oil and rub it into the skin for an enchanting scent that will inspire confidence and charisma. Or blend cardamom oil with jasmine and vanilla oil to become enchanting.

Cedarwood Essential Oil

Botanical Names: *Cedrus* spp. and *Juniperus* spp.

Magickal Properties: Communication, divination, healing, protection, purification, and summoning

Emotional Response: Both calming and uplifting. Helps diffuse anger and anxiety. Combats negative emotions and exhaustion.

Healing Benefits: Anti-inflammatory, antiseptic, antispasmodic, and antifungal properties. It is used to treat respiratory problems and reduce the pain of sore muscles and arthritis. Its antiseptic action helps fight infections.

. . . .

281. Clevely et al., *Cooking with Herbs and Spices*, 299.

282. Hajeski, *National Geographic Complete Guide to Herbs and Spices*, 210.

Warning: Not recommended for young children. Avoid using if you are pregnant or breastfeeding. Do not use if trying to conceive. When diffused, it is toxic to birds.

Blends Well With: Chamomile, clary sage, frankincense, juniper berry, lavender, lemon, patchouli, pine, rosemary, and vetiver

Cedarwood oil is steam distilled from a variety of trees in the *Cedrus* and *Juniperus* genera. It has a sweet, woodsy scent to elevate mood and calm anxiety. Add it to beauty baths to improve your skin's appearance, or burn it in a diffuser to dispel fear, anger, and frustration.

Cedars have a long history as sacred trees. Cultures around the world have used cedar wood to house their gods and its oil to heal, cleanse, and purify the body and spirit. The Hindu word for cedar is *deodar*, which translates to "timber of the gods."[283] The Egyptians used cedar wood for making coffins and cedar pitch to anoint the bodies to prepare the dead for rebirth, as they believed the scent facilitated entrance to higher realms.[284] The Babylonians held the cedar as a tree of life and employed it to restore strength and vigor to the body.[285]

Cedarwood oil has antiseptic and astringent properties. It is used to treat respiratory problems, skin irritations, and fungal infections.[286] A 2018 study on *Juniperus virginiana* found the cedrol in cedarwood oil to have a soothing effect on mice, suggesting it may be beneficial for reducing stress and anxiety symptoms.[287]

The cedar is associated with Mercury, Uranus, Virgo, and Odin and is known as a visionary tree. The scent promotes peaceful thoughts and helps carry messages from both the universe and the higher self. Anoint a candle with cedarwood oil and burn it during divination to improve intuition. Use the oil during meditation to deepen

· · · · · · · · · · · · · · · · ·

283. Elbert Luther Little, Susan Rafield, and Olivia Buehl, *National Audubon Society Field Guide to North American Trees: Western Region* (New York: Alfred A. Knopf, 1980), 257.

284. Folkard, *Plant Lore, Legends, and Lyrics*, 273.

285. J. H. Philpot, *The Sacred Tree: or, The Tree in Religion and Myth* (London: Macmillan, 1897; Project Gutenberg, 2014), 131.

286. Wilson, *Aromatherapy*, 57.

287. Kai Zhang and Lei Yao, "The Anxiolytic Effect of *Juniperus virginiana* L. Essential Oil and Determination of Its Active Constituents," *Psychology and Behavior* 189 (May 2018): 50–58, doi:10.1016/j.physbeh.2018.01.004.

the experience. Mix it with sweet almond oil and wear it as perfume to realize your dreams.

Use cedarwood oil to banish negativity, ease pain, calm nervous tension, and stop bad dreams. Blend 5 drops of cedarwood oil into a tablespoon of castile soap and add it to bathwater for a comforting soak to relax and unwind. Add it to a footbath after a hectic day to calm nervous tension. Anoint a candle with cedarwood oil and burn it for psychic protection.

Chamomile Essential Oil

Botanical Names: *Matricaria recutita* (German) and *Chamaemelum nobile* (Roman)

Magickal Properties: Abundance, communication, healing, peace, rest, and water elemental

Emotional Response: Soothing and calming. Chamomile helps keep emotions balanced. Use it to stem worry, calm anger, ease nervous tension, or encourage a peaceful outlook.

Healing Benefits: Analgesic, anesthetic, anti-inflammatory, antispasmodic, and relaxant properties. Its natural anti-inflammatory properties make it a wonderful remedy to soothe skin irritations. Chamomile strengthens the immune system and promotes rest.

Warning: Avoid using if you are pregnant or breastfeeding. May irritate the skin.

Blends Well With: Bergamot, cedarwood, clary sage, clove, cypress, eucalyptus, frankincense, grapefruit, jasmine, lavender, lemon, lemongrass, melissa, myrrh, neroli, patchouli, pine, rosemary, rose, sandalwood, sweet orange, yarrow, and ylang-ylang

Chamomile oil has a pleasant, soothing, apple-like aroma. German chamomile is sometimes called blue chamomile because the essential oil is deep blue or bluish-green in color. Both German chamomile and Roman chamomile belong to the botanical family *Asteraceae* and have similar properties. Chamomile oil has antiseptic powers to soothe skin discomfort and speed the healing process. It is used to reduce inflammation, ease muscle and joint pain, treat skin irritations, and speed the healing process.[288] Mix it with a carrier oil and massage it into the skin to soothe muscle pain or treat inflamed joints and rheumatism.

Chamomile is an Old World medicine plant. The ancient Egyptians valued chamomile as a remedy for malaria. In ancient Rome it was used to relieve headaches and disorders for the bladder, liver, and kidneys.[289] In the Middle Ages chamomile was a popular strewing herb.[290] It was mixed into potpourris and stuffed into sachets to scent linens and clothes. Early Teutonic tribes discovered chamomile growing in southern Europe and dedicated it to their sun god.[291]

Chamomile has sedative properties and is often prescribed as a stress reducer. Rub the oil into your forehead to relieve a headache. Or rub it into your hands to prepare the mind and body for magickal work. Blend chamomile oil with lavender oil to easy worry. Blend it with melissa oil to encourage a positive outlook.

Chamomile oil is associated with the sun and has energy to manifest abundance. An infusion of chamomile tea is a Hoodoo good luck fix used by gamblers to wash their hands to increase winnings. Mix chamomile oil with olive oil and rub into your hands to attract opportunities.

Chamomile also has energy for protection. Add 5 drops of chamomile oil to a tablespoon of castile soap and add it to bathwater to remove negative energy or soothe frazzled nerves. Add basil oil to remove a curse.

Cinnamon Essential Oil

Botanical Name: *Cinnamomum* spp.

Magickal Properties: Healing, love, luck, protection, strength, spirituality, success, and wealth

Emotional Response: Warm and energizing. The spicy scent of cinnamon stimulates and lifts mood and energy.

Healing Benefits: Antibacterial, antidepressant, anti-inflammatory, antiseptic, and astringent properties. This warming oil is used in massage oils to

. . . .

288. Wilson, *Aromatherapy*, 59.

289. Foster and Johnson, *National Geographic Desk Reference to Nature's Medicine*, 94.

290. Kruger, *The Pocket Guide to Herbs*, 49.

291. Reader's Digest, *Magic and Medicine of Plants*, 195.

enhance circulation and counter depression. Its antiseptic prosperities can speed healing.

Warning: This oil is very strong and can burn on contact. Avoid if pregnant or breastfeeding. Avoid if you are undergoing chemotherapy or radiation. When diffused, it is toxic to dogs, cats, and birds.

Blends Well With: Bergamot, cardamom, clove, frankincense, grapefruit, jasmine, lemon, lemongrass, melissa, neroli, peppermint, rose, rosemary, sweet orange, tea tree, vanilla, and ylang-ylang

Cinnamon essential oil is made by distilling the bark and leaves of trees in the *Cinnamomum* genus. It has a wonderful sweet, spicy, and slightly earthy scent and a very long history. The Hebrew priests of old used cinnamon oil as a holy anointing oil. The Chinese and Egyptians used it to purify their temples.[292] In Rome cinnamon was so prized it was used as currency.[293] Medieval doctors used cinnamon "to treat conditions such as coughing, arthritis, and sore throats."[294]

Cinnamon essential oil is a natural antiseptic that helps the healing process. It is used to soothe muscle aches, menstrual cramps, arthritis pain, and insect bites and stings. Mix it with a carrier oil to use topically to accelerate healing. Rub it into inflamed joints to treat arthritis pain.

Cinnamon oil is also used to relieve depression. Mix 7 drops of cinnamon oil into ¼ cup of salt. Pour it under running bathwater and soak to lighten your mood and lift your spirit. Add it to a footbath to revive a weary spirit. Add 2 drops of lavender to soothe anxiety. Mix 5 drops of cinnamon oil and 2 drops of rosemary oil to a tablespoon of castile soap and add it to bathwater to alleviate exhaustion.

Cinnamon oil is associated with the sun and Uranus. It holds a warming energy to empower, draw money, stimulate psychic abilities, kindle love, boost attraction, and increase general magickal energy. Add it to blends to instigate action or boost the energy of other oils. Use cinnamon oil to energize a spell. It will act as a spark

. . . .

292. S. Theresa Dietz, *The Complete Language of Flowers* (New York: Wellfleet Press, 2020), 59.

293. Hajeski, *National Geographic Complete Guide to Herbs and Spices*, 215.

294. Yvette Brazier, "What Are the Health Benefits of Cinnamon?" Medical News Today, January 3, 2020, https://www.medicalnewstoday.com/articles/266069.

of energy to get the manifestation moving. Use it in rituals to heal, draw love and riches, and invoke protection.

The scent of cinnamon registers deep within us to sharpen focus and open doors. Dress a candle in a blend of sweet almond oil and cinnamon oil and burn to raise energetic vibrations and deepen concentration. Or make a blend to open possibilities with cinnamon, bergamot oil, and sesame seed oil. Mix cinnamon oil with patchouli and vanilla to make a good luck oil blend. Mix the blend with olive oil and rub into your hands whenever you need a dose of good luck. Anoint candles with cinnamon and sweet orange oil to speed money magicks. Or mix cinnamon oil, basil, and nutmeg to empower abundance magick.

Clary Sage Essential Oil

Botanical Name: *Salvia sclarea*

Magickal Properties: Balance, calming, creative thought, communication, destiny, focus, growth, healing, protection, restoration, and wisdom

Emotional Response: Reviving, uplifting, and encouraging affection. The scent of clary is an aphrodisiac that balances emotions, lifts mood, and revives the weary.

Healing Benefits: Aphrodisiac, antidepressant, antiseptic, antispasmodic, carminative, and sedative properties. This uplifting oil is used to stimulate circulation, relieve minor aches, ease depression, and revive the weary.

Warning: Avoid if you are pregnant or breastfeeding. Should not be used by children.

Blends Well With: Bay, bergamot, cedarwood, chamomile, cypress, frankincense, grapefruit, jasmine, juniper berry, lavender, lemon, lemongrass, melissa, patchouli, pine, rose, sandalwood, sweet orange, vetiver, and yarrow

Clary sage oil is steam distilled from the leaves and flowers of *Salvia sclarea*, an herb in the mint family known as an Old World medicine. Clary sage oil has astringent and antifungal properties. It is used topically to treat skin conditions. A 2015 study showed that clary sage oil sped wound healing and prevented infection.[295] Mix 3 drops of clary sage oil with 1 teaspoon of coconut oil and use it as a salve to accelerate healing. Its rich, musky scent promotes relaxation and eases anger. Mix clary with lavender oil to ease headaches and soothe frazzled nerves. Mix clary and chamomile to soothe hysteria. Make a blend with 5 drops of clary and 8 drops of sweet orange. Burn it in a diffuser to end melancholy thoughts. Blend clary with bergamot to dispel anger.

Clary sage oil is associated with the moon and Mercury. It holds energy to enhance intuition and visionary states. Sprinkle a couple of drops of clary sage oil on a pillowcase to enhance dreamwork. Mix it with coconut oil and use it to anoint the third eye. Blend clary with frankincense. Inhale the scent to open communication channels with the universe. Blend it with frankincense and lavender oil and burn it to deepen awareness. Mix the blend into sweet almond oil and wear it as a perfume to inspire intuition.

Clove Essential Oil

Botanical Name: *Syzygium aromaticum*

Magickal Properties: Banishing, comfort, friendship, love, prosperity, protection, and romance

Emotional Response: Its warm scent calms and comforts.

Healing Benefits: Analgesic, antiaging, antiseptic, carminative, and stimulating properties. It is used to help heal the skin, clear congestion, and reduce anxiety.

Warning: This warm oil is very strong and can burn on contact. Avoid if pregnant or breastfeeding. Do not use if you take blood thinners. When diffused, it is toxic to dogs, cats, and birds.

Blends Well With: Bay, bergamot, cardamom, chamomile, clary sage, coriander, ginger, grapefruit, jasmine, lavender, lemon, lemongrass, melissa, myrrh, neroli, patchouli, sandalwood, sweet orange, tea tree, vanilla, and ylang-ylang

. . . .

295. Monika Sienkiewicz et al., "The Effect of Clary Sage Oil on Staphylococci Responsible for Wound Infections," *Postepy dermatologii i alergologii* 32, no. 1 (2015): 21–26, doi:10.5114/pdia.2014.40957.

Clove essential oil, also known as clove bud essential oil, is distilled from the aromatic flower buds of an evergreen native to the Spice Islands, *Syzygium aromaticum*. It has a warm, spicy scent and is loaded with eugenol, a compound that has both antiseptic and anti-inflammatory properties and is a common ingredient in mouthwashes, toothpastes, soaps, and insect repellents. The Greeks, Romans, and Chinese used cloves in their herbal medicines.[296]

Clove oil is used to protect and empower. It was customary for the people of the Spice Islands to plant a clove tree at the birth of a child. The child would wear a necklace made of strung cloves as a protection amulet from evil and illness.[297] Today clove oil is burned to drive away hostility, dispel negative energy, and stop gossip. Diffuse clove oil to provide psychic protection and dispel negative energy. Use it to empower binding rituals.

Clove essential oil imparts strength and support to help us beat troublesome behaviors. Add 9 drops of clove oil to a spray bottle of water. Spritz whenever you need help staying on track. Drip 7 drops of the oil onto a small piece of cloth and carry it with you. Breathe in the scent when you need strength to keep your resolve.

Clove oil is associated with Uranus and Aquarius and holds a warming energy to activate other energies. Add to formulas to move an action forward. Use it to boost creativity. The scent of clove lifts the spirit and heightens positive emotions. Use it to fortify formulas for love and friendship. Mix clove oil with olive oil and wear it as a perfume to draw love to you. Scent friendship gifts with clove oil to strengthen your bond.

Clove oil is also used to soothe painful joints and insect bites. The scent grants clarity of thought and bolsters self-esteem. Add 7 drops of clove oil to a spray bottle of water and spritz the air or yourself to inspire a fresh outlook. Blend clove oil into a carrier and wear it as a scent to enliven personality.

. . . .

296. Richard Craze, *The Spice Companion* (London: Quintet Publishing, 1997), 72.

297. Clevely et al., *Cooking with Herbs and Spices*, 300.

Coriander Essential Oil

Botanical Name: *Coriandrum sativum*

Magickal Properties: Adaptation, creativity, enthusiasm, healing, love, luck, and optimism

Emotional Response: Warm and calming. Coriander calms the spirits, eases nervous exhaustion, and increases a sense of well-being.

Healing Benefits: Aphrodisiac, analgesic, antimicrobial, antifungal, and antiseptic properties. This uplifting oil is used to improve mood, clear skin irritations, increase circulation, and relieve muscle and joint pain.

Warning: Avoid if pregnant or breastfeeding. Avoid if you have kidney disease.

Blends Well With: Bergamot, cardamom, clove, frankincense, grapefruit, lemon, lemongrass, melissa, neroli, ylang-ylang, pine, and sweet orange

Coriander oil is steam distilled from the seeds of the herb known as cilantro or Chinese parsley (*Coriandrum sativum*). Coriander is an herb of antiquity mentioned in the Ebers Papyrus, an Egyptian medical text from 1552 BCE, and in the *One Thousand and One Nights*, where it is cited as a love potion.[298] It was cultivated by the Egyptians and was a popular cooking herb of both the Greeks and Romans.[299] Its popularity spread through Europe by the Roman legions who used it to flavor their bread.[300]

Coriander was a medicinal plant. Both the plant and the seeds were used as a remedy to soothe digestive troubles.[301] It was also held to be an herb with magickal powers. The Egyptians used coriander for protection; to the Chinese it was an herb of immortality.[302] In European lore coriander was used to inspired love and boost fertility.[303] Coriander oil is associated with Mercury, the moon, and Mars. It is used to draw luck and new love and to encourage passion. Its warm, earthy, sweet scent

. . . .

298. Hajeski, *National Geographic Complete Guide to Herbs and Spices*, 32.

299. Hajeski, *National Geographic Complete Guide to Herbs and Spices*, 32.

300. Clevely et al., *Cooking with Herbs and Spices*, 292.

301. Craze, *The Spice Companion*, 61.

302. Picton, *The Book of Magical Herbs*, 89.

303. Picton, *The Book of Magical Herbs*, 89.

holds a positive, uplifting energy to elevate outlook and remedy lethargy and mental fatigue. Diffuse coriander oil with bergamot and lavender oil to boost mood and reduce anxiety. Mix the blend into a spoonful of castile soap and add to bathwater for a relaxing soak. Add the blend to a footbath to ease nervous tension.

The scent of coriander oil lifts and inspires. Use it to encourage a new way of thinking. Use it in meditation to gain insight when facing a crossroads. Mix it with olive oil and wear to ease fears and facilitate change. Burn coriander oil during divination to gain a deeper understanding. Anoint candles with olive oil and coriander oil and burn to empower love spells. Burn coriander oil and frankincense to promote positive energy flow.

Cypress Essential Oil

Botanical Name: *Cupressus sempervirens*

Magickal Properties: Comfort, healing, longevity, loss, protection, and truth

Emotional Response: Warm, soothing, and elevating. The healing properties of this oil are used to revitalize the mind and spirit to ease stress and fight mental fatigue.

Healing Benefits: Anti-inflammatory, antiseptic, and stimulating properties. This warm, uplifting oil is used to calm nervous tension, improve circulation, ease muscle aches, and accelerate wound healing to help maintain healthy skin.

Warning: Avoid if you are pregnant or breastfeeding. When diffused, it is toxic to birds.

Blends Well With: Bay, bergamot, cardamom, cedarwood, clary sage, chamomile, ginger, grapefruit, jasmine, lavender, lemon, lemongrass, melissa, neroli, pine, sweet orange, sandalwood, yarrow, and ylang-ylang

Cypress oil is steam distilled from the twigs and needles of an evergreen tree. It has a fresh and pungent aroma that lifts mood to create a brighter outlook. Diffuse cypress oil to soothe the psyche and clear away upset emotions. Blend it with melissa to ease sadness. Use cypress oil to ease transitions.

Since the earliest times, the cypress has been an emblem of mourning and grief.[304] Use cypress oil to provide comfort and help overcome loss. Blend cypress oil into a dish of salt and add it to bathwater for a comforting soak to balance emotions. Blend it with bergamot to elevate outlook. Add cypress oil to a footbath to revive tired feet.

Cypress oil has long been associated with the dead, passing between the worlds, and funeral rites. It is used at Samhain to honor ancestors and to aid in past-life workings. Make an invocation oil with a blend of cypress, patchouli, and sandalwood oil mixed into sweet almond oil. Use it to anoint candles and burn it to empower rituals.

Cypress oil also holds energy to empower defensive magick. Use it to strengthen rituals to bind or banish. Mix 3 drops of cypress oil with 2 drops of clove and 2 drops of cedarwood oil. Use it to empower banishing spells.

Eucalyptus Essential Oil

Botanical Name: *Eucalyptus globulus*

Magickal Properties: Cleansing, healing, health, protection, success, and vision

Emotional Response: A warm, stimulating oil that awakens thought, sharpens concentration, and alleviates feelings of depression.

Healing Benefits: Antiaging, antibacterial, antiseptic, and stimulating properties. This warm oil is used to treat headaches, make breathing easier, ease muscle and joint aches, and accelerate the healing of the skin.

Warning: This is a strong oil and may cause skin irritation. If inhaled, it may irritate the respiratory tract. Avoid if you are pregnant or breastfeeding. Avoid if you have high blood pressure. When diffused, it is toxic to cats and birds.

Blends Well With: Cedarwood, chamomile, cypress, ginger, grapefruit, juniper berry, lavender, lemongrass, melissa, myrrh, neroli, peppermint, pine, rosemary, sweet orange, tea tree, thyme, and yarrow

Eucalyptus oil is steam distilled from the leaves and twigs of the eucalyptus tree. The oil has a strong, fresh scent and a stimulating energy to boost the immune

. . . .

304. Folkard, *Plant Lore, Legends, and Lyrics*, 304.

system, protect against infection, relieve respiratory conditions, and aid in the healing of minor skin irritations. Its camphoraceous scent is known for its use in vapor rubs, inhalants, and household cleaners. Add eucalyptus oil to bath salts to bolster the spirit and banish negative energy. Add it to a salve to treat blisters, boils, burns, and scrapes.

Eucalyptus oil is associated with the moon and Pluto. The scent lifts the spirit, stimulates healing, and encourages emotional balance. Add eucalyptus oil to healing baths to boost well-being. Anoint a dinner candle with eucalyptus oil, place it in the center of the table, and light it to aid reconciling difficulties in a relationship. Blend eucalyptus oil with myrrh and thyme and use it to fight sickness, fortify health, or purify any space.

The scent of eucalyptus oil opens awareness. Burn eucalyptus oil to enhance meditation. Blend it with pine to inspire creative thought. Blend it with bay oil to enhance concentration and remove barriers.

Frankincense Essential Oil

Botanical Name: *Boswellia* spp.

Magickal Properties: Blessing, consecration, courage, exorcism, healing, protection, spirituality, and visions

Emotional Response: Uplifting, soothing, and calming. The scent of this oil calms anxiety, elevates outlook, and increases your sense of well-being.

Healing Benefits: Analgesic, anti-inflammatory, antiseptic, carminative, and sedative properties. It is used to support immune functions, heal the skin, open the chest to ease coughs, treat discomfort caused by arthritis, and reduce nervous tension.

Warning: None.

Blends Well With: Bergamot, chamomile, cinnamon, clary sage, cypress, ginger, grapefruit, jasmine, lavender, lemon, lemongrass, melissa, myrrh, neroli, patchouli, pine, rose, rosemary, sandalwood, sweet orange, vanilla, vetiver, and ylang-ylang

Frankincense oil is steam distilled from the resin of trees in the genus *Boswellia*. It is one of the oldest magickal resins and has been traded for more than five thousand years. Frankincense oil has a rich woodsy scent. It was burned as ceremonial incense by the Jews, the Assyrians, and the Egyptians.[305] Frankincense was one of the gifts of the Magi (gold, frankincense, and myrrh). Egyptian women made kohl to paint their eyelids out of charred frankincense and mixed it into a paste with other ingredients to perfume their hands.[306]

Frankincense oil is associated with the sun, Saturn, Adonis, Apollo, Demeter, and Ra. The resin is burned as incense for its pleasant, uplifting scent that lifts the spirit, alleviates sorrow, and promotes feelings of security and spirituality. Burn frankincense oil anytime you feel frightened, as the scent not only fills the space with positive vibrations, but it also banishes negativity. Diffuse it with lavender oil to calm frazzled nerves.

Frankincense is a traditional resin that is burned to carry prayers. Combine frankincense with myrrh oil and burn it during meditation to gain insight or foster spiritual growth. Make a sweet dream oil to anoint sachets and dream pillows by mixing frankincense oil, myrrh, and lemon oil. Add the blend to a tablespoon of sweet almond oil and wear it as a perfume to brighten outlook and sweeten prospects.

Frankincense oil has antianxiety properties. The scent is calming. Blend 9 drops of frankincense oil into 1 tablespoon of castile soap and add it to bathwater for a soak to calm the psyche and balance emotions. Burn frankincense oil in a diffuser whenever you feel overwhelmed.

Ginger Essential Oil

Botanical Name: *Zingiber officinale*

Magickal Properties: Abundance, courage, energy, inspiration, health, love, luck, prosperity, and success

Emotional Response: Warm and reviving. The scent of this oil energizes to lift mood and remedy fatigue.

Healing Benefits: Analgesic, anesthetic, anti-inflammatory, and antiseptic properties. Ginger oil is used to fight colds and flu, soothe a troubled stomach, and remedy both head and body aches.

. . . .

305. Folkard, *Plant Lore, Legends, and Lyrics,* 346.

306. Grieve, *A Modern Herbal,* vol. 1, 327.

Warning: Do not use if you take blood thinners.

Blends Well With: Bergamot, cardamom, cedarwood, clove, coriander, cypress, eucalyptus, frankincense, grapefruit, jasmine, juniper berry, lemon, lemongrass, melissa, neroli, patchouli, rose, sandalwood, sweet orange, and ylang-ylang

Ginger oil is derived from the dried roots of *Zingiber officinale*. It has a sweet, earthy, woody, warm aroma just like the hot, fragrant spice. Ginger oil is used to increase circulation, treat coughs and colds, and relieve muscle aches. The scent of ginger oil gives a pleasant lift to boost well-being. Burn it in a diffuser to protect against feelings of loneliness and depression. Blend 5 drops of ginger oil into 1 tablespoon of castile soap, add it to bathwater, and soak to relieve feelings of fatigue. Blend 5 drops of ginger oil into 1 tablespoon of sweet almond oil and massage it into skin to relieve muscle aches and migraines. Ginger oil holds a warming, energizing energy to amplify personal power and motivate action. Anoint a purple or yellow candle with ginger essential oil, sprinkle it with hemp or celery seeds, and burn it to increase psychic your abilities. Mix ginger oil with hemp oil and wear it during spellwork to get your personal power flowing.

Ginger is associated with the moon and Mars and holds energy to protect and to increase or "heat up" the action of any luck, money, or love spell. Add ginger oil to spells and formulas to boost the working. Anoint candles with a blend of ginger oil, basil oil, and bergamot oil to draw abundance. Or make a wealth-drawing oil blend with ginger oil, cinnamon, and sweet orange oil.

Grapefruit Essential Oil

Botanical Name: *Citrus ×paradisi*

Magickal Properties: Cleansing, communication, energy, inspiration, joy, psychic powers, and vitality

Emotional Response: Energizing, uplifting, and cleansing. The scent of grapefruit essential oil stimulates good mood, combats fatigue, and soothes aches and pains.

Healing Benefits: Antidepressant, antiseptic, detoxifying, and stimulating.
The invigorating scent remedies anxiety and depression as it lifts mood
and brightens outlook. It is used to treat headaches, stimulate circulation, and relieve muscle and joint aches.

Warning: May be phototoxic. May be toxic to cats if ingested.

Blends Well With: Bergamot, cardamom, chamomile, clary sage, clove,
cypress, eucalyptus, frankincense, juniper berry, lavender, lemon, lemongrass, melissa, myrrh, neroli, patchouli, peppermint, pine, rosemary, sandalwood, sweet orange, thyme, vanilla, vetiver, yarrow, and ylang-ylang

Grapefruit essential oil is cold pressed from fruit peels. It has a sweet, uplifting
aroma and is used to remedy headaches, hangovers, and seasonal affective disorder.
Mix 9 drops of grapefruit oil into 1 tablespoon of castile soap and add it to bathwater for a soak to revive and reenergize. Add peppermint oil to remedy a hangover.

Grapefruit oil holds a refreshing, joyful energy to soothe stress-related conditions, remedy fatigue, and ease depression. Burn grapefruit oil in a diffuser to reduce
mental fatigue. Fill a spray bottle with water, add 20 drops of grapefruit oil, and use
it to spritz away negativity and inspire creative thought. Add grapefruit oil to a footbath and soak tired feet to restore your spirit.

Grapefruit essential oil is associated with the moon. Wear it to awaken the senses,
promote mental clarity, encourage action, and stimulate psychic abilities. Add grapefruit oil to a spray bottle with water and use it to spritz the air above you before a
meeting to stimulate intellect and refresh ideas or grant resilience in adversity. Mix
grapefruit oil into olive oil and wear as a scent to boost confidence and feel positive.
The scent of grapefruit oil energizes the subconscious, facilitating communication
with the higher self. Wear the oil during meditation to deepen spiritual connection.
Blend grapefruit oil with sandalwood to inspire cooperation and generosity.

Grapefruit has a bright, bold energy to fortify spirit and stimulate energy flow.
Blend grapefruit essential oil with bergamot and sweet orange oil to increase positive energy for opportunities to manifest. Mix grapefruit oil into coconut oil and add
rose and rosemary oil. Wear it as a scent for a bright and flirty fragrance that exudes
benevolent, uplifting energy.

Jasmine Absolute Oil

Botanical Names: *Jasminum officinale* or *J. grandiflorum*

Magickal Properties: Attraction, hope, love, peace, prophetic dreams, and prosperity

Emotional Response: Relaxing and uplifting. This heady floral scent enhances well-being, as it encourages a positive outlook.

Healing Benefits: Aphrodisiac with analgesic and anti-inflammatory properties.

Warning: Do not ingest. Avoid if you are pregnant or breastfeeding.

Blends Well With: Bergamot, cardamom, chamomile, cinnamon, clary sage, clove, coriander, cypress, frankincense, ginger, grapefruit, lemon, melissa, myrrh, neroli, patchouli, peppermint, rose, sandalwood, sweet orange, vanilla, vetiver, and ylang-ylang

Jasmine absolute oil is extracted from the fragrant white flower of *Jasminum officinale* and *J. grandiflorum*. It is called an absolute because the oil cannot be produced by steam distillation but must be extracted using a solvent. Jasmine absolute oil has an intoxicating floral scent with the power to lift mood, stimulate mental creativity, attract abundance, and inspire love. The name comes from the Persian-Farsi word *yasamin*, which means "gift from god."[307]

Jasmine is associated with Jupiter, Cancer, the moon, the element water, Diana, Vishnu, and Quan Yin. It symbolizes beauty, love, good luck, and sensuality. Shakespeare wrote that Cleopatra used jasmine oil to seduce Antony, by scenting the sails of her ships so that he was enthralled before her ship reached the land.[308] Wear jasmine oil as perfume to increase your attraction. Pour a bit of olive oil into your palm. Add a few drops of jasmine oil and use your finger to trace the oil down the inside of both your wrists. Anoint your throat, your heart, and your belly. Anoint your lips to sweeten words.

. . . .

307. Bayton, *The Gardener's Botanical*, 170.

308. William Shakespeare, *Antony and Cleopatra*, 2.2.229, https://shakespeare.folger.edu/shakespeares-works/antony-and-cleopatra/act-2-scene-2/.

The scent of jasmine has been used for centuries to stir passions. Burn jasmine oil in a diffuser in the bedroom to infuse the space with a loving, harmonic energy. Add a few drops of jasmine oil to a cotton ball and tuck it into a love sachet to sweeten the working. Mix jasmine oil with sweet orange and ylang-ylang to inspire a flirty mood. Or mix jasmine oil with cardamom and cinnamon oil and wear it as a scent to encourage romance.

Jasmine oil holds a stimulating energy to open the mind, grant inspiration, and increase psychic abilities. Use jasmine oil as a hair rinse to invigorate thought and inspire new ideas. Blend jasmine oil with ginger and sandalwood to inspire a magickal outlook. Anoint a red candle with jasmine oil and use it to empower love spells. Anoint a green candle to draw prosperity. Anoint a yellow candle to inspire creativity or gain wisdom. Add a few drops to a dream pillow to inspire prophetic dreams. Use a blend of jasmine oil and bergamot to encourage happiness or mix jasmine oil with neroli to boost confidence.

Juniper Berry Essential Oil

Botanical Name: *Juniperus communis*

Magickal Properties: Anti-theft, cleansing, comfort, exorcism, love, protection, and visions

Emotional Response: Uplifting and soothing. The clean scent of juniper relaxes and soothes and helps release negative thinking.

Healing Benefits: Analgesic, astringent, antispasmodic, and sedative properties. The oil is used to regulate the menstrual cycle, ease cramps, treat skin conditions, and promote healing.

Warning: Avoid if pregnant or breastfeeding. Do not use if you have kidney disease. When diffused, it is toxic to dogs.

Blends Well With: Bay, bergamot, cedarwood, clary sage, cypress, eucalyptus, ginger, grapefruit, lavender, lemongrass, myrrh, neroli, peppermint, pine, sweet orange, and tea tree

Juniper berry oil is distilled from the fruit of *Juniperus communis*. Juniper berries are not actually berries but small cones. The oil has a sweet, crisp, woodsy scent and a long association with ritual cleansing. It was burned in temples in purification rites.[309] According to *Magic and Medicine of Plants*, "In the Middle Ages people thought juniper smoke gave protection against contagious diseases such as the plague and leprosy."[310] Parents burned juniper during childbirth in belief that the smoke would prevent fairies from stealing the child.[311] Juniper berries were also used in the Middle Ages for protection against evil.[312] In European folk medicine, the oil extracted from the berries was used to treat typhoid, cholera, dysentery, tapeworms, and other ills.[313] Use juniper berry oil for protection. Add 3 drops of juniper berry oil to a cotton ball and wear it in your left pocket when traveling to avoid accidents and stay safe. Blend juniper oil with rosemary oil and diffuse it to cleanse a space of negativity.

Juniper berry oil has a stimulating energy to ease mental exhaustion and strengthen fortitude. Diffuse juniper berry oil with grapefruit oil to chase away negativity and preserve a positive outlook. Mix juniper berry oil with bergamot and eucalyptus for a blend to alleviate sadness. Mix the blend into a small dish of salt and add it to bathwater for a soak to recharge your energy and elevate outlook.

Juniper berry oil is associated with Mars, Saturn, and Aries. It holds energy to cleanse, encourage healing, awaken the senses, and promote mental clarity. Mix juniper berry oil into coconut oil and rub it into skin to expand awareness. Diffuse it with bay to stimulate psychic abilities. Burn juniper berry oil in a tea light oil warmer to enhance divination or coax spirits to becoming visible. Mix juniper berry oil into hemp oil and wear it during meditation to sharpen focus. Wear the blend while hiking to increase awareness of the faery folk and nature spirits.

Lavender Essential Oil

Botanical Name: *Lavandula angustifolia*

Magickal Properties: Calm, clarity, communication, healing, love, protection, sleep, and transformation

· · · · · · · · · · · · · · · ·

309. Ody, *The Complete Medicinal Herbal*, 72.

310. Reader's Digest, *Magic and Medicine of Plants*, 227.

311. Reader's Digest, *Magic and Medicine of Plants*, 227.

312. Clevely et al., *Cooking with Herbs and Spices*, 305.

313. Ody, *The Complete Medicinal Herbal*, 72.

Emotional Response: Calming, centering, and rejuvenating. Lavender is renowned for its abilities to soothe emotions, relax the mind, and promote feelings of calmness.

Healing Benefits: Analgesic, antibacterial, and antispasmodic properties. It is used to treat anxiety, nervous tension, headaches, and insomnia and to heal the skin.

Warning: When diffused, it is toxic to cats.

Blends Well With: Bay, bergamot, cardamom, cedarwood, chamomile, clove, cypress, frankincense, ginger, grapefruit, juniper berry, lemon, lemongrass, melissa, patchouli, peppermint, pine, rosemary, sweet orange, vetiver, and yarrow

Lavender oil is steam distilled from the flowers of *Lavandula angustifolia*. It has a sweet floral scent that lifts mood and instills happiness. The scent of lavender is calming. It holds the power to relieve stress, instill tranquility, and soothe the weary. Wear lavender oil as perfume to calm the spirit and encourage clear thinking. Mix with bergamot and frankincense oil to deepen understanding. Blend lavender oil with chamomile oil to induce restfulness to a worried mind.

The word "lavender" comes from the Latin word *lavare*, which means "to wash," and lavender has been used for centuries to scent washwater.[314] Add lavender oil to washwater, then rinse the countertops or wash the floor to instill a peaceful atmosphere. Burn lavender oil in a diffuser to promote harmony in the home.

Lavender has long been a remedy to treat headache pain and cool anger. Staub tells us that it was the costly ointment Mary rubbed on Jesus's feet noted in John 12:3.[315] Seventeenth-century botanist John Parkinson prescribed lavender for headaches, and later Nicholas Culpeper advised lavender be applied to the temple or nostrils to ease "the tremblings and passions of the heart, and faintings and swoonings."[316]

....

314. Richard Folkard, *Plant Lore, Legends, and Lyrics* (London: Sampson Low, Marston, Searle, and Rivington; 1884), 71.

315. Staub, *The Illustrated Book of Edible Plants*, 172.

316. John Parkinson, *Theatrum Botanicvm* (London: Thomas Cotes, 1640), 74; Nicholas Culpeper, *Culpeper's Complete Herbal*, 85.

Lavender oil is an ingredient in many healing and beauty rituals. Its antibacterial and anti-inflammatory properties make it a useful treatment for many skin problems.[317] Apply a dose of lavender oil to banish pimples. Blend lavender oil into aloe to treat sunburn or relieve headache. Add it to jojoba oil and massage it into skin to relax and restore. Make a healing bath salts formula by mixing lavender oil, chamomile oil, and vetiver oil with salt. Add it to bathwater to relax the body and lift mood. Blend lavender oil with melissa oil and diffuse it to elevate outlook and calm the psyche.

In Tuscany, lavender was used to counter the evil eye.[318] Lore subscribes that if you stuff your pockets with lavender, you may gain the ability to see ghosts.[319] Burn lavender oil to enhance meditation. Place a drop of lavender oil on a tissue and place it beneath a pillow to make dreams memorable.

Lavender is associated with Mercury, Gemini, Virgo, and the element air, making it a good addition to any spell that requires fast, clear communication. The scent of lavender holds a calming energy to clear the mind and open awareness. Use lavender oil to enhance divination and dreamwork. Breathe in the scent to calm the spirit and encourage clear thinking. Anoint a candle with lavender oil and burn it to facilitate communication with the spirit world. Lavender is also used to empower love magick. Use it to anoint candles and burn it to empower love magick. Add lavender oil to bathwater to attract love. Blend it with rosemary and peppermint to make a moment memorable.

Lemon Essential Oil

Botanical Name: *Citrus ×limon*

Magickal Properties: Brightening, clarity, friendship, healing, love, purification, and success

Emotional Response: Uplifting, energizing, and stimulating. The refreshing scent of lemon fosters a sense of joy, clears thought, and improves concentration.

· · · · · · · · · · · · · · · · · ·

317. Cynthia Cobb, "How to Improve the Health of Your Skin with Lavender Oil," Healthline, March 2, 2022, https://www.healthline.com/health/lavender-oil-for-skin#fights-acne.

318. Folkard, *Plant Lore, Legends, and Lyrics*, 409.

319. Martin, *Garden Flower Folklore*, 169.

Healing Benefits: Analgesic, antibacterial, anti-inflammatory, and astringent properties. It is used to tone skin, improve mood, and deepen concentration.

Warning: Avoid if pregnant or breastfeeding. May cause photosensitivity and skin irritation.

Blends Well With: Bergamot, cardamom, cedar, chamomile, clove, eucalyptus, frankincense, ginger, grapefruit, jasmine, juniper berry, lavender, lemongrass, melissa, neroli, peppermint, pine, rose, rosemary, sandalwood, tea tree, vanilla, vetiver, and ylang-ylang

Lemon essential oil is cold pressed from lemon peels. It has a fresh, revitalizing lemony scent that stimulates, lifts, and inspires. Lemon oil is associated with the sun and has properties to empower thought and boost general well-being. A 2005 study in *The Irish Journal of Education* suggests that lemon essential oil improved perception, performance, and achievement when vaporized during lessons.[320] Burn lemon oil in a diffuser to improve learning. Add rosemary oil to improve memory retention.

Lemon oil holds a bright, sparkling energy to renew and cleanse. It is used to clean the spirit, the body, and the home. Mix a few drops of lemon oil with salt and add it to bathwater to cleanse away the gunk of the world and emerge renewed. The bright, cheery scent revives the weary and lifts the spirit as it instills a sense of calm and security to ease anxiety and hysteria. Use lemon oil to cool anger and ease fear. Blend with clary to balance emotions. Mix lemon oil with melissa oil and chamomile oil to calm and restore.

The scent of lemon oil inspires confidence and kindness. Blend lemon oil with bergamot oil and olive oil. Wear it as a scent to encourage love and friendship. Wear it when a friend is visiting to turn the friendship into a lasting one. Or blend 3 drops of lemon oil with 2 drops of lavender oil and 2 drops of rose oil. Mix the blend into 1 tablespoon of castile soap and add it to bathwater for a soak that encourages affection.

. . . .

320. Burhan Akpinar, "The Effects of Olfactory Stimuli on Scholastic Performance," *The Irish Journal of Education* 36 (2005): 86–90, http://www.erc.ie/documents/vol36chp5.pdf.

Lemongrass Essential Oil

Botanical Names: *Cymbopogon flexuosus* and *C. citratus*

Magickal Properties: Inspiration, mental clarity, psychic powers, purification, and wakefulness

Emotional Response: Refreshing and stimulating. Helps vanquish feelings of apathy and lethargy. Inspires actions and opens thought as it magnifies psychic awareness and enhances well-being.

Healing Benefits: Analgesic, antibacterial, anti-inflammatory, antiseptic, and astringent properties. It is used to aid healing, soothe headaches, aid digestion, and improve circulation.

Warning: Avoid if pregnant or breastfeeding. May cause skin irritation.

Blends Well With: Bergamot, cardamom, cedar, chamomile, clary sage, coriander, cypress, eucalyptus, frankincense, ginger, grapefruit, juniper berry, lavender, lemon, melissa, neroli, pine, rose, sandalwood, vanilla, vetiver, and ylang-ylang

Lemongrass oil is steam distilled from the scented grasses *Cymbopogon flexuosus* and *C. citratus*. It has a bright, citrus-like scent and an inspiring energy to lift and open. Lemongrass oil is known as a road-opening oil, as it clears away obstacles and opens the way for opportunities to manifest. Burn lemongrass oil to renew the energy of a room and instigate positive energy flow. Blend it with cardamom to boost mood and relieve anxiety. Mix the blend into a tablespoon of castile soap and soak for a restorative bath to soothe worry and calm the psyche.

The energizing scent of lemongrass boosts positive emotions and clears away negative energy. Add it to bathwater to brighten outlook, restore energy, and awaken the senses. Fill a spray bottle with 1 cup of water and 10 drops of lemongrass oil and spritz the room to open communication channels and inspire creativity. Add 5 drops of eucalyptus oil and use it as an air freshener to instigate fresh energy flow.

Lemongrass is used to wake intuition and stimulate psychic powers. Pour a dime-size portion of olive oil into your palm. Add 3 drops of lemongrass essential oil and trace the mixture over your third eye to empower your inner voice. Rub the oil blend into your hands before reading the tarot to strengthen your intuitive connection.

Melissa (Lemon Balm) Essential Oil

Botanical Name: *Melissa officinalis*

Magickal Properties: Friendship, happiness, healing, love, peace, and success

Emotional Response: Calm and relaxing. The lemony uplifting scent soothes away nervous tension and restores good spirits.

Healing Benefits: Antibacterial, anti-inflammatory, antihistamine, antiseptic, antispasmodic, carminative, sedative, and astringent properties. It is used to treat stings, remedy nausea, restore balance, and relieve tension.

Warning: Avoid if pregnant or breastfeeding. Do not use if you have thyroid disease.

Blends Well With: Bergamot, chamomile, cinnamon, clary sage, clove, cypress, eucalyptus, frankincense, grapefruit, jasmine, lavender, lemon, lemongrass, neroli, patchouli, rose, sandalwood, sweet orange, vetiver, and yarrow

Melissa or lemon balm is steam distilled from the leaves and flowering tops of the lemon balm plant. It has a fresh, lemony scent and a soothing energy to calm and cheer. Melissa oil is used to tone skin, treat minor skin irritations, relieve headaches, reduce anxiety, and aid breathing. It has a long history of medical use. Sixteenth-century English herbalist John Gerard wrote, "Bawme drunke in wine is good against the bitings of venomous beasts, comforts the heart, and driveth away all melancholie and sadnesse."[321] Grieve tells us, "The London Dispensary (1696) says: 'An essence of Balm, given in Canary wine, every morning will renew youth, strengthen the brain, relieve languishing nature and prevent baldness.'"[322] Melissa is one of the oils I use most often. It has a lovely, elevating citrusy scent that acts as a mild tranquilizer to restore balance, elevate mood, soothe anxiety, and ease nervous tension. Melissa also can help relieve headache pain and cold symptoms and remedy insomnia without the harsh side effects of prescription sedatives.

Melissa oil has a cheering energy with a sedative action, making it a lovely oil to calm and cheer. Make a blend with melissa oil, clary sage, and frankincense oil. Burn

· · · · · · · · · · · · · · · ·

321. Gerard, *The Herball*, 692.

322. Grieve, *A Modern Herbal*, vol. 1, 76.

it in a diffuser to elevate mood. Mix the blend into a tablespoon of castile soap and add it to bathwater for a calming soak to banish worry and balance emotions. Add equal parts of melissa oil and lavender oil to a spray bottle of water. Use it to spritz the air above you to balance emotions and lift outlook.

Myrrh Essential Oil

Botanical Name: *Commiphora myrrha*

Magickal Properties: Beauty, exorcism, healing, joy, protection, purification, and spirituality

Emotional Response: Grounding. The scent of this oil supports emotional balance to enhance well-being.

Healing Benefits: Antifungal, anti-inflammatory, antiseptic, carminative, and sedative properties. Myrrh oil is used to ease coughs and treat skin conditions.

Warning: Avoid if pregnant or breastfeeding. When diffused, it is toxic to birds.

Blends Well With: Bergamot, chamomile, clove, cypress, eucalyptus, frankincense, grapefruit, jasmine, lavender, lemon, lemongrass, melissa, neroli, patchouli, pine, rose, rosemary, sandalwood, sweet orange, tea tree, vetiver, and ylang-ylang

Myrrh essential oil is steam distilled from the resin of the desert tree *Commiphora myrrha*. Its soft, musky scent with its warm, sweet, and spicy notes has made it a prized resin since antiquity. The Chinese, Hindu, Bantu, Hebrew, and Bactrian cultures employed myrrh through the ages as a holy resin. It was prized by the Egyptians as an embalming oil and was one of the gifts of the Magi along with frankincense and gold.[323]

Myrrh oil is associated with beauty. Its earthy-spicy scent is comforting. It is used in antiaging formulas to heal the skin, reduce wrinkles, and diminish signs of aging. Mix myrrh oil into a dish of salt and add it to bathwater to accelerate healing. Mix it

....

323. Colin Michie, "Pharmaceutical Magic from the Magi," *New Scientist*, December 23, 1989, https://www .newscientist.com/article/mg12416963-800.

into a cup of milk for a luxurious, empowering bath to channel love goddess energy. Myrrh oil is associated with Isis as a resin of love. Use myrrh oil to anoint an amulet and wear it to attract love and happiness.

Myrrh is also used to increase intuition and deepen feelings of spirituality. Burn it with sandalwood oil during divination to empower intuition. Blend myrrh oil into a tablespoon of olive oil and wear it as a scent to sharpen insight and discernment. Mix it into almond or olive oil and wear it to aid your outlook when facing any transformation. Combine it with frankincense oil and burn it to raise vibration, gain insight, and foster spiritual growth. Or mix myrrh oil with lemon oil and frankincense oil for a sweet dream oil blend to anoint candles, sachets, and dream pillows.

Neroli Essential Oil

Botanical Name: *Citrus ×aurantium*

Magickal Properties: Attraction, calming, happiness, healing, love, and purification

Emotional Response: Calming restorative. It is used to soothe stress and ease grief, hysteria, mood swings, and anxiety.

Healing Benefits: Antibacterial, antifungal, anti-inflammatory, carminative, and sedative. Neroli is used to stimulate relaxation, treat skin irritations, sore muscles, ease shock, and help combat addictions.

Warning: Avoid using on children.

Blends Well With: Bergamot, cardamom, chamomile, clary sage, coriander, frankincense, ginger, grapefruit, jasmine, juniper berry, lavender, lemon, myrrh, patchouli, rose, sandalwood, sweet orange, yarrow, and ylang-ylang

Neroli essential oil is steam distilled from the flowers of the bitter orange tree. The pleasant, uplifting floral scent of neroli oil, with its citrusy-spicy undertones, has made it a staple in the perfume industry. The scent promotes relaxation and stimulates positive, feel-good energy. Mix neroli with a tablespoon of sweet almond oil and wear it to empower a sense of well-being.

Neroli oil instills emotional balance as it cools anger, soothes depression, quiets hysteria, and eases grief. Add a couple of drops of neroli oil to a cotton ball and tuck it into your pillowcase to remedy insomnia or into your pocket to fortify your spirit. Anoint a candle with a few drops of neroli oil and burn it during meditation to open communication channels. Add neroli oil to jojoba and use it as massage oil to relax and renew.

Neroli oil is used in therapies to reduce anxiety and fear and to help break addictive behaviors. Burn neroli in a diffuser to lift outlook and stop a negative thought loop. Blend it with melissa to calm and balance emotions. Add sweet orange to inspire happiness.

Neroli oil also has properties for attraction. It is used to empower love and beauty spells. Make an attraction oil by mixing 3 drops of neroli oil with 3 drops of clary sage oil and 3 drops of frankincense oil. Mix the blend into a tablespoon of sweet almond oil and use it to anoint candles in love spells or wear it as a scent to boost your charm.

Nutmeg Essential Oil

Botanical Name: *Myristica fragrans*

Magickal Properties: Clarity of vision, confidence, divination, friendship, love, luck, and prosperity

Emotional Response: Both calms and stimulates. Nutmeg oil balances emotions to boost confidence and enhance well-being. It helps us accept change and release doubt.

Healing Benefits: Aphrodisiac, analgesic, antispasmodic, carminative. Used to soothe sore muscles and improve sleep.

Warning: None.

Blends Well With: Bay, bergamot, chamomile, clary sage, coriander, grapefruit, lavender, lemon, melissa, neroli, rosemary, sweet orange, and tea tree

Nutmeg oil has a warm and spicy scent. It is distilled from the seed of an evergreen tree, *Myristica fragrans*. In China, nutmeg is known as *rou dou kou* and has been used as medicine since the seventh century. It traveled to Europe with Portuguese sailors in 1512 and quickly gained the reputation as a cure-all. Its hallucinogenic properties were discovered when the eaters became "deliriously inebriated."[324]

Nutmeg is a sedative with anti-inflammatory properties. It improves circulation and provides pain relief. Studies have shown nutmeg has anti-inflammatory compounds and can be an effective treatment for pain relief.[325] Nutmeg oil can bring emergency relief to a toothache and reduced joint and muscle pain. Mix it into jojoba oil for a warming massage oil that will help alleviate muscle aches and pains. Mix nutmeg oil with a tablespoon of castile soap and add it to a hot bath to remedy stress and fatigue. Add it to a footbath to relieve aching feet and renew energy.

Nutmeg oil is used to help someone accept change, ease depression, and make peace with uncertainty. Mix nutmeg oil into a small dish of salt and add the mixture to bathwater for an uplifting soak to encourage acceptance and let go of self-doubts. Blend nutmeg oil with sweet orange to boost confidence.

Nutmeg is also known for its ability to draw luck. Mix nutmeg oil with sweet almond oil and wear it as a scent when you need luck on your side. Take a cotton ball and drop nutmeg oil, grapefruit oil, and rosemary oil onto it. Tuck it into your left pocket and wear it when you need to find luck to figure your way through a tricky situation. Or make an oil blend to enhance psychic sight with nutmeg, bay, and lemongrass oil.

Nutmeg oil is associated with Jupiter and has energy to manifest and expand. It is used to draw luck and riches and empower prosperity spells. For quick money, take a green candle and carve the amount you desire into it. Anoint the candle with nutmeg oil, sprinkle some ground nutmeg over it, and place it on a firesafe dish. Arrange 4 silver coins around the candle and light. Visualize the money making its way to you. Nutmeg has properties to empower beginnings and boost creativity. Blend nutmeg oil with cedarwood, ginger, and sandalwood oils and use it to empower rituals to draw love, luck, and riches.

. . . .

324. Ody, *The Complete Medicinal Herbal*, 81.

325. Wei Kevin Zhang et al., "Nutmeg Oil Alleviates Chronic Inflammatory Pain through Inhibition of COX-2 Expression and Substance P Release in Vivo," *Food & Nutrition Research* 60 (2016): 30849, doi:10.3402/fnr .v60.30849.

Oregano Essential Oil

Botanical Name: *Origanum vulgare*

Magickal Properties: Added energy, dreams, joy, legal issues, love, protection, strength, and vitality

Emotional Response: Uplifting, courageous, helps facilitate change, and encourages releasing the past.

Healing Benefits: Antibacterial, antifungal, anti-inflammatory, and antiviral properties. Oregano oil is a remedy for headaches and helps the body fight colds and flu viruses.

Warning: This is a strong oil and may cause skin irritation or may irritate the respiratory tract if inhaled. Avoid if you are pregnant or breastfeeding. When diffused, it is toxic to dogs, cats, and birds.

Blends Well With: Bay, bergamot, cedarwood, chamomile, cypress, eucalyptus, lavender, lemon, lemongrass, melissa, neroli, peppermint, pine, rosemary, sweet orange, and thyme

Oregano essential oil is steam distilled from the flowering perennial herb also known as wild marjoram (*Origanum vulgare*). It has a strong minty scent. Oregano is a close relative to sweet marjoram (*O. majorana*), and like marjoram, it has a long history as a medicinal herb.[326] To the Egyptians and Greeks oregano was a medicine used to combat sadness and treat a range of illnesses from infections to poisoning. Its popularity continued into Shakespearean times, when it was used as a panacea.

Today oregano oil is used to boost immunity and fight flus and colds. It contains the antimicrobial component carvacrol, which fights infection and reduces redness and swelling. Blend oregano oil with pine oil to ease congestion. Blend oregano oil with lemon oil and peppermint oil to help clear a stuffy nose. Add oregano oil and witch hazel to a footbath to sweat out a cold.

Oregano oil is a potent antifungal remedy when diluted with a carrier oil and applied topically to treat mild skin and nail infections. It is a nervine that soothes anxiety and restores emotional balance. Blend it with lavender oil to ease irritability. Mix it into cypress oil to ease insomnia.

. . . .

326. Hajeski, *National Geographic Complete Guide to Herbs and Spices*, 59.

Oregano oil is associated with the moon, Juno, Venus, Aphrodite, and Diana, and it holds energy to foster happiness, harmony, love, and peace; encourage psychic development; and provide a barrier of protection. Use oregano oil to sweeten affections and encourage freedom of expression. Anoint a candle with oregano oil to empower a love spell. Use oregano oil in magicks to find comfort when faced with a separation from a loved one. Add a few drops of oregano oil to a dream pillow to induce psychic dreams. Ward a room by mixing oregano oil into olive oil. Trace the blend over the threshold to ward and protect. Use it in magickal work to repel a meddling neighbor or stop the interference of a troubling coworker.

Patchouli Essential Oil

Botanical Name: *Pogostemon cablin*

Magickal Properties: Beauty, fertility, healing, love, luck, protection, reversals, and wealth

Emotional Response: Heals, soothes, and cheers. The scent of patchouli relieves stress and alleviates nervous exhaustion.

Healing Benefits: Aphrodisiac, antibacterial, antidepressant, anti-inflammatory, antiseptic, carminative, and stimulating properties. Patchouli essential oil is added to a carrier oil and massaged into the skin to relieve tension and soothe away anxiety. It is used to treat exhaustion and stress and to enhance a sense of well-being.

Warning: None.

Blends Well With: Bergamot, cardamom, cedarwood, chamomile, cinnamon, clary sage, clove, coriander, frankincense, ginger, grapefruit, jasmine, lavender, lemongrass, melissa, myrrh, neroli, rose, sandalwood, sweet orange, vetiver, and ylang-ylang

Patchouli oil is steam distilled from the leaves of an herb in the deadnettle family, *Pogostemon cablin*. The oil has an earthy, herbaceous signature scent and has been used to make perfumes, soaps, incense, and insect repellent. Patchouli is native to Southeast Asia. It arrived in the Middle East along the silk trading routes, and supposedly it was Napoleon who introduced the exotic and intoxicating scent to Europe.[327] When the sixties counterculture embraced patchouli oil, it became associated with antiestablishment.

The scent of patchouli oil is deeply relaxing. It is used to increase focus and boost feelings of well-being. Burn patchouli oil in a tea light diffuser during meditation to focus thought. Blend patchouli oil with sweet orange and vanilla to inspire tranquility or mix it with chamomile oil for a restful night's sleep. Make a confidence-boosting blend by mixing patchouli oil with jasmine, chamomile, and sandalwood. Mix the blend into a carrier oil and wear it as a scent to boost self-esteem and expand sense of freedom.

Patchouli oil is known for its ability to heal. It contains antiseptic and anti-inflammatory properties to speed the healing of dry skin and fade scars. It is used to guard the body against infections, improve hair luster, and arouse sensuality. Add a few drops of patchouli oil to your conditioner to treat dandruff and scalp irritation. Blend it with sandalwood to make an effective treatment for nail fungus.[328]

Patchouli is associated with Saturn, the element earth, Scorpio, Aphrodite, Pan, and Osain. It holds a grounding energy to inspire love, draw wealth, and heat passion. Use patchouli oil to empower prosperity spells and promote fertility. Make a luck-drawing blend with patchouli oil, cinnamon, and vanilla. Blend it with jojoba oil and rub it into skin when you need to boost your own luck. Blend patchouli oil with bergamot, coriander, jasmine, and rose oils. Mix the blend into sweet almond oil and wear it as a scent to become irresistible.

Patchouli also holds protective power to boost defensive magick and bind or return negative energy to its source. Mix patchouli oil with sweet almond oil. Trace the blend over your threshold and windowsills to ward a room. Add patchouli oil to washwater and wash down the front door and steps after a run-in with an aggressive neighbor to keep their negative energy from entering.

. . . .

327. Amy Galper, "Patchouli Essential Oil: An Aroma with History," *Organic Spa Magazine*, March 11, 2014, https://www.organicspamagazine.com/patchouli-essential-oil-an-aroma-with-history/.

328. Ane Orchard, Sandy F. Van Vuuren, and Alvaro M. Viljoen, "Commercial Essential Oil Combinations against Topical Fungal Pathogens," *Natural Product Communications* 14, no. 1 (2019): n.p. doi:10.1177/1934578X1901400139.

Peppermint Essential Oil

Botanical Name: *Mentha ×piperita*

Magickal Properties: Purification, sleep, love, healing, and psychic powers

Emotional Response: Refreshing and stimulating. The uplifting oil has a buoyant affect to lift spirit and cheer the heart. It is used to chase away boredom or weariness as it sharpens focus and grants alertness.

Healing Benefits: Analgesic, antibacterial, anti-inflammatory, antiseptic, antispasmodic, and stimulating properties. This oil is used to treat skin irritations, respiratory infections, and headaches.

Warning: If inhaled, it may irritate the respiratory tract. Avoid if pregnant or breastfeeding. Should not be used by children. When diffused, it is toxic to dogs, cats, and birds.

Blends Well With: Basil, cypress, eucalyptus, grapefruit, juniper berry, lavender, lemon, melissa, neroli, pine, rosemary, and tea tree

Peppermint oil is steam distilled from the flowering herb *Mentha ×piperita*. It is prized for its pleasant, stimulating aroma and refreshing taste. It is used to flavor a variety of candy, gums, foods, and drinks and to scent soaps, shampoos, and cosmetics.

Peppermint oil holds an uplifting energy to energize mood and grant clarity of thought. Add peppermint oil to a spray bottle filled with water and spritz for a refreshing mental lift, or add the oil to a footbath for a restorative soak. Studies have shown that peppermint oil can be effective for preventing fatigue and improving exercise performance.[329] Use it to reduce fatigue and inspire clear communications.

Peppermint oil is associated with Venus, Zeus, Pluto, and the underworld. Use it to enhance psychic abilities. Blend peppermint oil with pine and vetiver to wake your magickal powers. Like pepper, peppermint holds energy to heat up action and warm feelings. Add a drop to the bills in your wallet to attract money. Use it to

. . . .

329. Abbas Meamarbashi, "Instant Effects of Peppermint Essential Oil on the Physiological Parameters and Exercise Performance," *Avicenna Journal of Phytomedicine* 4, no. 1 (2014): 72–78, doi:10.22038 /AJP.2014.1170; Abbas Meamarbashi and Ali Rajabi, "The Effects of Peppermint on Exercise Performance," *Journal of the International Society of Sports Medicine* 10, no. 1 (March 2013): 15, https://pubmed .ncbi.nlm.nih.gov/23517650/.

empower health and money spells. Add peppermint oil to a spray bottle filled with spring water and mist your place of business to attract customers. Burn peppermint oil in a diffuser when selling your home to make a buyer feel welcome.

Peppermint also has properties to protect. Dab peppermint oil onto a bracelet or pendant and wear it to avoid being cursed. Dab some on a crystal, stone, or small statue and keep it on your desk to protect against office jealousy.

Pine Essential Oil

Botanical Name: *Pinus sylvestris*

Magickal Properties: Abundance, banishing, fertility, health, prosperity, and purification

Emotional Response: This grounding oil opens the chest to ease breathing. It revitalizes energy and enhances a sense of well-being.

Healing Benefits: Analgesic, antibacterial, antifungal, anti-inflammatory, and antiseptic. Used to treat sore muscles, improve circulation, lessen congestion, and relieve cough and congestion.

Warning: May irritate the skin. Avoid if pregnant or breastfeeding. When diffused, it is toxic to dogs, cats, and birds.

Blends Well With: Bergamot, cedarwood, clary sage, cypress, eucalyptus, frankincense, grapefruit, juniper berry, lavender, lemon, melissa, myrrh, neroli, peppermint, rosemary, sandalwood, tea tree, thyme, and yarrow

Pine essential oil, sometimes called Scotch pine oil, is steam distilled from the needles of the conifer *Pinus sylvestris*, or Scotch pine. It has a fresh, crisp scent to wake the mind and arouse the senses. It is used to relieve mental and physical fatigue. Pine oil also has properties to sanitize and disinfect. It is an ingredient in cleaning products and air fresheners. Pine is also a spiritual cleanser. Burn pine oil in a tea light warmer before moving into a new home to drive out any residual energy left by the previous tenant. Add a few drops of pine oil to washwater and clean counters and floors to cleanse the space of negativity and ward off illness. Mix pine oil with cedarwood oil and juniper berry oil and burn to purify a ritual area.

The pine is a symbol of immortality and generation. Long ago the green boughs were brought into the home in the dead of winter to lift spirits, invite new life, and remind all that spring was only a few months away. We continue the tradition with the Christmas tree and the pine garland we use to decorate at Yule. The scent of pine oil holds a hopeful, comforting energy. Use it in spells to bless new beginnings or instigate necessary endings. Mix pine oil into salt and add it to bathwater for a cleansing bath that stimulates the senses.

Blend pine oil with juniper berry and grapefruit oil to make a soothing blend to calm frazzled nerves. Or adjust your mood with a blend of pine oil, cardamom, frankincense, and grapefruit oil. Blend pine oil with coriander and clove oil. Mix the oil blend into coconut oil and rub it into skin to bolster your spirit and make your thoughts receptive when facing a new job or an interview.

Pine has positive energy to attract abundance and good luck. Make a blend of pine oil, basil, and cinnamon oil to draw new opportunities. Use the blend to anoint a green candle to empower prosperity spells.

Rose Essential Oil

Botanical Name: *Rosa damascena*

Magickal Properties: Divination, dreams, joy, love, healing, protection, secrecy, and wish magick

Emotional Response: Calm and uplifting. The scent eases depression, reduces anxiety, and helps restore your sense of well-being.

Healing Benefits: Aphrodisiac, analgesic, antibacterial, antifungal, anti-inflammatory, antiseptic, and sedative properties. Rose oil is used to heal skin damage, fight infections, and relieve pain and nausea.

Warning: Avoid if pregnant or breastfeeding.

Blends Well With: Bergamot, chamomile, cinnamon, clary sage, clove, cypress, frankincense, ginger, jasmine, lavender, lemon, melissa, myrrh, neroli, patchouli, sandalwood, sweet orange, vanilla, vetiver, and ylang-ylang

Rose oil, also known as rose otto, is extracted from rose petals. It has a sweet floral scent and contains antibacterial and antifungal properties.[330] A 2015 study concluded that using rose oil is an effective way to ease pain in patients who have undergone surgery.[331] Blend rose oil into jojoba and massage it into the skin to ease aches and pains and accelerate healing. Add rose oil to bathwater to lift your outlook and cheer the spirit.

The heady romantic scent of rose oil can help alleviate depression and stimulate the brain to release endorphins, or "feel-good" hormones.[332] Blend rose oil with a spoon of castile soap and add it to bathwater for a luxurious soak that lifts vibration and encourages happiness. Power up your feel-good energy with a blend of rose oil, lavender oil, and sweet orange oil. Mix the blend into a tablespoon of sweet almond oil and wear it as a scent to remain positive. Wear a blend of rose oil, frankincense, and sandalwood oil to deepen spirituality.

Rose oil is associated with Venus, Aphrodite, Bacchus, Dionysus, the moon, Taurus, peace, empowerment, attraction, and love. Use it to enhance beauty and amplify attraction magick. Channel a love goddess with a blend of rose oil, jasmine, and patchouli oil. Use it as a massage oil to promote affection. Use the blend to anoint candles to empower love magicks. Burn a blend of rose oil and frankincense in a tea light diffuser to inspire a deepening of emotions. Or make an attraction oil with a blend of rose oil, patchouli, and ylang-ylang. Mix it into olive oil and wear it as a scent to boost charisma and increase sex appeal. Blend rose oil with bergamot, coriander, jasmine, and patchouli oils. Mix the blend into sweet almond oil and wear it as a scent to become irresistible.

· · · · · · · · · · · · · · · ·

330. Mohamed Shohayeb et al., "Antibacterial and Antifungal Activity of *Rosa damascena* MILL. Essential Oil, Different Extracts of Rose Petals," *Global Journal of Pharmacology* 8, no. 1 (January 2014): 1–7, doi:10.5829/idosi.gjp.2014.8.1.81275.

331. Maryam Marofi and Motahareh Sirousfard, "Evaluation of the Effect of Aromatherapy with *Rosa damascena* Mill. on Postoperative Pain Intensity in Hospitalized Children in Selected Hospitals Affiliated to Isfahan University of Medical Sciences in 2013: A Randomized Clinical Trial," *Iranian Journal of Nursing and Midwifery Research* 20, no. 2 (2015): 247–54, https://www.ncbi.nlm.nih.gov/pmc/articles/PMC4387651/.

332. Rebecca Joy Stanborough, "The Benefits of Rose Oil and How to Use It," Healthline, last modified August 8, 2019, https://www.healthline.com/health/rose-oil#1.

Rose energy is nurturing. The sweet scent encourages acceptance. Use rose oil in grief and healing rituals. Add rose oil to a dream sachet to encourage prophetic dreams.

Rosemary Essential Oil

Botanical Name: *Salvia rosmarinus*

Magickal Properties: Beauty, communication, friendship, love, protection, purification, remembrance, and rest

Emotional Response: Clears the mind, improves memory, and acts as a restorative.

Healing Benefits: Analgesic, antibacterial, antifungal, anti-inflammatory, antiseptic, sedative, and nervine properties. Rosemary is a cleansing oil used to fight germs, relieve cramps, enhance concentration, and improve circulation.

Warning: Avoid if pregnant or breastfeeding. Should not be used by children. Avoid if you have high blood pressure or a history of seizures. May be toxic if ingested.

Blends Well With: Basil, bergamot, cedarwood, cinnamon oil, chamomile, clary sage, cypress, eucalyptus, frankincense, grapefruit, juniper berry, lavender, lemon, lemongrass, melissa, neroli, oregano, peppermint, pine, sweet orange, tea tree, and thyme

Rosemary essential oil is steam distilled from the leaves of an evergreen perennial native to the Mediterranean, *Salvia rosmarinus*. It has a fresh, woodsy scent. Rosemary oil is used to heal the mind and body, empower memory, improve athletic performance, and cleanse and purify.[333] In French hospitals rosemary was burned with juniper berries to cleanse the air and prevent infection.[334]

The scent of rosemary eases headaches and calms the psyche. A 2013 study determined that not only did rosemary oil impact mood, but it also affected brain wave

333. Zhiyue Li et al., "Does the Fragrance of Essential Oils Alleviate the Fatigue Induced by Exercise? A Biochemical Indicator Test in Rats," *Evidence-Based Complementary and Alternative Medicine* (2017): 5027372, doi:10.1155/2017/5027372.

334. Grieve, *A Modern Herbal*, vol. 2, 682.

activity, the autonomic nervous system responses, and mood states.[335] Add 9 drops of rosemary oil to a bowl of cool water. Drop in a cloth. Wring out the water and lay the cloth over the forehead to ease suffering. Breathe in the scent to calm racing thoughts. Add rosemary oil to sweet almond oil and massage it into muscles to ease jet lag and alleviate aches and pains. Use rosemary oil to speed the healing process. Add rosemary oil to hot water and breathe in the steam to gain relief when a stubborn thought persists.

The Greeks wore rosemary to improve memory, and a 2018 study supported that rosemary oil does increase human short-term memory.[336] Blend rosemary oil and lemon oil to improve learning. Burn it in a diffuser to improve test performance. Blend rosemary oil with patchouli oil and lemon oil to enhance mental ability.

Rosemary is both a wedding herb and a funeral herb. Rosemary sprigs were distributed to mourners and tossed into the grave in fond remembrance.[337] Blend rosemary oil with lavender and peppermint oil to make a moment memorable. Blend rosemary oil with cypress oil and burn it in a diffuser to honor the dead.

Rosemary oil holds energy to bless and purify and protect. In Spain and Italy rosemary was used to drive away evil.[338] Blend rosemary oil with lemongrass oil. Add to your washwater and scrub to cleanse a room of negative energy. Add 1 drop each of rosemary oil, grapefruit oil, and nutmeg oil to a cotton ball. Tuck the ball into your left pocket and wear it when you need help finding your way through a tricky situation.

Rosemary is associated with the sun and Leo and holds energy to activate. The fragrant oil holds a versatile energy that can be used to empower many kinds of workings. Use it to draw good luck and empower love spells. Rosemary is also a faery favorite. Folkard shares, "It was a common saying in Sicily, that Rosemary is

. . . .

335. Winai Sayorwan et al., "Effects of Inhaled Rosemary Oil on Subjective Feelings and Activities of the Nervous System," *Scientia Pharmaceutica*, 81, no. 2 (2013): 531–42, doi:10.3797/scipharm.1209-05.

336. Kruger, *The Pocket Guide to Herbs*, 148; O. V. Filiptsova et al., "The Effect of the Essential Oils of Lavender and Rosemary on the Human Short-Term Memory," *Alexandria Journal of Medicine* 54, no. 1 (2018): 41–44, doi:10.1016/j.ajme.2017.05.004.

337. Grieve, *A Modern Herbal*, vol. 2, 682.

338. Grieve, *A Modern Herbal*, vol. 2, 682.

the favorite plant of the fairies, and that the young fairies, under the guise of snakes, lie concealed under its branches."[339]

Sandalwood Essential Oil

Botanical Name: *Santalum album*

Magickal Properties: Blessing, communication, healing, hospitality, love, opening doorways, peace, protection, security, spirituality, and wishes

Emotional Response: The grounding scent of this oil promotes a sense of inner calm. This is a helpful remedy to ease depression, reduce anxiety, release the past, and enhance intuition.

Healing Benefits: Aphrodisiac, antidepressant, antiseptic, calming, and sedative properties. Used to combat infection, heal the skin, restore mood, and foster sleep.

Warning: Do not use if you have kidney disease. When diffused, it is toxic to birds.

Blends Well With: Bergamot, cardamom, chamomile, clary sage, clove, cypress, frankincense, finger, grapefruit, jasmine, lavender, lemon, lemongrass, melissa, myrrh, neroli, patchouli, rose, pine, sweet orange, vetiver, and ylang-ylang

Sandalwood essential oil is steam distilled from trees in the genus *Santalum*. It has a complex scent that is spicy, woody, and earthy. It has been revered as a sacred oil since ancient times by cultures in India, Egypt, Greece, Rome, and China, who used it in both ceremony and medical practices.[340]

The scent of sandalwood is welcoming and calming. It is known to lift mood and spiritual vibrations. Sandalwood oil is traced on the forehead to focus thought and inspire intuition. It is burned to promote awareness and deepen spirituality. Wear sandalwood oil as a scent when you go out into the world to open to opportunities. Burn it in a diffuser to open meditation and communication channels. Burn it with myrrh or frankincense to carry your wishes up to the heavens.

. . . .

339. Folkard, *Plant Lore, Legends, and Lyrics*, 526.

340. Wilson, *Aromatherapy: Essential Oils for Vibrant Health and Beauty*, 120.

Sandalwood has energy to protect and banish. Burn it in a diffuser to clear a room of negativity. Use sandalwood oil to support rituals for death and dying. Mix sandalwood oil with frankincense oil for a comforting blend to balance emotions and ease transitions. Blend sandalwood with ylang-ylang oil to counter stress.

Sandalwood is associated with the moon, the element water, Venus, and Jupiter. It holds energy to support love magick. Make an attraction oil by mixing sandalwood oil with patchouli and vetiver oil. Wear it as a scent to elicit affection and draw interest. Or use it as a candle anointing oil to empower any love spell. Make a "love me, love me" oil blend by mixing sandalwood with rose and jasmine oil. Wear it as a scent to boost charm and persuasion abilities.

Sweet Orange Essential Oil

Botanical Name: *Citrus ×sinensis*

Magickal Properties: Abundance, clarity, divination, fertility, health, happiness, love, luck, money, and weddings

Emotional Response: Revitalizing, calming, and grounding. Restores energy and invigorates thought. This is a helpful remedy for reducing shock and easing depression.

Healing Benefits: Antidepressant, antiseptic, antispasmodic, and sedative properties. It is rich in antimicrobial properties to heal the skin and helps reduce inflammation and pain while supporting the immune system.

Warning: May be toxic to cats.

Blends Well With: Basil, bergamot, cinnamon, clary sage, clove, coriander, eucalyptus, frankincense, ginger, grapefruit, jasmine, juniper berry, lavender, lemon, lemongrass, melissa, myrrh, neroli, nutmeg, patchouli, rose, sandalwood, vanilla, vetiver, and ylang-ylang

Sweet orange essential oil is cold pressed from the peels of *Citrus ×sinensis*. It has a bright citrusy scent and an energizing, uplifting energy. The scent lifts mood and inspires joy. Use it to promote happiness, joy, and good fortune. Blend sweet orange oil with jojoba. Rub it into skin to elevate outlook and lighten your mood. Blend sweet orange oil with frankincense and cinnamon and diffuse to feel blessed. Or mix sweet orange with patchouli, sandalwood, and vanilla to make a blend to instill inner peace.

The bright, vibrant energy of sweet orange oil is associated with the sun, making it ideal for self-purification, inspiring creativity, and lifting the spirit. Blend it with peppermint oil to improve lung capacity and boost athletic ability.[341] Blend sweet orange with frankincense, sandalwood, and vetiver oil to boost magickal abilities. Or mix sweet orange oil with cardamom, ginger, sandalwood, and ylang-ylang to boost personal power.

Sweet orange oil is used to empower works for beauty, love, luck, and money. Mix sweet orange oil into a small dish of salt and add to bathwater to enhance beauty. Blend sweet orange with jasmine and ylang-ylang to channel love goddess energy. Burn sweet orange oil to inspire creativity. Anoint a green candle with a blend of sweet orange and cinnamon oil to work a quick money spell. Burn sweet orange oil with frankincense and myrrh to increase energy flow for beginnings and new opportunities. Anoint a green candle with sweet orange oil and honey. Roll the candle in ground cinnamon and burn it to draw prosperity.

Tea Tree Essential Oil

Botanical Name: *Melaleuca alternifolia*

Magickal Properties: Balance, courage, inspiring, healing, and rejuvenating

Emotional Response: Revitalizing, calming, and grounding. Restores energy and invigorates thought. This is a helpful remedy for reducing shock and easing depression.

Healing Benefits: Antibacterial, antifungal, antiseptic, antiviral, and stimulant properties. Supports the immune system and is a treatment for skin conditions, bites, and infections.

Warning: May cause skin irritation. When diffused, it is toxic to dogs, cats, and birds. Toxic when taken internally.

. . . .

341. Nidal Amin Jaradat et al., "The Effect of Inhalation of *Citrus sinensis* Flowers and *Mentha spicata* Leave Essential Oils on Lung Function and Exercise Performance," *Journal of the International Society of Sports Nutrition* 13, no. 36 (September 2016): n.p., doi:10.1186/s12970-016-0146-7.

Blends Well With: Chamomile, cinnamon, clary sage, clove, lavender, lemon, lemongrass, melissa, myrrh, neroli, nutmeg, peppermint, rose, rosemary, pine, and thyme

Tea tree essential oil is not related to *Camellia sinensis*, the plant from which we get drinking tea, nor the edible oil tea seed oil (*C. oleifera*). In fact, tea tree oil is toxic when taken internally.

Tea tree oil, also known as melaleuca oil and ti tree oil, is derived from a small tree native to Australia called *Melaleuca alternifolia*. It has a spicy, pungent scent and is valued for its antiseptic properties, used to treat skin conditions, kill germs, and fight infections. The leaves are loaded with terpene hydrocarbons, monoterpenes, and sesquiterpenes, which give the oil antibacterial, antiviral, and antifungal properties. It is used as a topical oil to relieve minor skin irritations. Apply a drop of tea tree oil to remedy the itch and swelling of insect bites. A drop of tea tree oil placed on a pimple can speed its healing time. Use tea tree oil to heal fungal infections. Mix tea tree oil with sweet almond oil and massage it into aching joints to relieve pain.

Tea tree essential oil is a wonderful cleanser known for its antiseptic properties. Add tea tree oil to a diffuser to avoid illness during cold and flu season. Add a few drops to water and diffuse it in a sickroom to curb germs and gently scent the room. But use with caution, as this process is toxic to dogs and cats. Add a few drops of tea tree oil to water and use it to wipe countertops, doorknobs, and light switches to kill germs and avoid sickness. Mix tea tree oil and lemon oil into jojoba oil and wear it on your fingernails to strengthen the nails and discourage fungal infections. The crisp scent of tea tree essential oil has a reassuring calming effect. Use tea tree oil to empower spells when action calls for you to be courageous. Anoint candles with tea tree oil and use them in spells for health and valor. Anoint candles with tea tree oil and roll them in crumbled sage to banish negative energy or empower a protection spell. Add a few drops of tea tree oil to a cotton ball and wear it in your left pocket to banish fear. Anoint a talisman or amulet with tea tree essential oil to boost its power.

Thyme Essential Oil

Botanical Name: *Thymus vulgaris*

Magickal Properties: Communication, courage, dreams, healing, love, luck, psychic powers, purification, sight, and success

Emotional Response: Refreshing, stimulation, and reviving. Thyme oil is used to stimulate fresh thought, invigorate mood, and enhance your sense of well-being.

Healing Benefits: Antibacterial, antiseptic, antifungal, anti-inflammatory, and antispasmodic properties. Thyme oil is used fight fungal infections, clear acne, improve circulation, and relieve sore muscles.

Warning: Avoid if pregnant or breastfeeding. Do not use on children. Do not use if you have high blood pressure. May cause skin irritation. When diffused, it is toxic to dogs and birds.

Blends Well With: Bergamot, clary sage, clove, eucalyptus, grapefruit, lavender, lemon, lemongrass, melissa, pine, rosemary, sweet orange, and tea tree

Thyme essential oil is steam distilled from the aerial portion of *Thymus vulgaris,* an aromatic perennial herb with a long history of culinary, medicinal, and magickal uses. It has a stimulating, spicy scent. The Egyptians used thyme to embalm the dead. The Greeks used it as an offering and burned it on the altars of their gods.[342] In Germany and Holland thyme was home to the faery folk.[343] Add thyme oil and lemongrass oil to a diffuser and burn for a visionary blend to open intuition.

Thyme is associated with Mercury, Venus, water, Taurus, Libra, bravery, and courage. Roman soldiers were known to bathe in thyme water before battles to bolster their valor, and in the Middle Ages it was customary for ladies of the court to present sprigs of thyme to their favorite knights.[344] Thyme oil is used to clear the mind, calm the nervous system, and encourage creativity, intuition, and psychic abilities. Blend thyme oil into olive oil and wear it as a scent to aid in clear seeing,

. . . .

342. Staub, *The Illustrated Book of Edible Plants,* 172.

343. Hajeski, *National Geographic Complete Guide to Herbs and Spices,* 85.

344. Picton, *The Book of Magical Herbs,* 103.

increase the power of attraction, or to fortify confidence. Blend thyme oil with bay oil and use to draw luck. Blend thyme oil with rosemary and peppermint to refresh thought.

Thyme essential oil is a strong germicide used to make cleansing formulas to combat infection. It contains thymol, which "exhibits antimicrobial, antioxidant, anticarcinogenesis, anti-inflammatory, and antispasmodic activities."[345] It also contains carvacrol, an effective anti-inflammatory agent that protects cells against viruses and bacteria. Add thyme oil to a footbath and soak the feet to remedy aches and restore the spirit. Blend thyme oil with bergamot, clary sage, and rosemary oil to treat a cold. Mix thyme oil with equal amounts frankincense, peppermint, and vetiver oil. Stir it into a carrier oil to make a soothing massage oil to treat back, foot, or neck pain.

Vanilla Essential Oil

Botanical Name: *Vanilla planifolia*

Magickal Properties: Affection, beauty, comfort, love, luck, lust, mental powers, and trust

Emotional Response: Soothing and relaxing. It is often diffused to ease anxiety and instill a sense of calm.

Healing Benefits: Aphrodisiac, analgesic, antidepressant, anti-inflammatory, antiseptic, carminative, and sedative properties. Vanilla essential oil is used to relieve muscle cramps, reduce anxiety, treat acne, and repair damaged skin.

Warning: None.

Blends Well With: Bergamot, frankincense, grapefruit, jasmine, lemon, lemongrass, melissa, neroli, patchouli, rose, sandalwood, sweet orange, vetiver, and ylang-ylang

Vanilla essential oil is extracted from the pods of an orchid native to Mexico (*Vanilla planifolia*). It is one of the world's most beloved scents and flavors. Both

....

345. Bahar Salehi et al., "Thymol, Thyme, and Other Plant Sources: Health and Potential Uses," *Phytotherapy Research* (May 2018): 1688–1706, doi:10.1002/ptr.6109.

vanilla and chocolate were foods of the Aztecs. They were both introduced to Europe in the 1520s.[346] The delicious fragrance of vanilla oil heightens citrus and floral scents.

The scent of vanilla is soothing. Breathe in vanilla to calm anxiety, quiet worry, or dispel negative feelings. Add 7 drops of vanilla oil to a tablespoon of castile soap and add it to bathwater to lift mood and encourage happiness. Make an oil blend to heal emotions by mixing vanilla oil with rose and ylang-ylang oils. Add to jojoba and wear it as a scent to encourage acceptance and move thought forward. Or blend vanilla oil with patchouli and sweet orange to inspire tranquility.

Vanilla oil holds energy to calm the spirit, grant clear thinking, and increase good luck. Use vanilla oil in rituals to bring clarity to a situation. Blend vanilla oil with jojoba oil and rub it into your hands. Touch someone when you wish to gain their trust or encourage them to speak the truth.

Vanilla is associated with Venus, Libra, Pisces, and the element water. The scent of vanilla induces feelings of affection. Use it to energize love charms and beauty spells or wear as an aphrodisiac. Use vanilla oil to empower friendship spells and attraction magick. Make an attraction oil with a blend of vanilla oil, patchouli, and rose oil. Mix the blend into coconut oil and wear to foster affection. The heat of your body will activate the oil scent and make you smell irresistible. Blend vanilla oil with cardamom and jasmine to become enchanting.

Vetiver Essential Oil

Botanical Name: *Chrysopogon zizanioides*

Magickal Properties: Antitheft, hex breaking, love, luck, and money

Emotional Response: Calm, grounding, and healing. Stimulates libido and fights fatigue and mental fog.

Healing Benefits: Aphrodisiac, analgesic, antibacterial, antiseptic, antifungal, anti-inflammatory, and antispasmodic properties. Used to treat cramps, ease muscle pain, heal skin inflammation and wounds, and treat depression and ADHD.

. . . .
346. Rebecca Rupp, "History of Vanilla," *National Geographic*, October 23, 2014, https://www.national geographic.com/culture/article/plain-vanilla.

Warning: None.

Blends Well With: Bergamot, cardamom, cedarwood, clary sage, frankincense, ginger, grapefruit, jasmine, lavender, lemon, lemongrass,
myrrh, patchouli, rose, sandalwood, sweet orange, vanilla, yarrow, and
ylang-ylang

Vetiver essential oil is steam distilled from the roots of a perennial clumping grass
native to India. It has a sweet grassy scent and has been grown through the ages for
perfume, to prevent crop erosion, to thatch roofs, to make hats, and to make mats
that are hung in doorways to cool and scent the rooms of the home. Vetiver oil
acts as a natural tranquilizer to calm nervousness, reduce hyperactivity, and encourage a restful sleep. Burn it to soothe the psyche, reduce absentmindedness, and ease
depression.

Vetiver oil has a positive drawing energy that can be used to draw opportunity
and protect against malice. Mix it into a carrier oil and wear it as a scent to boost
your confidence. Blend vetiver oil with rose oil and ylang-ylang oil to encourage
positivity and empower self-esteem. Or energize your mood with an uplifting blend
of vetiver, bergamot, neroli, and sweet orange oils. Stir the blend into a small dish of
salt and add it to bathwater to elevate your mood and encourage a positive outlook.
Add the blend to a footbath for a soak to comfort the soul, quiet thought, and alleviate worry.

Use vetiver oil to empower love, luck, and money rituals. Anoint a bay leaf with
vetiver oil and wear it in your left pocket to draw good luck to you. Mix vetiver oil
with patchouli and sandalwood oils to empower love magick. Make an enchantment
oil with a blend of vetiver, bergamot, lavender, and patchouli. Mix the blend with
olive oil and wear it as a scent to boost charisma and empower charm.

Yarrow Essential Oil

Botanical Name: *Achillea millefolium*

Magickal Properties: Banish, courage, exorcism, healing, love, protection, and
psychic powers

Emotional Response: Soothing and clearing. The scent of this oil promotes tranquility to ease worry, cool anger, and support overall mental wellness.

Healing Benefits: Antiarthritic, antibacterial, antifungal, anti-inflammatory, antiseptic, antispasmodic, carminative properties. It is used to ease sinus headaches and arthritis pain, heal the skin, and treat anxiety and sleep disorders.

Warning: Avoid if pregnant or breastfeeding. May cause photosensitivity and skin irritation. When diffused, it is toxic to dogs.

Blends Well With: Bay, bergamot, cedarwood, chamomile, clary sage, cypress, eucalyptus, grapefruit, lavender, melissa, neroli, pine, sweet orange, vetiver, and ylang-ylang

Yarrow essential oil is steam distilled from the flowering tops of *Achillea millefolium*. It has a sharp herbaceous scent that promotes feelings of tranquility. It is used to ease troubled thoughts, calm frustration, dispel anger, and treat insomnia. Burn yarrow oil in a diffuser to instill feelings of harmony. Mix yarrow oil into a spoon of castile soap and add to bathwater for a soak to relax the body and ease tension headaches.

Yarrow has a long history as a wound healer. Some of its names, like knight's milfoil, soldier's woundwort, stanch weed, and carpenter's grass, relate to its ability to stanch bleeding. The healers Hippocrates, Dioscorides, Pliny, and Hildegard von Bingen included yarrow in their medical works.[347] Yarrow oil has antiseptic properties to treat minor skin irritations and accelerate healing. Add yarrow oil to bathwater to treat abrasions and soothe itchy skin, or massage it into aching joints to reduce pain. Blend 3 drops of yarrow oil, 3 drops of lavender oil, and 5 drops of nutmeg oil into a tablespoon of castile soap and soak for a soothing bath to reduce inflammation. Use yarrow oil to reduce skim blemishes.

Yarrow oil is associated with Venus, Mars, and Libra. It holds energy to instill harmony and foster affection. Burn yarrow oil to attract lovers and friends. Add yarrow and lavender oil to bathwater and soak to heighten beauty. Diffuse yarrow oil

. . . .

347. Arrowsmith, *Essential Herbal Wisdom*, 292.

to fill a space with energy, harmony, and cooperation. Use yarrow oil to empower love spells.

Yarrow oil has energy to stimulate psychic abilities, clear away negative energy, and banish things you want to be gone. Blend yarrow oil with lemongrass to enhance psychic sight. Use yarrow oil to eliminate negativity from a person, place, or thing. Mix 9 drops of yarrow oil into a small dish of olive oil and use it to anoint a threshold to keep negative influences, unwanted guests, and pests away.

Ylang-Ylang Essential Oil

Botanical Name: *Cananga odorata*

Magickal Properties: Aphrodisiac, beauty, cheer, fertility, health, love, power, and social power

Emotional Response: Uplifting and arousing. The scent of this oil awakens the senses. It is used to treat trauma, anxiety, insomnia, and depression.

Healing Benefits: Antidepressant, anti-inflammatory, antiseptic, antispasmodic, and sedative properties. Use it to tone skin, help clear complexion, and restore hair. Use it as a massage oil to stimulate libido.

Warning: None.

Blends Well With: Bergamot, cardamom, chamomile, cinnamon, clary sage, clove, cypress, eucalyptus, ginger, grapefruit, jasmine, lemon, lemongrass, melissa, myrrh, neroli, patchouli, rose, sandalwood, sweet orange, vetiver, and yarrow

Ylang-ylang oil is a rich, fragrant oil extracted from the flowers of the cananga tree, a tropical tree native to Asia and the South Pacific islands. It has a sweet floral scent that acts as an aphrodisiac to inspire positive feelings about the self. A 2014 study found that students exposed to ylang-ylang essential oil experienced higher self-esteem.[348] Blend ylang-ylang oil into coconut oil and rub it into skin to boost self-confidence. As your skin warms the oil, the sweet scent will deepen to increase

. . . .

348. Juliana Rizzo Gnatta et al., "Aromatherapy with Ylang-Ylang for Anxiety and Self-Esteem: A Pilot Study," *Revista da Escola de Enfermagem da USP* 48, no. 3 (June 2014): 492–99, doi:10.1590/s0080-6234201 40000300015.

feel-good energy. Anoint candles with ylang-ylang oil and burn to promote happiness. Or blend ylang-ylang with lavender and rose oils and wear as a scent to keep your wits when you have to meet with someone who makes you feel insecure.

Ylang-ylang oil has both antiseptic and anti-inflammatory properties, and its scent is a natural antidepressant.[349] Add to bathwater to improve complexion, tone skin, and boost self-image. Add ylang-ylang oil to a footbath for a relaxing soak that encourages positivity and lifts outlook. Add ylang-ylang oil to a spray bottle of water and use it to spritz away negativity, induce cheer, and encourage a positive vibe. Or blend ylang-ylang oil with cinnamon and melissa oil to enhance cognitive performance.

Ylang-ylang is associated with Venus, Libra, and the element Water. It holds energy to empower love and sex magicks. Wear it as a scent to channel divine feminine energy. Diffuse a blend of ylang-ylang, clary sage, and cypress to turn a moment sexy or blend ylang-ylang oil with cypress and sweet orange oil. Mix the blend into olive oil and rub into skin to boost your ability to charm. Diffuse ylang-ylang oil with sandalwood and vanilla oil to inspire romance.

· · · · · · · · · · · · · · ·

349. Loh Teng Hern Tan et al., "Traditional Uses, Phytochemistry, and Bioactivities of *Cananga odorata* (Ylang-Ylang)," *Evidence-Based Complementary and Alternative Medicine* 2015 (2015): n.p., doi:10.1155/2015/896314.

BIBLIOGRAPHY

Books

Anthis, Christina. *The Beginner's Guide to Essential Oils*. Emeryville, CA: Althea Press, 2019.

Arrowsmith, Nancy. *Essential Herbal Wisdom: A Complete Exploration of 50 Remarkable Herbs*. Woodbury, MN: Llewellyn Publications, 2009.

Ashe, William Willard. *Shade Trees for North Carolina*. Raleigh, NC: North Carolina Geological and Economic Survey, 1908.

Ayales, Adriana. *Adaptogens*. New York: Sterling Ethos, 2019.

Bayton, Ross. *The Gardener's Botanical*. Princeton, NJ: Princeton University Press, 2020.

Bellebuono, Holly. *An Herbalist's Guide to Formulary*. Woodbury, MN: Llewellyn Publications, 2017.

Bennett, Robin Rose. *This Gift of Healing Herbs: Plant Medicines and Home Remedies for a Vibrantly Healthy Life*. Berkeley, CA: North Atlantic Books, 2014.

Brewer, Ebenezer Cobham. *Dictionary of Phrase and Fable*. London: Cassell and Company, 1895.

Bruton-Seal, Julie, and Matthew Seal. *Backyard Medicine for All: A Guide to Home-Grown Herbal Remedies*. New York: Skyhorse Publishing, 2017.

———. *Backyard Medicine: Harvest and Make Your Own Herbal Remedies*. New York: Skyhorse Publishing, 2009.

———. *The Herbalist's Bible*. New York: Skyhorse Publishing, 2014.

Burke, Nancy. *The Modern Herbal Primer*. Dublin: Yankee Publishing, 2000.

Callery, Emma. *The Complete Book of Herbs: A Practical Guide to Cultivating, Drying, and Cooking with More Than 50 Herbs*. Philadelphia, PA: Courage Books, 1994.

Chevallier, Andrew. *Encyclopedia of Herbal Medicine*. New York: DK Publishing, 2016.

———. *Herbal Remedies Handbook*. New York: DK Publishing, 2018.

Cichoke, Anthony J. *Secrets of Native American Herbal Remedies*. New York: Avery Books, 2001.

Clevely, Andi, and Katherine Richmond. *The Complete Book of Herbs*. London: Smithmark Publishers, 1998.

Clevely, Andi, Katherine Richmond, Sallie Morris, and Lesley Mackley. *Cooking with Herbs and Spices*. Leicester, UK: Anness Publishing, 1997.

Cohen, Bevin. *The Artisan Herbalist*. Gabriola Island, Canada: New Society Publishers, 2021.

Conway, DJ. *By Oak, Ash, & Thorn*. St. Paul, MN: Llewellyn Publications, 2004.

Cook, Michelle Schoffro. *Be Your Own Herbalist*. Novato, CA: New World Library, 2016.

Coppock, Robert W., and Margitta Dziwenka. "Nutraceuticals: Efficacy, Safety and Toxicity." In *Nutraceuticals,* edited by Ramesh C. Gupta, 619–31. London: Elsevier, 2016.

Craze, Richard. *The Spice Companion*. London: Quintet Publishing, 1997.

Culpeper, Nicholas. *The Complete Herbal*. Manchester, UK: J. Gleave and Son, 1826.

De la Forêt, Rosalee. *Alchemy of Herbs*. Carlsbad, CA: Hay House, 2017.

DK. *Home Herbal: Cook, Brew and Blend Your Own Herbs*. New York: DK Publishing, 2011.

Dietz, S. Theresa. *The Complete Language of Flowers*. New York: Wellfleet Press, 2020.

Evelyn, John. *Acetaria: A Discourse on Sallets*. London: B. Tooke, 1699.

Falconer, Randle Wilbraham. *The Ancient History of the Rose*. [London]: [Longman, Orme, Brown, Green, and Longmans], 1839.

Farrell, Kenneth T. *Spices, Condiments, and Seasonings*. Gaithersburg, MD: Aspen Publishing, 1999.

Folkard, Richard. *Plant Lore, Legends, and Lyrics*. London: Sampson Low, Marston, Searle, and Rivington, 1884.

Foster, Steven, and James A. Duke. *A Field Guide to Medicinal Plants: Eastern and Central North America*. Boston, MA: Houghton Mifflin, 1990.

Foster, Steven, and Rebecca L. Johnson. *Desk Reference to Nature's Medicine*. Washington, DC: National Geographic, 2006.

Gagliano, Monica. *Thus Spoke the Plant: A Remarkable Journey of Groundbreaking Scientific Discoveries and Personal Encounters with Plants*. Berkeley, CA: North Atlantic Books, 2018.

Gerard, John. *The Herball: or the Generall Historie of Plantes*. London: John Norton, 1597.

Gladstar, Rosemary. *Rosemary Gladstar's Herbal Recipes for Vibrant Health*. North Adams, MA: Storey Publishing, 2008.

Green Moyer, Betsy, and Ken Moore, eds. *Paul Green's Plant Book: An Alphabet of Flower Folklore*. Chapel Hill, NC: Botanical Garden Foundation, 2005.

Gregg, Susan. *The Complete Illustrated Encyclopedia of Magical Plants*. Beverly, MA: Fair Winds Press, 2014.

Grieve, Maud. *A Modern Herbal*. Vols. 1 and 2. New York: Dover Publications, 1971.

Groves, Maria Noel. *Grow Your Own Herbal Remedies*. North Adams, MA: Storey Publishing, 2019.

Hajeski, Nancy J. *National Geographic Complete Guide to Herbs and Spices: Remedies, Seasonings, and Ingredients to Improve Your Health and Enhance Your Life*. Washington, DC: National Geographic, 2016.

———. *Nature's Best Remedies*. Washington, DC: National Geographic, 2019.

Harrar, Sari, and Sara Altshul O'Donnell. *The Woman's Book of Healing Herbs*. Emmaus, PA: Rodale Press, 2000.

Harrison, Lorraine. *Latin for Gardeners: Over 3,000 Plant Names Explained and Explored*. Chicago: University of Chicago Press, 2012.

Hatfield, Gabrielle. *Hatfield's Herbal: The Curious Stories of Britain's Wild Plants*. London, UK: Penguin Books, 2009.

Homer. *Iliad*. Translated by Stephen Mitchell. New York: Simon & Schuster, 2011.

Johnson, Rebecca L., Steven Foster, Tieraona Low Dog, and David Kiefer. *National Geographic Guide to Medicinal Herbs*. Washington, DC: National Geographic, 2010.

Kaufer, Lanny. *Medicinal Herbs of California*. Guilford, CT: Falcon Guides, 2021.

Keniston-Pond, Kimberly. *Essential Oils 101*. Avon, MA: Adams Media, 2017.

Kruger, Anna. *The Pocket Guide to Herbs*. London: Parkgate Books, 1992.

Landon, Rachel. *Superherbs*. London: Piatkus, 2017.

Lawless, Julia. *The Encyclopedia of Essential Oils*. San Francisco, CA: Conari Press, 2013.

Lehner, Ernst, and Johanna Lehner. *Folklore and Symbolism of Flowers, Plants and Trees*. New York: Tudor Publishing Company, 1960.

Little, Elbert Luther, Susan Rafield, and Olivia Buehl. *National Audubon Society Field Guide to North American Trees: Western Region*. New York: Alfred A. Knopf, 1980.

Macculloch, J. A. *The Religion of the Ancient Celts*. New York: Charles Scribner's Sons, 1911.

Martin, Laura C. *Garden Flower Folklore*. Guilford, CT: Globe Pequot Press, 2009.

McFarland, Ben. *World's Best Beers: One Thousand Craft Brews from Cask to Glass*. New York: Sterling, 2009.

Morgan, Diane. *The Charmed Garden: Sacred and Enchanting Plants for the Magically Inclined Herbalists*. Scotland, UK: Findhorn Press, 2004.

Ody, Penelope. *The Complete Medicinal Herbal*. London: Dorling Kindersley, 1993.

Orozoff, Petr Ivanovich. *The Rose: Its History*. Kazanlik, Bulgaria: Petko Iv. Orozoff and Sons, 1908.

Oster, Maggie. *Flowering Herbs*. New York: Longmeadow Press, 1991.

Ovid. *Metamorphoses*. The Ovid Project. University of Vermont. Accessed January 13, 2022. https://www.uvm.edu/~hag/ovid/.

Parkinson, John. *Theatrum Botanicvm*. London: Thomas Cotes, 1640.

Pharr, Danny. "Winter Solstice-Sown Herbs." In *Llewellyn's 2010 Herbal Almanac*, 41–50. Woodbury, MN: Llewellyn Publications, 2009.

Philpot, J. H. *The Sacred Tree: or, The Tree in Religion and Myth*. London: Macmillan, 1897. Project Gutenberg, 2014. https://www.gutenberg.org/files/47215/47215-h/47215-h.htm.

Picton, Margaret. *The Book of Magical Herbs: Herbal History, Mystery, and Folklore*. London: Quarto, 2000.

Pliny the Elder. *Natural History: The Empire in the Encyclopedia*. Translated by John Bostock and Henry T. Riley. London: H. G. Bohn, 1855. Perseus Digital Library.

Reader's Digest. *Magic and Medicine of Plants.* New York: Reader's Digest, 1986.

Rhind, Jennifer Peace. *Fragrance and Wellbeing: Plant Aromatics and Their Influence on the Psyche.* London: Singing Dragon, 2014.

Romm, Aviva. *Botanical Medicine for Women's Health.* St. Louis, MO: Elsevier, 2010.

Sanders, Jack. *The Secrets of Wildflowers.* Guilford, CT: Lyons Press, 2003.

Shakespeare, William. *Antony and Cleopatra.* Folger Shakespeare Library. Accessed April 15, 2022. https://shakespeare.folger.edu/shakespeares-works/antony-and-cleopatra/.

———. *A Midsummer Night's Dream.* Folger Shakespeare Library. Accessed April 15, 2022. https://shakespeare.folger.edu/shakespeares-works/a-midsummer-nights-dream/.

Silverstein, Sara-Chana. *Moodtopia.* New York: Da Capo Press, 2018.

Simard, Suzanne. *Finding the Mother Tree.* New York: Alfred A. Knopf, 2021.

Small, Ernest. *North American Cornucopia.* Boca Raton, FL: Taylor & Francis, 2014.

Starhawk. *The Earth Path: Grounding Your Spirit in the Rhythms of Nature.* San Francisco, CA: HarperCollins, 2004.

Staub, Jack. *The Illustrated Book of Edible Plants.* Layton, UT: Gibbs Smith, 2016.

Thomas, Pat, Inna Duckworth, Victoria Plum, and Daphne Lambert. *Mental Wellness: A Holistic Approach to Mental Health and Healing.* New York: DK Publishing, 2021.

Tobyn, Graeme, Alison Denham, and Midge Whitelegg. *The Western Herbal Tradition.* Philadelphia, PA: Jessica Kingsley Publishers, 2016.

Willoughby, Jean. *Nature's Remedies: An Illustrated Guide to Healing Herbs.* San Francisco, CA: Chronicle Books, 2016.

Wilson, Roberta. *Aromatherapy: Essential Oils for Vibrant Health and Beauty.* New York: Avery, 2002.

Winston, David, and Steven Maimes. *Adaptogens: Herbs for Strength, Stamina, and Stress Relief.* Rochester, VT: Healing Arts Press, 2007.

Winston, David. *Herbal Therapeutics.* Broadway, NJ: Herbal Therapeutic Research Library, 2017.

Zak, Victoria. *The Magic Teaspoon: Transform Your Meals with the Power of Healing Herbs and Spices.* New York: Berkley Books, 2006.

Journal Articles

Abascal, Kathy, and Eric Yarnell. "Nervine Herbs for Treating Anxiety." *Alternative and Complementary Therapies* 10, no. 6 (December 2004): 309–15. doi:10.1089/act.2004 .10.309.

Akhondzadeh, Shahin, Hamid Reza Naghavi, M. Vazirian, Anooshirvan Shayeganpour, H. Rashidi, and M. Khani. "Passionflower in the Treatment of Generalized Anxiety: A Pilot Double-Blind Randomized Controlled Trial with Oxazepam." *Journal of Clinical Pharmacy and Therapeutics* 26, no. 5 (October 2001): 363–67. doi:10.1046/j.1365-2710 .2001.00367.x.

Akpinar, Burhan. "The Effects of Olfactory Stimuli on Scholastic Performance." *The Irish Journal of Education* 36 (2005): 86–90. http://www.erc.ie/documents/vol36chp5.pdf.

Ames, B. N., M. K. Shigenaga, and T. M. Hagen. "Oxidants, Antioxidants, and the Degenerative Diseases of Aging." *Proceedings of the National Academy of Sciences of the United States of America* 90, no. 17 (September 1993): 7915–22. doi:10.1073/pnas.90.17.7915.

Apaydin, Eric A., Alicia R. Maher, Roberta Shanman, Marika S. Booth, Jeremy N. V. Miles, Melony E. Sorbero, and Susanne Hempel. "A Systematic Review of St. John's Wort for Major Depressive Disorder." *Systematic Reviews* 5, no. 1 (September 2016): 148. doi:10.1186/s13643-016-0325-2.

Batool, Saima, Rasheed Ahmad Khera, Muhammad Asif Hanif, and Muhammad Adnan Ayub. "Bay Leaf." *Medicinal Plants of South Asia* (2020): 63–74. doi:10.1016/B978-0-08 -102659-5.00005-7.

Bhattacharyya, D., T. K. Sur, U. Jana, and P. K. Debnath. "Controlled Programmed Trial of *Ocimum sanctum* Leaf on Generalized Anxiety Disorders." *Nepal Medical College Journal* 10, no. 3 (September 2010): 176–79. https://pubmed.ncbi.nlm.nih.gov/19253862/.

Bokelmann, Jean M. "Motherwort (*Leonurus cardiaca*): Above-Ground Parts." In *Medicinal Herbs in Primary Care: An Evidence-Guided Reference for Healthcare Providers*, 511–14. Philadelphia, PA: Elsevier, 2022.

Brock, Christine, Julie Whitehouse, Ihab Tewfik, and Tony Towell. "American Skullcap (*Scutellaria lateriflora*): An Ancient Remedy for Today's Anxiety?" *British Journal of Wellbeing* 1, no. 4 (July 2010): 25–30. doi:10.12968/bjow.2010.1.4.49168.

————. "American Skullcap (*Scutellaria lateriflora*): A Randomised, Double-Blind Placebo-Controlled Crossover Study of Its Effects on Mood in Healthy Volunteers." *Phytotherapy Research* 28, no. 5 (May 2014): 692–98. doi:10.1002/ptr.5044.

Crego, Antonio, José Ramón Yela, María Ángeles Gómez-Martínez, Pablo Riesco-Matías, and Cristina Petisco-Rodríguez. "Relationships between Mindfulness, Purpose in Life, Happiness, Anxiety, and Depression: Testing a Mediation Model in a Sample of Women." *International Journal of Environmental Research and Public Health* 18, no. 3 (February 2021): 935. doi:10.3390/ijerph18030925.

Davison, Karen M., Shen Lin, Hongmei Tong, Karen M. Kobayashi, Jose G. Mora-Almanza, and Esme Fuller-Thomson. "Nutritional Factors, Physical Health and Immigrant Status Are Associated with Anxiety Disorders among Middle-Aged and Older Adults: Findings from Baseline Data of the Canadian Longitudinal Study on Aging (CLSA)." *International Journal of Environmental Research and Public Health* 17, no. 5 (2020): 1493. https://doi.org/10.3390/ijerph17051493.

Emmons, Robert A., and Michael E. McCullough. "Counting Blessings versus Burdens: An Experimental Investigation of Gratitude and Subjective Well-Being in Daily Life." *Journal of Personality and Social Psychology* 84, no. 2 (February 2003): 377–89. doi:10.1037//0022-3514.84.2.377.

Filiptsova, O. V., L. V. Gazzavi-Rogozina, I. A. Timoshyna, O. I. Naboka, Y. V. Dyomina, and A. V. Ochkur. "The Effect of the Essential Oils of Lavender and Rosemary on the Human Short-Term Memory." *Alexandria Journal of Medicine* 54, no. 1 (2018): 41–44. doi:10.1016/j.ajme.2017.05.004.

Froh, Jeffrey J., William J. Sefick, and Robert A. Emmons. "Counting Blessings in Early Adolescents: An Experimental Study of Gratitude and Subjective Well-Being." *Journal of School Psychology* 46, no. 2 (April 2008): 213–33. doi:10.1016/j.jsp.2007.03.005.

Ghazizadeh, Javid, Saeed Sadigh-Eteghad, Wolfgang Marx, Ali Fakhari, Sanaz Hamedeyazdan, Mohammadali Torbati, Somaiyeh Taheri-Tarighi, Mostafa Araj-Khodaei, and Mojgan Mirghafourv. "The Effects of Lemon Balm (*Melissa officinalis* L.) on Depression and Anxiety in Clinical Trials: A Systematic Review and Meta-Analysis." *Phytotherapy Research* 35, no. 12 (December 2021): 6690–705. doi:10.1002/ptr.7252.

Gnatta, Juliana Rizzo, Patricia Petrone Piason, Cristiane de Lion Botero Couto Lopes, Noemi Marisa Brunet Rogenski, and Maria Júlia Paes da Silva. "Aromatherapy with

Ylang-Ylang for Anxiety and Self-Esteem: A Pilot Study." *Revista da Escola de Enferma-gem da USP* 48, no. 3 (June 2014): 492–99. doi:10.1590/s0080-623420140000300015.

Haviland-Jones, Jeannette, Holly Hale Rosario, Patricia Wilson, and Terry R. McGuire. "An Environmental Approach to Positive Emotion: Flowers." *Evolutionary Psychology* 3, no. 1 (January 2005): n.p. doi:10.1177/147470490500300109.

Jamshidi, Negar, and Marc M. Cohen. "The Clinical Efficacy and Safety of Tulsi in Humans: A Systematic Review of the Literature." *Evidence-Based Complementary and Alternative Medicine* (2017): n.p. doi:10.1155/2017/9217567.

Janda, Katarzyna, Karolina Wojtkowska, Karolina Jakubczyk, Justyna Antoniewicz, and Karolina Skonieczna-Zydecka. "*Passiflora incarnata* in Neuropsychiatric Disorders—A Systematic Review," *Nutrients* 12, no. 12 (2020): 3894. doi:10.3390/nu12123894.

Jaradat, Nidal Amin, Hamzeh Al Zabadi, Belal Rahhal, Azmi Mahmoud Ali Hussein, Ja-mal Shaker Mahmoud, Basel Mansour, Ahmad Ibrahim Khasati, and Abdelkhaleq Issa. "The Effect of Inhalation of *Citrus sinensis* Flowers and *Mentha spicata* Leave Essential Oils on Lung Function and Exercise Performance." *Journal of the International Society of Sports Nutrition* 13, no. 36 (September 2016): n.p. doi:10.1186/s12970-016-0146-7.

Khalid, Sundus, Katie L. Barfoot, Gabrielle May, Daniel J. Lamport, Shirley A. Reynolds, and Claire M. Williams. "Effects of Acute Blueberry Flavonoids on Mood in Children and Young Adults." *Nutrients* 9, no. 2 (February 2017): 158. doi:10.3390/nu9020158.

Khan, Abdul Waheed, Arif-Ullah Khan, and Touqeer Ahmed. "Anticonvulsant, Anxiolytic, and Sedative Activities of *Verbena officinalis*." *Frontiers in Pharmacology* 7, no. 499 (December 2016): n.p. doi:10.3389/fphar.2016.00499.

Latif, R. "Chocolate/Cocoa and Human Health: A Review." *Netherlands Journal of Medicine* 71, no. 2 (March 2013): 63–68. https://pubmed.ncbi.nlm.nih.gov/23462053/.

Li, Zhiyue, Fengzhi Wu, Haozhen Shao, Yu Zhang, Angran Fan, and Feng Li. "Does the Fragrance of Essential Oils Alleviate the Fatigue Induced by Exercise? A Biochemical Indicator Test in Rats." *Evidence-Based Complementary and Alternative Medicine* (2017): 5027372. doi:10.1155/2017/5027372.

Ma, Xiao, Zi-Qi Yue, Zhu-Qing Gong, Hong Zhang, Nai-Yue Duan, Yu-Tong Shi, Gao-Xia Wei, and You-Fa Li. "The Effect of Diaphragmatic Breathing on Attention, Negative Affect and Stress in Healthy Adults." *Frontiers in Psychology* 8, no. 874 (2017): n.p. doi:10.3389/fpsyg.2017.00874.

Mahboubi, Mohaddese, and Leila Mohammad Taghizadeh Kashanib. "A Narrative Study about the Role of *Viola odorata* as Traditional Medicinal Plant in Management of Respiratory Problems." *Advances in Integrative Medicine* 5, no. 3 (December 2018): 112–18. https://doi.org/10.1016/j.aimed.2017.12.003.

Mao, Jun J., Qing S. Li, Irene Soeller, Kenneth Rockwell, Sharon X. Xie, and Jay D. Amsterdam. "Long-Term Chamomile Therapy of Generalized Anxiety Disorder: A Study Protocol for a Randomized, Double-Blind, Placebo-Controlled Trial." *Journal of Clinical Trials* 4, no. 5 (November 2014): 188. doi:10.4172/2167-0870.1000188.

Marofi, Maryam, Motahareh Sirousfard, Mahin Moeini, and Alireza Ghanadi. "Evaluation of the Effect of Aromatherapy with *Rosa damascena* Mill. on Postoperative Pain Intensity in Hospitalized Children in Selected Hospitals Affiliated to Isfahan University of Medical Sciences in 2013: A Randomized Clinical Trial." *Iranian Journal of Nursing and Midwifery Research* 20, no. 2 (2015): 247–54. https://www.ncbi.nlm.nih.gov/pmc/articles/PMC4387651/.

Meamarbashi, Abbas. "Instant Effects of Peppermint Essential Oil on the Physiological Parameters and Exercise Performance." *Avicenna Journal of Phytomedicine* 4, no. 1 (2014): 72–78. doi:10.22038/AJP.2014.1170.

Meamarbashi, Abbas, and Ali Rajabi. "The Effects of Peppermint on Exercise Performance." *Journal of the International Society of Sports Medicine* 10, no. 1 (March 2013): 15. https://pubmed.ncbi.nlm.nih.gov/23517650/.

Möykkynen, T., M. Uusi-Oukari, J. Heikkilä, D. M. Lovinger, H. Lüddens, and E. R. Korpi. "Magnesium Potentiation of the Function of Native and Recombinant GABA(A) Receptors." *Neuroreport* 12, no. 10 (July 2001): 2175–79. doi:10.1097/00001756-2001 07200-00026.

Nikfarjam, Masoud, Neda Parvin, Naziheh Assarzadegan, and Shabnam Asghari. "The Effects of *Lavandula angustifolia* Mill. Infusion on Depression in Patients Using Citalopram: A Comparison Study." *Iranian Red Crescent Medical Journal* 15, no. 8 (August 2013): 734–39. doi:10.5812/ircmj.4173.

Orchard, Ane, Sandy F. Van Vuuren, and Alvaro M. Viljoen. "Commercial Essential Oil Combinations against Topical Fungal Pathogens." *Natural Product Communications* 14, no. 1 (2019): n.p. doi:10.1177/1934578X1901400139.

Pattanayak, Priyabrata, Pritishova Behera, Debajyoti Das, and Sangram K. Panda. *"Ocimum sanctum* Linn. A Reservoir Plant for Therapeutic Applications: An Overview." *Pharmacognosy Reviews* 4, no. 7 (2010): 95–105. doi:10.4103/0973-7847.65323.

Rahbardar, Mahboobeh Ghasemzadeh, and Hossein Hosseinzadeh. "Therapeutic Effects of Rosemary (*Rosmarinus officinalis* L.) and Its Active Constituents on Nervous System Disorders." *Iranian Journal of Basic Medical Sciences* 23, no. 9 (September 2020): 1100–1112. doi:10.22038/ijbms.2020.45269.10541.

Salehi, Bahar, Abhay Prakash Mishra, Ila Shukla, Mehdi Sharifi-Rad, María Del Mar Contreras, Antonio Segura-Carretero, Hannane Fathi, Nafiseh Nasri Nasrabadi, Farzad Kobarfard, and Javad Sharifi-Rad. "Thymol, Thyme, and Other Plant Sources: Health and Potential Uses." *Phytotherapy Research* (May 2018): 1688–706. doi:10.1002/ptr.6109.

Sayorwan, Winai, Nijsiri Ruangrungsi, Teerut Piriyapunyporn, Tapanee Hongratanaworakit, Naiphinich Kotchabhakdi, and Vorasith Siripornpanich. "Effects of Inhaled Rosemary Oil on Subjective Feelings and Activities of the Nervous System." *Scientia Pharmaceutica*, 81, no. 2 (2013): 531–42. doi:10.3797/scipharm.1209-05.

Sharma, Anup, Marna S. Barrett, Andrew J. Cucchiara, Nalaka S. Gooneratne, and Michael E. Thase. "A Breathing-Based Meditation Intervention for Patients with Major Depressive Disorder Following Inadequate Response to Antidepressants: A Randomized Pilot Study." *Journal of Clinical Psychiatry* 78, no. 1 (2017): e59–e63. doi:10.4088/JCP.16m10819.

Shohayeb, Mohamed, El-Sayed S. Abdel-Hameed, Salih A. Bazaid, and Ibrahim Maghrabi. "Antibacterial and Antifungal Activity of *Rosa damascena* MILL. Essential Oil, Different Extracts of Rose Petals." *Global Journal of Pharmacology* 8, no. 1 (January 2014): 1–7. doi:10.5829/idosi.gjp.2014.8.1.81275.

Sienkiewicz, Monika, Anna Glowacka, Katarzyna Poznańska-Kurowska, Andrzej Kaszuba, Anna Urbaniak, and Edward Kowalczyk. "The Effect of Clary Sage Oil on Staphylococci Responsible for Wound Infections." *Postepy dermatologii i alergologii* 32, no. 1 (2015): 21–26. doi:10.5114/pdia.2014.40957.

Tala, Álvaro. "Gracias por todo: Una revisión sobre la gratitud desde la neurobiología a la clínica [Thanks for Everything: A Review on Gratitude from Neurobiology to Clinic]." *Revista Medica de Chile* 147, no. 6 (2019): 755–61. doi:10.4067/S0034-98872019000600755.

Tan, Loh Teng Hern, Learn Han Lee, Wai Fong Yin, Chim Kei Chan, Habsah Abdul Kadir, Kok Gan Chan, and Bey Hing Goh. "Traditional Uses, Phytochemistry, and Bioactivities of *Cananga odorata* (Ylang-Ylang)." *Evidence-Based Complementary and Alternative Medicine* 2015 (2015): n.p. doi:10.1155/2015/896314.

Tuenter, Emmy, Kenn Foubert, and Luc Pieters. "Mood Components in Cocoa and Chocolate: The Mood Pyramid." *Planta Medica* 84, nos. 12–13 (August 2018): 839–44. doi:10.1055/a-0588-5534.

Veits, Marine, Itzhak Khait, Uri Obolski, Eyal Zinger, Arjan Boonman, Aya Goldshtein, Kfir Saban, Udi Ben-Dor, et al. "Flowers Respond to Pollinator Sound within Minutes by Increasing Nectar Sugar Concentration." *Ecology Letters* 22, no. 9 (September 2019): 1483–92. doi:10.1111/ele.13331.

Woelk, Helmut. "Comparison of St John's Wort and Imipramine for Treating Depression: Randomised Controlled Trial." *British Medical Journal* 321, no. 7260 (September 2000): 536–39. doi:10.1136/bmj.321.7260.536.

Zeinoddini, Shirin, Mohammad Nabiuni, and Hanieh Jalali. "The Synergistic Cytotoxic Effects of Doxorubicin and *Viola odorata* Extract on Human Breast Cancer Cell Line T47-D." *Journal of Cancer Research and Therapeutics* 15, no, 5. (2019): 1073–79. doi:10.4103/jcrt.JCRT_990_17.

Zhang, Kai, and Lei Yao. "The Anxiolytic Effect of *Juniperus virginiana* L. Essential Oil and Determination of Its Active Constituents." *Physiology & Behavior* 189 (2018): 50–58. doi:10.1016/j.physbeh.2018.01.004.

Zhang, Wei Kevin, Shan-Shan Tao, Ting-Ting Li, Yu-Sang Li, Xiao-Jun Li, He-Bin Tang, Ren-Huai Cong, Fang-Li Ma, and Chu-Jun Wan. "Nutmeg Oil Alleviates Chronic Inflammatory Pain through Inhibition of COX-2 Expression and Substance P Release in Vivo." *Food & Nutrition Research* 60 (2016): 30849. doi:10.3402/fnr.v60.30849.

Zhang, Zongpai Wen-Ming Luh, Wenna Duan, Grace D. Zhou, George Weinschenk, Adam K. Anderson, and Weiying Dai. "Longitudinal Effects of Meditation on Brain Resting-State Functional Connectivity." *Brain Sciences* 11, no. 10 (September 2021): 1263. doi:10.3390/brainsci11101263.

Zorich, Zach. "Neanderthal Medicine Chest." *Archaeology*. January/February 2013. https://www.archaeology.org/issues/61-1301/features/top-10/266-top-10-2012-neanderthal-medicine.

To Write to the Author

If you wish to contact the author or would like more information about this book, please write to the author in care of Llewellyn Worldwide Ltd. and we will forward your request. Both the author and the publisher appreciate hearing from you and learning of your enjoyment of this book and how it has helped you. Llewellyn Worldwide Ltd. cannot guarantee that every letter written to the author can be answered, but all will be forwarded. Please write to:

Laurel Woodward
⅟ Llewellyn Worldwide
2143 Wooddale Drive
Woodbury, MN 55125-2989
Please enclose a self-addressed stamped envelope for reply,
or $1.00 to cover costs. If outside the U.S.A., enclose
an international postal reply coupon.

Many of Llewellyn's authors have websites with additional information and resources. For more information, please visit our website at http://www.llewellyn.com.

NOTES

NOTES

NOTES